D1083083

THE LAST PARTY

THE LAST PARTY

Scenes from My Life with Norman Mailer

Adele Mailer

BARRICADE BOOKS INC. / New York

Published by Barricade Books Inc.
150 Fifth Avenue
New York, NY 10011

Printed in the United States of America.

Book design by Cindy LaBreacht

Library of Congress Cataloging-in-Publication Data
Mailer, Adele.
    The last party : scenes from my life with Norman Mailer / Adele Mailer.
        p.   cm.
    Includes index.
    ISBN 1-56980-098-7
    1. Mailer, Norman—Marriage. 2. Authors, American—20th century—
Biography. 3. Authors' spouses—United States—Biography. 4. Mailer,
Adele—Marriage. I. Title.
PS3525.A4152Z755   1997
813'.54—dc21
[B]   96-47445
                                           CIP

10 9 8 7 6 5 4 3 2 1

A NOTE FROM THE AUTHOR

All of the events in this book are recounted as I remember them. None have been invented. The dialogue, where not word-for-word, reflects my honest recollection of what occurred at the time.

Prologue

Before I started this book about my marriage to Norman Mailer, I talked to my daughters, trying to explain why I felt compelled to write it. Over the years, I was sick of reading about the stabbing from people who didn't know what they were talking about. It is my story, and I've decided to tell it how it was. I have tried to separate my girls as much as I can from the book and have not discussed any aspect of it with them.

Although they are both in their thirties, the stabbing is still very painful to them. The three of us decided that they should never read the book, making it easier for them to be as neutral as possible considering the circumstances, because I know from experience that Norman would dump his anger at me on my kids, trying to get at me through them.

I've toiled and I've troubled over this book, wailing and cackling like one of Macbeth's witches stirring up a cauldron full of mixed memories, spiced with an event so catastrophic, it was to alter my life forever. It is a simmering stew of the most hateful, the most painfully sweet, and the most ridiculous of my life's recollections, peppered with a splash of brutal honesty burning my tongue and heart.

Having inherited my Spanish gypsy grandmother's psychic sensibility, I think of myself as part witch, susceptible to visits by the shades of various members of my Spanish family, coaxed from the grave by my fervent prayers and meditations. I pray standing, lying down, walking, and even when sitting on the toilet, making the sign of the cross to excuse my irreverence. Because of my arthritic knees, kneeling is not my favorite position. It hurts too much. So I save that for the heavier stuff like my hypochondriacal cancer scares or my own or my family's financial welfare. The more pain, the more God would know that what I was praying for I really wanted. It was usually at those moments of supplication when my father's ghost would appear, speaking to me as if I were seven years old. "You're such a worrywart. You know that your daddy and the Big Feller up here will never let anything happen to you or the kids."

What follows evolved from a one-woman show about my family that I'd written in 1988. I played all the characters, trying it out in a few places, including living rooms and La Galleria, an annex of La Mama Theatre. In 1990, I did it in Provincetown, Massachusetts, with my ex-husband and his sixth wife, Norris, in the audience. Norman liked it enough to suggest I send it to the Actors Studio in New York where I performed it and was accepted as a member.

Much encouraged, I decided to write act two which would cover age nineteen to the present, an ambitious project considering my age. One draft later, I had my second act. As far as my chances of getting it produced, the hook, naturally, would be my life with Norman from 1951 to 1962.

I wrote about myself as honestly as I could, treading rather cautiously through the more sensational aspects of my marriage. It wasn't solely out of caution that I did so, but also out of necessity since a play could not hold as much pertinent detail as a book.

But I had more fear about the project than I realized, in conflict about how much I wanted to reveal, unconsciously tapping my brakes when it came to writing about the brutal realities contributing to the disintegration of a marriage that ended tragically in 1962, when Norman Mailer almost stabbed me to death during a psychotic break.

I took it into my head to read it to Norman, and I was not quite sure why. Since the material was painful for me, how would it be for him to listen to my account of his psychological deterioration? I knew I wasn't doing it for revenge. In fact, I thought I was doing him a favor by letting him hear it before it became a public reality. While I was writing, I thought of Hamlet's words, "The play's the thing wherein I'll catch the conscience of the King." Was I trying to catch the conscience of my ex-husband? Whatever my reason, nervous or not, I decided to call him.

I said that I wanted to read the second half of my script to him because the center of the play was about everything that happened before and after our divorce, and I thought it only fair that I read it to him before it made the rounds. "I do have a producer," I said, "who's interested, but I don't know what's going to happen. Since I've written it as a one-woman show, rather than sending you a copy to read yourself, I'd like to perform it for you, especially since you were impressed by the first part."

"I don't know, Adele, I am kind of busy." His tone was a shade less than enthusiastic. "How long will it take?" he asked.

"About an hour and a half," I said, "but I don't want to rush it."

There was a long pause before he answered, and I knew he was struggling with his curiosity.

"What about Tuesday?" I pressed.

"This week isn't great. I'm really busy," he repeated.

At this point, I almost backed out. Fuck it, I thought, I'm doing it for his sake, but if he doesn't want it, to hell with it. I can always say I offered.

"Well, okay," he said. "Tuesday it is. Do you want to come here, or should I come to your place?"

"Yours," I said.

It was a long subway ride to Brooklyn Heights, and I was nervous, not looking forward to carving our past down to the bloody bone.

When I arrived, he seemed uncomfortable and a bit gloomy.

"Do you want a drink?" he asked, forgetting that I had been in AA for twenty years. Norris was friendly, as always, and aware of the tension of this rather strange situation. She understood about my reading for Norman alone. After all, it all happened a long time ago, and as far as she was concerned, it bore no relationship to her life or the man she knew today.

I blabbered nervously, repeating how it was only fair that I read the play to him first, before it went anywhere.

"All right," he growled, "you made your point. Let's get on with it."

So here we were, both of us in our sixties facing what neither of us really wanted to do, and why the hell were we doing it? I knew I wasn't going to get his approval on any level since he obviously hated the idea of my writing about the stabbing and what preceded it. Neither did I want a critique of the writing, only because I was not sure he could be objective.

"Let's go downstairs to my secretary's office. It's quieter there."

It was a small room crowded with a desk, a computer, an armchair, and a couch cluttered with the pages of his new manuscript. He pushed some aside to make room for himself. I settled into the chair, took a deep breath, and began my reading. After my initial nervousness, I was beginning to enjoy performing, letting my characters take over.

Norman was the one character I had difficulty with, feeling inhibited about trying to catch his voice and mannerisms. I started to giggle, self-conscious at my bad imitation. "Oh God," I said. "You're impossible to do, just impossible."

"Yeah," he said, "you gotta work on it."

But then I tensed up again as I got more deeply into the play, the coming apart of our marriage, and our wild ride into one destructive situation after another until the bloody ending. I tried to avoid looking at him as I read, but when I did, I could see him frowning, his mouth set against anything he may have been feeling.

I was re-creating some painful scenes for us both. At one point, I thought I saw tears start in his eyes. But they were immediately covered over by a sullen mask.

It ended, and there was a silence in the darkening room, neither of us wanting to look at the other, the fine dust of the memories disturbed by my explosion sifting down upon our heads.

I struggled with a myriad of feelings, none of which were clearly defined for me. Forty-nine years of my life in two hours and now I was feeling a sadness, a deep sense of loneliness, sitting in that little room opposite a figure carved in stone. Wanting to warm that stone, I touched his shoulder. "C'mon Norman," I said tentatively and bent to kiss his cheek. He scowled, turning his head away from me.

In all those years, he had never brought up the stabbing, at least not in any meaningful way. Now I was reaching out to him in that charged silence for a sign of affirmation, some acknowledgment of the past, that our pain and suffering wasn't for nothing. I wanted to hear words like, "Yes, I know what you must have gone through in those years, and I'm sorry for that terrible time. We've lived our separate lives, but we *did* love each other once. We made beautiful children out of that love, and they in turn made beautiful children. So there has to be some sense to it all. Else why are we still on this earth and in this room together?"

I waited for his comment. When Norman was nervous, he had a way of clearing his throat before he spoke. "It was a good reading," he mumbled, "some powerful writing. But there's just one thing." Uh-oh, I thought, here it comes, the big ax. He's going to pick it apart, deny this or that. Instead he said, somewhat to my relief, "Everything is okay except I never said 'fuck' to the maid."

he story of Adele and Norman really begins several years before girl met boy.

When I was nineteen, someone in my art class gave me a New School catalog. I had passed the building a few times in my jaunts through the Village, and I thought about taking a course there. After all, one of my girlfriends said there were a lot of guys studying on the GI Bill. Leafing through, I was impressed by the diversity of the courses listed, fascinated by some of the titles. I decided to pick something by someone I knew nothing about. For me, an easy task.

Anthropological studies, that was it, I thought. Margaret Mead was giving a series of six lectures entitled, "The First Communication, Visceral Sounds of Grunts, Belches, Farting, and Spitting"—at least that's how it came across to me.

The first lecture was in the auditorium. I quickly noticed that there were more women than men in the audience, and that dampened my enthusiasm. One night, before class, I was having coffee in the cafeteria, looking at my reflection in the large mirror behind the counter (I never passed one by). I was aware of a guy sitting next to me, and I watched him in the mirror. Sandy haired, with fair skin and even features, wearing a GI regulation jacket with sergeant's stripes. There was something manly about him, with a bit of the teddy bear at the same time.

Unaware of my staring, he was totally concentrated on blowing and poking at his nose with a tent-sized handkerchief, unfurling it to examine the contents. I was both fascinated and repelled. Was he poking clear up to his brain? I wished he'd stop because he was ruining my fantasy.

But then our eyes met, and he stopped in embarrassment. He laughed apologetically, bobbing his head. "One of those summer colds. I can't get rid of it." He took a sip of his coffee. "Would you pass the sugar, please?"

I smiled. "Cubes or granulated?"

"Cubes, thank you."

I studied my coffee cup, trying to think of an opener. Then I saw him twist around in his seat to stare at a pretty girl walking by. That's that, I thought. He turned towards me, and I was happy to have his attention again.

"Been coming here long?" he asked.

"Not really. This is only my second class."

"Who with?"

"Margaret Mead, she's very good, only she looks like somebody's maiden aunt, not an anthropologist. Imagine that little woman going into all those wild places by herself. What are you taking?"

"I'm a clinical psychology major."

God, I thought, this guy must really be smart. "Really," I said. "You don't look the type."

That seemed to amuse him. He was adorable when he laughed. There was something so good natured and likable about him. I laughed with him. "Oh, you know, steel-rimmed glasses and a long grey beard like those pictures of Freud."

He nodded. "Well, I may have one yet. It could be a long haul. But since I'm on the GI Bill, it could take forever."

"You're lucky," I said, thinking of my little salary. "I have to pay my own way. Whose class are you in tonight?"

"Erich Fromm. He wrote *Escape from Freedom*. Have you read it?"

"I've never heard of Fromm. And why would anyone want to escape from freedom?" I could have bitten my tongue. Why did I say that? He'll think I'm stupid.

"It's a little complicated. I'll explain it to you sometime. I could lend you the book, and we could discuss it." His voice had an intimate coaxing quality, and he looked at me as if I were the only person in the room.

"Yeah, sure, I'd like to read it." I glanced into the mirror again as we talked. We looked good together, his fair handsomeness a foil for my dark good looks. I smiled at him, aware of my sexuality. I knew he wanted me.

"You've got the most beautiful white teeth," he said.

"Oh, thank you. I guess brushing them three times a day helps. It runs in the family, 'cause Daddy has great teeth, too. He likes to crack steak bones, that's why they're so strong and white."

He leaned towards me, looking directly into my eyes. "You look Italian. Are you?"

"No, but you're close. I'm half Spanish. Peruvian Indian on my father's side."

"Really? That's fascinating." He paused. "I bet you get passionate about a lot of things."

I didn't answer. We stared at each other. I laughed nervously and looked away. Oh God, I thought, if he only knew. "Well, it's what they say about Latins, but that's silly. There are all kinds, you know."

I wanted to know more about him. "Where do you live? Are you here in the Village?"

"Just a few blocks away on Eleventh Street, between Sixth and Seventh Avenue."

I brightened. "Oh," I said. "That's one of my favorite blocks in the Village. It looks like the pictures I've seen of New Orleans, with all those white wrought-iron balconies."

"Yeah," he said, "I've got a room in one of those houses."

"Oh, I envy you. I still live with my family in Brooklyn. It's not so bad, except my mother gives me a pain, especially when it comes to my wanting to leave and live in the Village. She won't let me." I looked at my watch. "Wow, I'll be late to my class." I held out my hand. "Well, it's nice meeting you." I laughed. "I don't know your name."

"Ed Fancher," he said. "What's yours?"

I gathered up my books. "Adele Morales."

"Listen," he said, "could I call you sometime? Maybe we can get together for a movie or something?"

I was pleased, but I tried to be cool. "Yeah, I'd like that."

We chatted a bit more, and when it was over, he had my phone number, and I had my hopes he would call.

Chapter 2

About a week after I met Ed Fancher, I went to a New School folk dance with a friend. We got some Cokes and sat down at a corner table. It was a small, crowded dance floor, couples swinging around to a hot polka. I tapped my feet to the rhythm, scanning the room for a likely partner. I hadn't heard from Ed yet, and I was hoping he would be here. A man came toward our table, wearing a black-leather flight jacket, plaid shirt, and dungarees and, with a courtly little bow, asked me to dance.

"I just came in," he said, taking off his jacket. "I saw you, and I wanted to get to you before anyone else did."

He could have been a movie star with that kind of dark good looks. Short and stocky, not fat, but solid with a strong body and good shoulders. He had even features, black hair and grey eyes and a beautifully shaped mouth.

Without introducing himself, or even asking my name, he lifted me from my chair, grabbed me around my waist, giving a loud cowboy yahoo. I waved goodbye to my friend, and off we galloped. He danced furiously, whirling me about the room so fast my feet were off the ground, my energy matching his.

"I'm Jack," he said above the din. "Let's go somewhere quiet."

By now I'd had enough of the polka, so I nodded. "Adele's my name, and I feel the same."

He laughed. "Are you a poet?"

"Yes," I said, "but I don't know it."

He finished, "because your feet are Longfellows." We laughed together, and I liked him immediately.

I looked around for my friend, but she was dancing, so we left, heading for San Remo on MacDougal Street. Like me, he knew his way around the Village. He ordered a beer, and a Coke for me. Now that we were away from the noise and the dancing, we had to make conversation.

"So, what's your last name, Jack?"

"Kerouac," he said.

"Oh, really? You don't look like an Eskimo."

He laughed. "Why did you say that?"

"Because your name has an Eskimo sound to it, especially the last three letters."

"How many Eskimos do you know?"

"Well," I said, "not any, but a friend of mine had an Eskimo girlfriend by the name of Rachel Inactook."

"Well, you're not too far off. I'm a Canuck."

"What's a Canuck?" I asked.

"That's what they call a French Canadian. What the hell, there are a few Eskimos running around in northern Canada, so maybe you're right. You know, I like that name."

Picking up two spoons, he began drumming on the table, chanting the three names over and over to the rhythm of the beat, "Kerouac, Inactook, Canuck," like he was going into a trance. Then he got up from his seat, shuffling his feet in the sawdust in an odd little dance, repeating the names in the same beat.

God, I thought, looking around the bar, why doesn't this nut sit down? But this was the Village and nobody cared.

Finally he did sit down, pleased with himself. "I just invented an Eskimo dance."

Without asking me if I wanted another Coke, he got himself another beer. He's cheap, I thought. Either that or he's down to his last nickel and really needed that drink. So I didn't mention I was still thirsty. He took a small notebook from his jacket and began to write. I sat there watching him, trying to read upside down. He took a long time, and I got annoyed at his rudeness. I wanted him to concentrate on me. "Man," I said, "what are you writing? Is that about me?"

"No, I just got an idea for my book."

"You didn't tell me you were a writer."

"So, now you know," he said, putting the notebook back in his pocket. I looked at him with new interest.

"Have you ever published?"

"No, this is my first novel, and I know someone will publish it, because I'm a damn good writer." I admired his conviction, envying that belief he seemed to have about his writing. "You haven't told me your last name," he said.

"It's Morales."

"What nationality are you?"

"You gotta be kidding, Jack. I'm Spanish, at least half of me is."

"And what else?"

"Peruvian, Indian." I had never liked to admit to my Indian heritage before, but it seemed to go over in the Village. It must have intrigued him. Leaning across the table, he framed my face in his hands. I closed my eyes and waited for him to kiss me.

"Now I see the Indian. It's there in the slant and the sadness of your eyes. You're very beautiful, you know, like an exotic tropical flower."

Not too original, I thought, for a writer, but the compliment pleased me. That was the last bit of attention I got because Jack talked incessantly about himself. Then he told me about his friend, Lucien Carr, whom he'd met at Columbia. Carr had stabbed another student to death in a park on Riverside Drive. Afterward, he had gone to Jack for help. The first thing Jack told him was to get rid of the knife by dropping it down a subway grate. As a result, Jack was picked up and booked as an accessory and released on bail. That all happened about a year before our meeting. It should have been a warning to me to stay away from this guy, but I didn't take it seriously, and for me, it added to his glamour.

Jack talked a lot about his mother. Memére, he said, was a wonderful woman who believed in his writing. He could always go home to her when he was broke or tired or needed a quiet place to cool down and work. She would clean for him and tirelessly cook his favorite dishes. He talked about her the way a guy would go on and on about a woman he'd fallen in love with.

By now I began to think of the long subway ride home. "Jack, I gotta go. It's getting late."

"Don't worry, I'll see you home. Where do you live?"

"In Brooklyn, with my parents, but I hope not for long."

"Why not? Don't you like them?"

"Yeah, they're okay."

It was late, and I didn't want to get into my long list of complaints, so I just said that it was too far from my life in the Village.

When the Sea Beach Express got to the bridge, Jack acted as if he'd never crossed over before, getting all excited about the river view. He jumped out of his seat—Jack never rose from a sitting position as much as he goosed himself into the air. Rushing up and down the subway car, looking out the windows, rambling incoherently in that nonstop poetic, Thomas Wolfe style. I wondered if he wrote like that. I had just started reading Wolfe and really loved him.

Jack had seemed pretty calm all night until now. Could he have popped something when I wasn't looking? People were staring at him, and I was embarrassed, but I did look at the view with new eyes, having been jaded out with all the dreary crossings every day. He even got some passengers to look up from their newspapers and out the window.

We walked down the dark, quiet, tree-lined streets to my door.

"Jesus, where the hell am I?" It was late, and his poetry was gone. "I'll never find my way back."

"You can't go home again, Jack."

He laughed. "Well, in that case, can I come in for a cup of coffee?"

"God, no, Jack. Everyone is asleep." Lucky for him, I thought. He kissed me good night, and I decided I wanted to see him again.

"I'll call you," he said. "And by the way, I like Brooklyn."

Laughing, I said "You would, you don't have to live here."

He did call, inviting me to a lecture at the New School. He said he would bring his manuscript of "The Town and the City" for me to read. I would be the first woman to read it. Before his mother? I thought. True or not, I was flattered and excited about seeing this strange young man again.

I took the manuscript home after the lecture. Mama saw me reading. "Where did you get that?"

"From a friend of mine, it's his first novel."

She leafed through it. The pronouncement came in three seconds. "He ain't no Dickens." She handed it back. "A writer, that's all you need, you'll live in poverty the rest of your life. Does he do anything else?"

"He's a merchant seaman."

"Oh my God, another one, it's gettin' worse. By the way, Louis Scalia called. Aren't you going to see him again? He's so nice, so well mannered, and he's got a good job."

"Ma, you call running a cement mixer a good job?"

"But he's crazy about you."

"Ma, he bores me. He's a jerk."

"So at least he's a nice jerk, and an ex-marine to boot."

"Who cares, just leave me alone," and I went to bed.

Obviously Jack had talent as a writer, with a lyrical sense of language, but sometimes I got impatient with his overblown prose. If Thomas Wolfe was his influence, he should have sat down and had a couple of drinks with Hemingway. Jack had played football at Columbia, and his descriptive passages of the game were the best writing in the book, I thought. That I could even read about football was a real compliment from me, since I disliked the game so much.

A few days later, we met at the San Remo. "So, what did you think?" he asked.

I decided to be as honest as I could. "It's a good first effort, Jack." I liked this phrase, which I had heard somewhere, but when I said it, it sounded condescending. I went on to say why I was bored by most of it, enjoying the sound of my own voice, not noticing how dark his face was getting.

He slammed his beer mug down on the table so hard he broke the handle. "Fuck you," he said, picking up the manuscript. "What do you know. Allen Ginsberg thinks it's a great novel."

"Who's Allen Ginsberg?"

"Only the greatest poet in the world."

"You're a sore loser, Jack. You can't take criticism."

His face reddened.

"And you're a bitch." He was up from the table and out the door, leaving me to pay the check.

I felt badly. Maybe I should have lied, but the words would have stuck in my throat. I was tempted to run after him, to apologize. Apologize for what? I thought. I didn't say I disliked the whole book. Anyway, he shouldn't have called me a bitch, so fuck him, let him go, he'll get over it.

Two weeks went by, and I didn't hear from him. I was conceited enough to believe that it wasn't his dented ego, but another trip out to sea that kept him from calling.

I had begun seeing Ed Fancher, so I wasn't sitting by the phone. With Jack and me, it had been a few dates and some kisses, nothing beyond that.

He said he was in love with me, which was pretty quick for so short a time together. True or not, it satisfied my vanity. I might have even said the same to him. I don't recall. He never really pushed it, and I had the feeling he was afraid of a really passionate involvement then. Jack's self-absorption bored me. I felt there was so much of an innocent in Jack. He tried so hard to be hip, but he was basically a nice guy.

As young as I was, I recognized his talent. I was on my own road, though, so his vision didn't interest me, nor did his over-heated prose.

Chapter 3

I became more and more involved with Ed Fancher, and it would be a few more years before I would see Jack again. Ed was my first real love.

The first time I slept with Ed, it was in his rented room on Eleventh Street. I had to tiptoe up the five flights because his landlady had said no to women visitors. I trusted Ed, making the decision to give myself completely to him. That first time, I pressed down on him, oblivious of the pain, wanting only to come with him, loving him inside me. He was wonderful, patient, and understanding, holding me afterward, telling me how beautiful I was.

Even more than sex, I needed tenderness, and Ed was that and more. Afterward I looked at myself in the mirror, without shame, liking what I saw, a woman in love who had given her virginity, passionately and fully. Looking at my mouth, I thought of Ed tracing it with his fingers, loving the shape and the pleasure it gave him.

We saw each other as much as we could, without arousing my mother's suspicions. She knew I was seeing Ed, but she had no idea how serious it was. We usually met at the Waldorf Cafeteria on Sixth Avenue and Eighth Street. In a way, it was the first coffeehouse in the Village, before the Rienzi. It was a hangout for me and my best friend, Sylvia Roseni.

Sylvia was an artist. She hung out with some Communist pals at the Waldorf. It was a gathering place for painters, would-be painters, writers, intellectuals of every type, who could argue for hours over a nickel cup of coffee.

My mother heard me on the phone one day. "See you at the Waldorf, Ed."

"Well," she said, "this guy must have money. He's taking you to the Waldorf-Astoria. What're you gonna wear, honey?"

"Ma," I said, "it's not the Waldorf-Astoria. It's the Waldorf Cafeteria."

She was disappointed. "I might have known. He's a cheapskate."

Ed helped me make some major changes in my life. He got me my first diaphragm and picked my first therapist, Dr. Gotthard Booth. He even found me a cold-water flat for sixteen dollars a month. I was making thirty-five a week at Gimbels, but with some careful budgeting, I could manage.

Living at home was now impossible, especially since I was really in love. I couldn't get along with my kid sister or my father, and my mother least of all. In desperation, I had talked to her about seeing Dr. Booth. She had already decided to hate him, but I was willing to try anything with the hope that he could persuade her that moving out was the right thing for me to do. At first she refused, but I threatened, cajoled, and nagged her until she relented.

The day of her appointment, she got all dressed up, passing my inspection. She had her hair marcelled and had gotten a manicure. Mama was proud of her long red-painted fingernails, nagging me about my bitten-down ones. She picked out her nicest frock, a Gloria Swanson-type turban, and her black ankle-strap shoes, pinning on her favorite cameo pin.

"You look nice, Ma, but the charm bracelets don't go with the rest of your outfit. Take them off."

"Certainly not, whither I goest, they goest."

I laughed. "Is that supposed to be Shakespeare?"

"Of course, don't you know it when you hear it?" Fortified by a couple of shots of whiskey, she was ready to go into enemy territory.

I couldn't wait for her to get back, but the minute I saw her face, I knew it hadn't worked. Doctor Booth was probably no match for her. "Well," she said, "I gave that frog-faced Nazi a piece of my mind, and it cost me ten bucks, too. Gotthard? I'll bet. Ha, ha."

In spite of this, I made up my mind to leave home. I took the apartment Ed had found for me. I would give my mother only a day's notice. When the moment came, I took a deep breath.

"Ma, with or without your permission, I'm leaving. I'm going to be an artist, and that means living on my own."

She took a puff from her cigarette, blowing smoke into my face. Here we go again, I thought. "You think you're finally going to get your own way." I could see one of those rages that had frightened me so as a child. Not until years later did I realize that they were fueled by her drinking.

"Well, you're not. Where is it? Goddamn it, tell me."

"I can't, Ma, not just yet, but I promise I'll call you as soon as I get settled."

"Settled," she yelled, "settled," and she took a plate and smashed it against the wall. "Don't make me laugh. The only dump you'll settle in is your own room. You're not capable of living by yourself, you're so goddamn naive. And you know what? You're under legal age, that's what." By now she was screaming. "Wait till your father gets home. He'll lock you up." The screaming slid into sobs, and her hands were shaking as she lit another cigarette. "Between your father's floozies and you, I'm goin' crazy."

That's another thing, I thought, I won't have to live in a chimney anymore. Look at her puffing away, she hasn't finished the last one. I wondered where she left the other butt. Maybe she'd burn the place down, that would fix everything.

She swept up the smashed pieces, sobbing uncontrollably. I felt sorry for her, and I started to cry myself. "Mama, please don't cry. It's not that I don't love you, but you just gotta let go. I'll be all right."

She wiped her eyes on her apron and blew her nose. She looked at me, and her face was set. "Joanie's the only daughter I got left."

The next afternoon, I packed one suitcase, my portable record player, which was a Christmas present from my parents, my collection of Glenn Miller and Harry James, most of them presents from my father. I took my Mozart and Bach recordings and a small chintz-covered armchair from my bedroom. I took my paints and easel, my roller skates, Shirley Temple doll, and finally, Teddy, my beautiful Persian with his carrying case. That day I was wearing my Village uniform, dungarees, a Mexican peasant blouse, and my new diaphragm. Ed was coming to get me in his pickup truck.

He ran a small moving business in spite of the fact that his father owned part of the Middletown, New York, Telephone Company and got a sizable allowance. He neglected to tell me this, so I always assumed he was a struggling student like myself, gladly sharing expenses, paying my half for movies and our Sunday lamb dinner at the Automat.

Ed had never met my family, but I prepared him for the worst, still hoping by some miracle, that they would behave. I just wanted to get it over with. Not only did I have to contend with my parents, there were my grandparents, too. What a picture.

Grandma was on her knees praying for me. "Aye, aye, aye, Dios mío. Qué pasa con este, muchacha, me aguelita. Vas a volver una puta y romper el corazón de tu Madre. Ave María Sanctissima," and she crossed herself.

She was saying that I would become a whore and break my mother's heart. It made me angry that all their objections had to do with sex, instead of being concerned about whether I'd be able to support myself. They worried that I'd become a whore and, God forbid, have a good time doing it. What a bunch of actors, I thought. "Please, Grandma, get up. You're making things worse."

Mama had mixed herself a pitcher of martinis, pacing the length of the apartment with a drink in her hand. "You can put that stuff back cause you're not going."

"Yes I am, Dr. Booth says . . . "

She cut me off. "You better not mention that Nazi's name to me. It's all his fault my baby's leaving the nest. I'm gonna sue him."

"Ma, it's got nothing to do with Booth. I do have a mind of my own. Besides, Ed and I love each other."

She turned from speaking to me to addressing the wall. "Get her, she's in love. Ain't that sweet," and back to me, "You'll find out about love. That bum Ed, he's to blame for all this," forgetting she had already put all the blame on Dr. Booth.

"Make up your mind, Ma, who's to blame?" By that time, Ed had arrived with his truck. There was a huge scene, and everybody joined in—my mother, my sister Joanie, Daddy, and even Grandpa, who actually turned out to see things my way.

We finally got everything loaded up and drove off. I looked back at the house until it was out of sight. My negativity started to operate again. Am I doing the right thing? Suppose I lose my job? Suppose I can't pay the rent? Suppose we break up, what then? I wouldn't blame him after this scene, but I'm not my family, I thought. I'm different. Ed put his arm around me. There was something so solid about him, so reassuring.

"You'll be all right, darling. You're with me." I snuggled against him. "They sure are excitable," he said.

I laughed. "Excitable? They're crazy."

"Well, I can see why you had to do it, and I'm proud of you, Delski." When we crossed the bridge, I knew it was final and that I could never go home again. But Ed was there, and we loved each other. I could take care of myself, and Ed, of course, would take care of me.

That night I sat in my three-room apartment, my few belongings looking lost in the center of the room. Teddy was warm and comforting in my lap. I felt badly about taking him away from my sister, but after all, I was going to be by myself, and I needed him. He let out a hungry meow. He felt the strangeness, too.

I looked around the grungy rooms. "This apartment is all mine, Teddy, and I can do anything I want."

I was thrilled, thinking about how I would fix it up. It was a cold-water flat all right, because it was freezing. "I'll have to buy a kerosene stove tomorrow." I had to pee, and then I remembered, "Oh God, the fucking john is in the hall." It was dim, and the bathroom was dirty. "Ugh, how many people are using it? Well, I'll clean it tomorrow, and from now on, no drinking water before bedtime."

I tried the stove. It was ancient, but it worked. Mama should see this big bathtub in the kitchen. It was one of those old-fashioned claw-footed ones. She'd have a fit, but I loved it. I could eat and bathe at the same time. My neighbors' bedroom was about six feet away from mine, separated by a garbage-littered courtyard.

There was the sound of a violent argument between a couple.

I slammed the window shut, but I could still hear them. Oh my God, what am I going to do? Am I going to hear that all the time? I might as well have stayed home. In a few minutes, it was quiet. Either they had passed out or he had murdered her. What's the difference, I thought? I'll be at Ed's most of the time, but just the same, I was depressed, and the apartment suddenly looked impossibly dreary. Even having a bathtub in the kitchen had lost its charm.

The only sound was the ticking of the clock on the floor. I sighed. Seven o'clock, they're just sitting down to supper. I thought of my mother crying in the doorway, but then I remembered that she'd thrown my easel out like a piece of garbage. "Fuck 'em," I said. "I don't care if I never see them again. Come on, Teddy, we're going over to Ed's."

I climbed two flights to the roof, crossing over to the connecting building into Ed's apartment. For the first time, I could spend the night and make him breakfast. He was so sweet, and being with him, I was happy again. I loved him so much. It would be all right, and tomorrow I would start to fix up my apartment. My Village life had begun for real. Brooklyn and my family were behind me.

Chapter 4

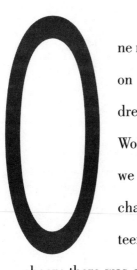ne night, after work, I met Ed at the San Remo
on McDougal Street, a hangout for artists,
dreamers, and drunks. He was bringing Dan
Wolf, his best friend, to meet me. Afterward,
we were going to supper at La Bilbaina, a
charming little Spanish restaurant on Four-
teenth Street. The food was plentiful and
cheap; there was even a dessert cart, and you could order a
three-course meal for two dollars.

Dan arrived, and I shook hands with a very thin, dark young man with a face that was difficult to read. We instinctively liked each other. Dan was another intellectual, in the true sense of the word, and I loved his wry sense of humor, often directed at himself. He was a warm and a marvelous listener, and even made me feel that what I had to say was important. Dan hated phoniness, and I think he sensed the real person in me, and I felt he was special.

We knew a lot of bright, articulate people, and there were interesting discussions. I was shy and unsure of myself, so I rarely expressed my own ideas. That is, when I had them. I heard names I didn't know—Philip Wylie, author of *Generation of Vipers*, Nietzsche, Schopenhauer, Kant, Kafka, Sartre, Aldous Huxley, Theodore Reik, and a dizzying number of others. When it came to discussing painters, I was more knowledgeable, so I was less shy.

Alone with Ed and Dan, I felt cared for, and I blossomed and could be my funny, rather ingenuous, self. We were comrades, going to Village parties, art openings, and movies, sharing classics like Carl Dreyer's, *The Passion of Joan of Arc*, and of course *Les Enfants du Paradis* with the beautiful Arletty. Dan was a tireless walker, like myself, and we enjoyed strolling the Wall Street area on Sundays when the streets were deserted.

It was my first ménage à trois, but not sexual, or at least not overtly sexual. Later on, it seemed that most of the men I fell in love with always had a close friend, and luckily we liked each other. The friends were always a little in love with me, not enough to cause trouble, but enough to make me feel good.

Everything seemed to be falling into place. I was the happiest I had ever been. I had left Gimbels, and I liked my job as a papier-mâché artist in a display studio. At the end of each day,

I would change from my paint and paste-spattered work clothes into my Village uniform, to which I had added silver hoop earrings. In the winter, I wore black Capezios and in the summer, my handmade Grecian sandals from Raymond Duncan, Isadora's brother, whose shop was on MacDougal Street. I would see him walking around the Village often with movie actor Lionel Stander, and poet and writer Maxwell Bodenheim. Winter or summer, Raymond wore a flowing white toga with a silver band encircling his shoulder-length white hair.

One morning, I came to work, and there was a new girl there, an actress and painter, Emily Stevens. We became friends, and she invited me to her own cold-water flat to meet her roommate, José Quintero. He was a tall, handsome Panamanian, with beautiful dark eyes that looked at you from a deep, painful past and a smile that lit up his face. He was rather shy, with an inner elegance, and one felt he came from an aristocratic background.

He shared Emily's passion for the theater and having been in New York for just a few years, still spoke English with a strong Spanish accent. I tried my Spanish on him. My accent was good, but my vocabulary sadly limited.

When I was leaving, he gave me a little gift, one of those old seven-inch records. It was a current hit in Latin America, titled "Adelita." He played it, swaying me into a meringue, singing the words to me. I only remember the first line "Adelita con quien se fueron . . . Adelita who did you run away with."

I laughed and flirted back. "Why, with José, of course."

I knew Ed would like Emily and José, so I invited them, along with other artist friends I wanted Ed to meet, to a party at his apartment.

I offered to cook, but I was just a beginner and not very good. Naturally I was nervous. Fish was cheap, so I decided on flounder, rolling the fillets in cornflakes and throwing them into a pot of melted lard. I used the same oil to deep-fry the bananas, serving them as a side dish, a mistake since they tasted fishy. It didn't seem like enough, so I made chili, hot enough to make people gasp.

The food was awful, but no matter, there was plenty of wine to cool off with, and it didn't spoil the party. Nobody got drunk or high on drugs. This was a companionship of artists and intellectuals with a few bums who didn't do anything but be amusing. I remember how vital we all were, interested participants in the life around us, in the urgency of the moment. The high point of the party was the sound of José's beautiful reading in Spanish of García Lorca's poem "En el Cinco de la Tarde" about Spain's most famous bullfighter Manolete, who was gored to death in the ring at five in the afternoon.

The poem had a special meaning for me. When I was sixteen, I had made a trip with my family, to see my relatives in Lima, Peru. It was there I saw my first bullfight, feeling an immediate passion for the spectacle. We were lucky to see Manolete fight that day, and I remember shouting "Olé" with the crowd as he made one brilliant pass after another.

At that time, or shortly after, Quintero was directing an unknown actress by the name of Geraldine Page in Tennessee Williams's *Summer and Smoke*, in a little theater in Woodstock, New York. He and Ted Mann, a lawyer friend, had not yet started the Village theater, Circle in the Square. José asked Ed to move some sets upstate. I went along with Emily, helping to paint the set and making papier-mâché trees. At the time, none of us could know, José included, how far he was to go as the definitive director of the work of Eugene O'Neill.

ost nights I stayed with Ed, but I kept my own apartment. A friend needed a place to live so we split the rent. Eight dollars a month each for a three-room apartment! Like me, she was with her boyfriend most of the time. So the very few nights I slept there rarely coincided with hers, and our only contact was through notes we wrote and pinned on the door.

Those early times with Ed were happy. This was my first, passionate love affair, and we couldn't get enough of each other. I thought he was wonderful, sexually and in other ways, but then again, he was the only man I'd ever had.

There were all those attractive guys on the GI Bill at the New School, and being a flirt by nature, I was tempted. But for me, loving someone meant being faithful. My father had been something of a philanderer, and I had seen what it did to my family. I wanted no part of it.

I would tell Ed how much I loved him, but it was months before he could do the same, though I never doubted he loved me back. When the stubborn bastard finally said it, we went out and celebrated. It was an intense relationship, and like all lovers, there were occasional fights, nothing serious, not at that time anyway.

Ed was a calm and rational foil for my excitable, or should I say hysterical, nature. I had a short fuse and a need for drama, and like my favorite heroine, Carmen, I switched my hips around, screamed, and threw things, usually at Ed, both of us laughing afterward. And, of course, there was that special lovemaking after the fight.

I knew it was serious when he suggested we drive up to Middletown to meet his parents and his sisters, Ginny and Cynthia. I was a little nervous about it, but Ed gave me a reassuring hug. "Delski, you'll be fine. They'll like you."

So, off we went in his rattly pickup truck. He wore his baggy army fatigues and I, my cleanest dungarees, a plaid blouse instead of my blue denim work shirt, and my new penny loafers.

We arrived at a setting from out of all those forties Andy Hardy movies I had cut my teeth on. When I was a kid, I dreamt of living in a white gingerbread-trimmed Victorian house with a cupola, a front porch, and a white picket fence, on a street lined with ancient elms.

When we arrived, it was all there for me. I oohed and ahhed, envying Ed the times he had growing up there. When I met his parents, I'm sure they didn't quite know what to think of me since my background was so different. But I was Ed's girl, so I was accepted, a black dahlia in a field of daisies.

The family was definitely "Waspy," but Ed wasn't, and I wondered how he'd escaped it. The house was comfortably furnished, with lots of polished mahogany, some beautiful oak knickknack cabinets, antimacassars placed carefully on all the chairs and the overstuffed chintz-covered couch. I felt a sense of order and calm about the place.

We sat down to dinner, the table set with his mother's company china. I was careful of my table manners, trying not to gulp my food nervously, remembering to use a piece of bread instead of my fingers to push peas onto my fork. I was quiet, feeling shy, answering an occasional polite question from his parents. Ed did most of the talking. I looked at him as he spoke, thinking how handsome he was, how smart, and how much I loved him, feeling safe in this place where he had been a little boy.

I liked his sister Ginny, who was about my age, and her all-American boyfriend, Don. I talked to them about my painting and the Village, not about my family.

Mrs. Fancher was an agreeable, mild-mannered lady, speaking in a soft voice with an air of being somewhere else. She rarely disagreed with anything that was said, and if she did, it was in a tentative voice. But I sensed the anger beneath her crown of beautiful red hair. "Junior," she said, "would you like some more roast beef?" My God, I thought, Ed was a Junior? I almost laughed out loud.

Ed resembled his father, who was a rotund, balding Buddha-like figure with a secret little smile playing at the corner of his mouth as if he were laughing inwardly at some mysterious joke. He was cordial, and when he spoke to me, he had that same glint in his eye as his son. He didn't pinch my rear, but I'll bet he thought about it.

I was impressed by the way the family spoke to each other, and though I sensed some tension between Ed and his dad, they were all so polite. Nobody yelled, and everyone was calm. Ed's biggest complaint was that he came from a repressed family. I should have been so lucky.

As the evening ended, I wondered about the sleeping arrangements. Ed had never suggested we share a room, since, obviously, his family would have been shocked. So I sneaked into his room that night.

We continued to visit Middletown, and most weekends we would stay at an unfinished shack his family was building in the woods. I loved going there, driving up from the city with our friends piled in the truck. We would rough it, sleeping on cots, no sheets, just army blankets and no bathroom, just an outhouse in the woods.

Everyone had a good time. There was laughter and talk among some bright people, with very little drinking. We all pitched in to do the cooking, enjoying a huge pot of great macaroni salad that was often Mrs. Fancher's weekend contribution. To this day, my daughters and I use the same recipe.

Ed enjoyed camping and hiking, and so did I. We both were Scouts when we were kids. I remember the first mountain we climbed in the Poconos and the first time I'd ever made love in a sleeping bag under the stars. It was magic, and even as I write this, I have an intense longing to have those days back, when we were young and in love and in some ways so innocent.

Ed was still working toward his masters in psychology, and I was busy with my job and painting. We had many friends, painters, writers, psych majors, and perpetual students on the GI Bill, trekking though Ed's apartment, bringing their problems to Daddy Fancher. Sometimes Ed would get so involved, I would be jealous.

"Why don't you get yourself a leather couch?" I said. "You're already in practice."

I could only afford a weekly visit to Dr. Booth whereas Ed was getting the works, a Freudian depth-charge analysis four times a week on the couch with Dr. Berger, a walking, tight-lipped zombie with a thick German accent.

I was jealous of the couch. I had to sit up like all the proletariat and face Dr. Booth. I wanted to know why I couldn't lie down.

"It's preferable for you," he said, "to be in a more confrontational position." Sure, I thought, and less work for him. I liked to wear low-cut dresses to my sessions, because it was fun to watch his eyes slide toward and away from my cleavage.

Between Ed and me, we totaled twenty hours a month of agonizing soul searching. We were really into it, analyzing everything and everybody. I would laugh, saying that I could put out a shingle. My approach would be unique since I didn't know anything, but still thought of people as human beings.

Wilhelm Reich was giving a series of lectures at the New School and, of course, Ed and Dan were going. They invited me, and I sat between them not understanding much, since the language was highly technical.

At the time, Reich's "orgone" boxes were fashionable, and a few people in the Village had them. A good friend, Dick Williams, had built one, and if Ed wanted, he would give him the formula. It was made up of alternate layers of zinc, wood, and other odds and ends. Dick gave an orgone-box party. We were to take turns sitting in a rectangular box, locked from the outside. Why I don't know, but I volunteered to be first, sitting there in my bra and panties for half an hour.

There was nothing to read. "Hey guys," I yelled, "this is boring. Get me a magazine."

"Forget it," Dick said. "If you open the door, you'll lose orgone energy. Just stay with your own thoughts." Good thing I'm not claustrophobic, I thought, stifling an impulse to scream.

It seemed like more than half an hour, and I could hear the clink of glasses and the sound of laughter in the other room. I wondered if they had forgotten about me. So far, I felt nothing. No one, including Dick, knew exactly what you were supposed to feel.

I knocked on the box. "Is it time yet?" No one answered. I was getting nervous. What the hell were they doing? I guess they didn't hear me. "Hey," I shouted, "my time must be up."

"Five more minutes," Dick answered.

"This is silly," I said, and at that moment, I felt a slight tingle in my arms and legs, and my face got hot. Was it anxiety or was it the box? I banged again. "Okay, I'm ready, let me out."

"How was it, how do you feel?" Ed asked.

"Hungry," I said. "You got any bagels?"

I was totally committed to our relationship, but I was not so sure that Ed was. For four years, we had practically lived together, but I still had my apartment. I wanted him to ask me to give it up and move in with him. Ed had had a brief marriage before he met me. If he did it once, he could do it again and do it better with me. I wanted that, but he didn't.

We began to quarrel more often, presumably over silly things, but we both knew what those fights were really about. He was busier at school, or so he said, and there were other women. I found a strand of blonde hair under the couch cushions. I was upset, but I tried to rationalize it. After all, we had a lot of people up there.

I didn't know it at the time, but he'd been seeing a very attractive girl behind my back, someone I was acquainted with. I think she was a social worker or something of that sort. She was a blonde, so I guess that the hair was hers. The worst of it was when I found a pair of panties under the bed. I knew they weren't mine.

"Whose are these, you bastard?" I wanted to take a scissors and slash the panties and his face.

"Now Delski, calm down," he said. "They're yours."

"Mine, like hell, look at the size of them. They belong to some big fat ugly woman, like Sandra." He knew who I was talking about. Sandra had been sucking around Ed at the New School, insinuating herself into our crowd. She wasn't even an artist.

Ed's voice lost that warm timbre that I loved. It was a cold voice now that I'd heard quite often in the last few months. "Delski," he said, "we'll discuss it later. I'll be late for my class."

"No, I want to talk about it now," I said, "or I won't be here when you get back. I mean that."

Ed took a deep breath. "Delski, it's not working out between us. Maybe it would be better if we took some time off."

I stood there, feeling as if I'd been punched in the stomach. Tears filled my eyes. True, we had been quarreling a lot, but I couldn't believe he had said that. "I thought you loved me." And then came his usual rationalizations.

"I still do," he said, "but you know how I've been trying to work through my oedipal fixation and my fear of commitment."

The pain I'd been feeling turned to rage, and I said, "How about anal retentive, don't leave that one out. You and your jargon, I'm bored to death with it. Speaka da English. If you love someone, you get married, and you don't fuck around. I haven't, but don't kid yourself, Ed. You have no idea how many guys I could have had, including a few so-called pals of yours. But I didn't, not loyal little Adele."

"Like who?" he said.

"Boy, oh boy," I smirked, "wouldn't you like to know? You know what your problem is, Ed? You're dead inside, you can't feel anything, but you sure can pretend." I was really digging in. "My God, you've been with the same shrink, lying on that fucking couch for six years. What the hell do you talk about three times a week? Einstein's theory of relativity?" By now I was yelling, and I could barely keep from hitting his smug, psychoanalyst's face, looking at me as if I were some crazy patient. "Why don't you try being honest for a change and tell Berger about your stinginess, your pornography collection, and the way you still blow your nose and wave the snot under people's faces?"

He walked out the door and down the stairs. I ran into the hall after him. "That's right, run away. What's the matter, can't you take the truth, you fucking coward? I hate you, and I'm leaving." I slammed the rickety door after him with such force I almost broke it.

My legs felt weak, the pain in my gut was intolerable. I sat down at the kitchen table, and my darling Teddy jumped on my lap. It was very still, and the only sound was his purring vibrating through my legs. He looked at me with his beautiful green eyes, and I could see the love in them.

Oh God, I forgot to feed him, and I broke down and wept and wept into Teddy's warm grey fur. I gathered my things and put

Teddy in his case. I've had enough of four in our bed—Berger, Booth, Fancher, and Morales—except for my name, it sounded like a law firm. I was angry all over again, remembering how I still had to pay my half of everything, even after three years.

Every day was the same, I would awaken in the morning, my being flooded with a sense of loss. The same dull ache in my gut would return. I wanted to go back to sleep, blot it all out. But there was my job, and my rent to pay. I missed Ed terribly, and I couldn't believe he was no longer a part of my life. The thought that he was with someone else and that she might be with him at that very moment drove me from thoughts of suicide to thoughts of murder.

Ed lived next door, but might as well have been on the moon. How could he let four years go just like that? What did I do wrong? Was it because I wasn't smart enough, pretty enough, too dependent, too insecure? Was it because I was so quiet during all those intellectual discussions, not daring to open my mouth because I might say something stupid? The tape would play endlessly, and in my mind, I was getting smaller and smaller and he, bigger and bigger. The anger would alternate with my sorrow, and I hated him. But still, I wanted him back.

Dan Wolf tried to comfort me. He was still my friend. "Don't worry, kid. This isn't a permanent breakup." But my soul knew it was over.

I was all cried out. I had to get away from the apartment, even if it was for a dinner by myself. I was dressed, but I had to repair my face. I looked at myself, and in spite of my anguish, I was reassured by what I saw in the mirror. He hadn't taken away my looks. I splashed my face with cold water and put on my lipstick. The pain was replaced by anger, a much more welcome emotion. I thought, the next one will find out what he's really like, the cheap son of a bitch. I locked the door behind me.

Dan Wolf called, asking me to meet him one evening at the New School. He was with a friend, Steve Sanchez, from Mexico City. Latin men did not interest me, but I liked Steve as I liked most of Dan's friends. He had the dark, brooding beauty of an Aztec priest, slender with an aquiline nose and luminous dark eyes. When he looked at me, I could feel that anything was possible.

Like me, his face showed a mixture of Indian and Spanish. In fact, Steve resembled my father, both in looks and temperament. Unlike my father, he rarely laughed, but when he did, one sensed the pain and rage beneath the laughter, a rage that was easily triggered.

He was very bright, but essentially humorless. He took himself too seriously. If he had been an actor, he would have been cast as the tragic matador in *Blood and Sand*, overnight a new Valentino.

Having been told by Dan about my Latin background, Steve was surprised that I didn't speak more Spanish. But his English was quite good, so there was no problem. When he asked to see me again, I found it easy to say yes because I was seeing as many guys as I could, trying to still the hurt that was gnawing at me— patching up my damaged ego at the same time.

That first night he came back to my apartment, and we made love. I felt a desperate heat, a need to drown myself in a fuck, to have the hurt and anger pounded out of me. I had orgasm after orgasm, but I gave nothing from deep inside. We were well matched, Steve and me, two desperadoes riding out the night.

A few days later, over morning coffee, I told him quite gently that I loved having him stay over, but he snored all night, and I couldn't sleep. That released a tirade. "Why do you bring that up?

So what does something like that matter between a man and a woman who have made love all night? Besides, you exaggerate."

"I'm sorry, Steve, I didn't mean to offend you. It's not a crime, maybe you have a deviated septum." But he sulked anyway, and I was bleary eyed when I left for work.

We met another night at Dan's apartment where Steve was staying. Dan was having dinner with Ed, so we were alone, and we went to bed. Afterward, Steve asked me if I would mind if he did some important errand, saying it would take a couple of hours because he had to go all the way up to the Bronx to pick up something from a friend of his.

"The Bronx? Why don't you take a quick trip to Mexico while you're at it? Can't I go with you?"

"Adela, it is just business. You would be bored."

"You should have let me know yesterday," I said.

He sighed. "I didn't know about it till today. Do you want to wait here or at your place?"

I was really annoyed and tempted to tell him to forget the whole thing. But I didn't want to be alone for the night. "I'm sorry," he said, "but it cannot be helped. When I get back, we'll have dinner out."

"Okay," I pouted, "if you must, you must. I'll wait here, but come back as soon as you can." He kissed me and was gone.

I sat on the edge of the bed staring at the rumpled sheets, thinking about Steve. He's a nice guy, really bright and sexy, so why do I feel so empty, so depressed? My thoughts switched to Ed who was having dinner with his new girlfriend and Dan. That fucking Dan, why is he still friends with Ed? You're my friend, where's your loyalty? I knew I was being unreasonable, but I didn't care. Jesus, I have to stop thinking about all that, or I'll go nuts.

The apartment was quiet, too quiet. I thought of calling my girl-friends, but it was Saturday night, and I was sure they were out. I told myself there was no reason for me to feel lonely. After all, I had been with my lover, and everything was wonderful. He was coming back, and we were going out for dinner, and I wouldn't have to pay my half. But I was still lonely, terribly lonely. "Come on," I said to myself, "get dressed, you'll feel better."

There was no shower or tub. I took a whore bath, standing in a basin, pouring water over my body from the kitchen sink. There was a small mirror on the wall. I put on my makeup, speaking aloud to my reflection, grimacing at myself. "Grandma, what sharp white teeth you have. Yes, Ed, the better to tear out your cheating heart. Oh shit, what the hell am I doing here anyway?" I said to the girl in the mirror.

"Fucking your brains out," she answered. A temporary solution to a permanent situation. I should get out of here. Why did I tell Steve I would wait for him? Fuck it. I should just go. But I didn't want to go back to my apartment, and I didn't want to go to a movie or hang around the San Remo by myself. I was afraid I might run into Ed. Maybe Dan would come back soon, and even that was painful because he'd been out with him. It was all so incestuous. It made me dizzy.

I turned on the radio, blasting the sound in an effort to drown out my panicky feelings. "Don't cry," I said, "for God's sake, don't cry. You'll spoil your makeup." But the tears came anyway, and the more I tried to stop, the worse it was.

For the first time, I thought of a drink. Booze had always been an incidental if not a nonexistent part of my life. It had never occurred to me that I could use it to numb myself.

Dan kept a bottle of Scotch in his closet. I poured myself a shot glass, not bothering with ice. After the first awful taste, it got easier, so I slugged it from the bottle. It didn't take too much to make me drunk, and since I hadn't eaten since morning, the process was speeded up.

Pain gave way to rage, alternating with sniveling self-pity. "That lousy bastard and that bitch of a social worker, she's not even pretty. But she's been to college, and I haven't, that's why he doesn't love me anymore, the fucking intellectual snob. Where the hell is that Mexican? He's been gone for hours." The room, like my apartment, was depressing in its shabbiness. "I'm here alone, and no one gives a shit whether I live or die, not Ed or Dan or Steve. He's up in the Bronx, so he doesn't give a shit, neither does my friend Phyllis, my boss, my family, the butcher, the baker, or the fucking candlestick maker."

The radio was blasting big-band jazz. I took another swallow. "Hey everybody," I said to nobody, "it's party time." Stomping around the room in a drunken rhythm, singing, laughing, and crying at the same time.

"Who cares, who cares?" I said. "So why don't I kill myself? That'll shake Ed up. I don't have a gun, I don't have any poison. I don't wanna turn the gas jets on. After all, Dan is my friend, and I don't wanna blow up his apartment. I could cut my wrists. Nah, that's too messy. I guess it'll have to be aspirins. If I take about twenty mixed with all the Scotch I drank, that should be a lethal combination." I looked in Dan's medicine chest for a bottle of aspirin. "I'll show him."

Showing Ed meant washing down six aspirins with the Scotch. By now I was very drunk, my hysteria making me clumsy. I dropped the bottle, and it broke. There was glass all over the place.

"Oh shit, what a mess," I said. Then, picking up the pieces, I accidentally cut myself at the bottom of my palm near the wrist. It was a small cut, but it bled terribly and didn't stop.

I panicked. "Oh Christ, maybe I hit a vein. This wasn't part of the plan." The aspirins did nothing, I didn't feel sleepy, just dizzy.

I called Ed, screaming incoherently into the phone. "I'm bleeding to death from my wrist, and I don't care. It's all your fault, you bastard."

He tried to get through my hysterics. "Honey, just listen to me, you'll be all right."

"Oh, Ed, I'm so scared."

"It's all right, baby. I'll be right there. Where are you?"

"At Dan's place."

He came right away. He paled when he saw the bloody rag wrapped around my wrist.

"Jesus, Delski, what's the matter? What did you do?"

I held it up to him, like a puppy holding out a hurt paw. By then the bleeding had stopped, and he was relieved when he saw it wasn't serious. I didn't say it was not self-inflicted, letting him believe anything he wanted.

"Ed," I blubbered. "I took six aspirins," and with perfect timing, I threw up at his feet.

He laughed, and then he made me clean up. He bandaged my wound, brewed some black coffee, and scolded me for being a bad girl.

"Ed, I've missed you so much."

"I know, Delski. I guess I still love you, but I told you, it's not fair to you for us to go on the way we were. I just can't commit myself at this point of my life. It's not you. It's me."

"Stop it, I don't want to hear that anymore." I knew in my innermost self that if he could say those words at this moment, then it was really over and I had to accept it and get on with my life. I left a note for Steve and went home.

Chapter 6

Coming out of the New School one night, I heard someone call my name. It was Jack Kerouac. I hadn't seen him for a couple of years, and in spite of the way we parted, he seemed glad to see me. His manner was as exuberant as always, and he looked really handsome in his preppy tweed jacket. He asked me how my life was.

It had been a year since my breakup with Ed. My immediate hurt had faded; my young enthusiastic nature had taken over. I skipped the downs and recited the ups. "I moved out of Brooklyn since I saw you last."

"Hey, that's great," he said. "How did your folks feel about that?"

I laughed. "They weren't too happy. Anyway, I'm working hard at my painting, and everything's fine How's it going with you?"

"Great," he said. "And by the way, Harcourt Brace is publishing my novel."

"That's wonderful, Jack," and I hugged him. "I'm really happy for you. When's it coming out?"

"Not for a while yet. I'm working on another book. Look, why don't you give me your number, and we can go out and celebrate."

Why not, I thought, it can't hurt. Besides, I knew very few about-to-be-published writers. Maybe this was a new chapter for me. "Yes, I'd like that."

I'd not met any of his friends before, so he took me to the West End Cafe the first time we went out. This was the Columbia University pub and new territory for me. A new scene was what I needed, away from the Village and its painful memories.

Jack introduced me to John Clellon Holmes, another writer, rather shy and bookish looking, who seemed to be more an observer than a participant. I supposed it would all end up as material for his new book. Besides John, I met other members of Jack's clique. There was Allen Ginsberg; Peter Orlovsky, Allen's longtime lover; Gregory Corso; and William Burroughs, a quiet, dour man, older than the rest of us, all part of the West End scene.

One night I sat nursing my one beer while Jack pointed out the various other characters. A midget sat across the room with a six-foot, good-looking blonde. "You see that little guy?" Jack asked. "He's a second-story man, and that's his wife."

"What's a second-story man?" I asked.

"He breaks into apartments from the fire escape." I was fascinated on two counts. I'd never seen a midget with a six-foot wife. Their sexual possibilities or impossibilities together challenged my imagination. And I'd never seen a real robber.

By now, Jack and I were lovers. Sex was not his major thrust in more ways than one. He rushed the act, the same way he hurried through everything else. It seemed to me he was only interested in the big event. What led up to it was of minor interest. Nevertheless, I liked him, and through him, I was meeting some interesting characters in a new setting.

It was always party time at Holmes's apartment. I can't recall exactly where it was, but I remember a rat-infested walk-up practically under the Manhattan Bridge. The area looked like a set from Maxwell Anderson's forties play, *Winterset.*

Unlike my other Village friends, this group smoked a lot of pot, used other drugs, and got very drunk on cheap wine, Jack especially. I had no interest in booze or drugs. Since that abortive suicide attempt, and except for an occasional beer, I had not touched liquor again.

I was an onlooker, not because I felt superior, but because I couldn't be one of them, acting drunk and crazy. It was an intelligent, gifted group, especially Ginsberg. The conversation was entertaining, then I would watch the evening gradually disintegrate. But I was very young, and I thought that these were brilliant people and this was the way it was supposed to be. I especially liked John's wife, Marion, but their violent, hysterical, alcoholic fighting both frightened and bored me.

Jack was staying with his friend, Neal Cassady, from Salt Lake City, and Neal's girl Luanne, a sweet blonde airhead. Neal was twenty-five and very attractive, looking like a mix of Paul Newman and Sean Penn.

When we met, I sensed he didn't like me. He was possessive of Jack and jealous because I was Jack's girl. Neal made me nervous. He was always high on something, booze, bennies, or whatever he could get his hands on. He was never still, hopping from one foot to another, his body jerking, his arms flailing the air in an involuntary spastic dance. He giggled nervously, endlessly talking, talking about everything and nothing. I realized then where Jack had picked up his stream-of-consciousness style.

Luanne and I soon ran out of girl talk. She was nice, but except for our gender, we had zero in common. We watched Jack and Neal, hugging, pummeling, and punching each other while talking nonstop, neither of them listening to the other. There was a curious lack of ideas in what they were saying.

Given my potential alcoholic psyche, I don't understand why I didn't do bennies, booze, or anything else then. But I sure made up for it later.

Sometimes, after a night at the West End Cafe, we would stay over at Neal's. He and Luanne lived in a filthy tenement walkup in Spanish Harlem. My flat was a palace by comparison. There was no bed, so we slept on a thin pad on the floor, and I was awakened a few times by roaches crawling across my legs.

"Jack," I said, "I'm not staying here anymore. You can stay with me at my place."

Every time we went out with them, Neal would pick us up in a different car. "Jack, Neal hasn't a pot to piss in. How come he has all those cars?"

Jack laughed. "He steals them just for joyriding."

"That's terrible," I said. "He's a car thief, supposing we get caught?"

"Don't worry," Jack said. "He just picks them up when he feels like driving and dumps them after he's done."

I disapproved, but at the same time, it was exciting to me, an adventure. There must have been two of me, one the daughter of a conservative Spanish Catholic family who thought I shouldn't be doing these things and the wild one, who enjoyed every minute of it. Basically, I was really an innocent, nice girl who wasn't out to get anybody or their money. I was just out to have a good time. I loved sex, and I always wanted to be in love.

One night, when Jack stayed over, I told him it would be good for our relationship if we would just sleep together for one night without having sex. At first he objected, but then he agreed. It was a very narrow bed, and he tossed all night, neither of us got any sleep. The next day he was furious and sulked all morning. No woman had ever treated him like that, he said.

"There are other things in a relationship besides fucking."

"Like what?" he asked.

"Well, if you don't know, I'm not going to tell you, and I think you're being childish."

We also had a big fight about my using Orthocreme on my diaphragm. I used it sparingly, washing myself carefully after I inserted it. He said he hated getting it on his cock and told me not to use it. I refused. I wasn't going to risk getting pregnant. We began arguing over silly things, but the truth of the matter was that I was getting bored. We gradually drifted out of the relationship, and I began to see other men. For all I knew, he was doing the same those times he went to sea.

Chapter 7

It was 1951, and I was living on Sixteenth Street with my cat, and Ed Fancher was living in the building next door. We rarely ran into each other, and when we did, I would look at him and think, how is it I feel almost nothing at all? All that love and rage and now only a small twinge of pain.

Dan was still in my life, and my social circle had stayed more or less the same. Though I was between lovers, I was not lonely. My life was full and as always sustained by my painting.

I had exhibited in some group shows and sold a few canvasses. There's nothing like the thrill of your first sale. I was so happy, and I wished I had framed the check. I enjoyed my job in the display studio, where I had been put in charge of a small group of talented artists. Papier-mâché was my specialty, and I was one of the few people of a very small group in New York who knew how to do this kind of work. I really was on my own now, and to my surprise, I liked it.

It was a Saturday night, and I had been to a movie. When I got home, the apartment was cold. I lit the kerosene stove, made myself some hot cocoa, and got into bed with an early edition of the Sunday *Times* and Teddy curled at my side.

Since breaking up with Ed, I had fixed up my apartment, painting those ugly dark green walls white and hanging my pictures. Instead of looking like a storage room, it looked like a place where a real person lived. I was just drifting off into sleep when the phone rang.

"Who the hell is this?"

It was Dan. "Del, how are you, kid?"

"I'm fine." He sounded like he'd been drinking heavily. "Dan, it's two o'clock. Are you okay? You must be at some kind of party."

"No, it's not a party. I'm at Norman's apartment." He was mumbling.

"Dan, I can't hear you, whose apartment?"

"Norman Mailer, we're just sitting around having a few drinks."

"I thought you said he was living in Vermont."

"Not anymore. He split up with his wife." Dan hesitated a moment. "Why don't you come up here for a drink?"

"Well, where exactly is 'up here'?"

"Sixty-fourth between Second and Third."

"Are you kidding? I'm not going up there at this hour."

"Come on, Adele, why don't you get rid of whoever is there and get up here. Norman really wants to meet you."

"Dan, I happen to be alone."

"Hah, that's a switch."

I laughed, both pleased and annoyed. "Meaning what?"

"Adele, I was only teasing. Look, he's a great guy, you'll like him."

"Dan, for the tenth time, I'm not getting dressed and schlepping up to the Sixties. Besides, I don't have money for a taxi."

"Where's your spirit of adventure? Just a minute, hang on."

I looked at the clock. It was almost two twenty. "Okay, but hurry up." There was such a long pause that I thought we were disconnected. Finally a voice came on the line, and it wasn't Dan's.

"Hello, Adele."

"Oh, hi Norman, how are you?"

"You know you're disappointing me," he said.

"I'm sorry. I'm in bed, or I was."

"I hope we didn't wake you."

I laughed. "No, no, it's okay. I was half-awake anyway."

"You know," he said, "Dan's told me so much about you."

"Yeah, he's talked about you, too."

He had a nice voice, deep, with just a hint of a purr. There was a pause. "Look, Adele, I know it's late, but why don't you come up here. I really would like to meet you. Put yourself in a cab, it's on me."

God, I thought, what a nice voice. I glanced out the window, the street looked cold and dark. Maybe they could come here, I thought, but the apartment was a mess. Besides, why should I run up there? If he's so eager to meet me, let him ask me for a date.

"Norman, I just can't. It really is too late. But I'd love to another time." Another longish pause.

"Listen, have you read *The Last Tycoon?*" His question took me off guard.

"No, I haven't. Well, I mean not lately."

"Can I read something to you?"

I hesitated. I've always disliked being read to, especially at two thirty in the morning.

"Well . . . sure," I answered.

There was a pause.

"Here it is." He cleared his throat. "'Coming down the hill, he listened inside himself as if something by an unknown composer, powerful, strange and strong was about to be stated presently, but because the composer was always new, he would not recognize it as a theme right away.'"

"That's beautiful," I said, "especially the way you read it. What does it mean?"

"I'll tell you when you get here," he said.

I heard myself saying, "Okay, I'll come, but just for a little while."

"That's fine," he sounded pleased. "Let me give you the address. It's 224 East Sixty-fourth Street, apartment 6B."

"Okay, Norman, see you in awhile."

I looked at the clock. It was 2:45. I'd better hurry. What should I wear? I chose a cream-colored silk blouse and a black, velveteen skirt. After searching frantically, I found a pair of stockings with no runs, hooking them onto my garter belt. There were no such things as pantyhose then. I wore very little makeup, so that didn't take much time. As an afterthought, I knotted a flowered chiffon scarf around my neck and screwed on my silver hoop earrings.

It was cold outside, and I waited, shivering in the deserted street, for a cab, thinking, "This is madness!"

But nevertheless, I was excited. How could I know that Scott Fitzgerald, Norman Mailer, and that cab ride would change my life forever? My trip into the light fantastic with a nice Jewish boy genius, newly famous and rich, my fatal attraction.

he cab stopped in front of a seedy old brownstone, a shade better than my tenement. The stairs seemed endless. The hall was so dim I could barely see the numbers on the doors. I walked in the wrong direction. Where the hell is 6B? At that moment, I heard a door opening, and I saw Dan.

"You made it, kid," and he gave me a welcoming hug.

I was glad to see him. "Yeah, your crazy friend made it uptown."

He laughed. "Forget it. We're all nuts. Welcome to the party," he said, taking my coat.

"You said it wasn't a party."

He thought that was funny, but to me he was just drunk. "Ha, well it is now."

I looked around. "This reminds me of my place." There was a mirror near the coat closet. Dan waited while I combed my hair and fixed my lipstick.

"Okay," I sighed, "where's the boy wonder?"

I followed Dan down the hall along a string of rooms, through a kitchen with a bathtub like mine, into a parlor with a lot of dark brown furniture. I saw a skinny little guy sitting on the couch. I knew he was twenty-eight, but he looked much younger. Dan hugged me again. He was being more affectionate than usual. Maybe it was the drink.

"She made it, she's here," he said to Norman. I felt shy and strange, but the presence of Dan reassured me.

"What, no trumpets?" I asked, making a little curtsy. They laughed.

The boy wonder was wearing a plaid flannel shirt and dungarees, baggy on his slender frame. He looked at me, and his eyes were beautiful, not only in their blue color, but for their soft, almost melancholy expression. He was good looking, with a strong nose, a beautifully shaped sensual mouth, and a delicate chin with a small indentation. He had a lot of dark brown curly hair that I immediately wanted to touch and a warm smile that crinkled his eyes. There was a sensitivity in his face that I responded to. He half rose from his seat.

"Oh, hi Adele, did you recognize the theme yet?"

I said, "Not yet, you may have to read it to me again." I sat on the couch.

"Can I get you a drink? We only have Scotch."

I made a face. "I really hate Scotch."

"Well," he said, "I could run out for something else."

The voice matched the one on the phone, deep, slightly nasal, sexy, but a bit artificial. I knew that, like me, he had made the decision that no one would hear the Brooklyn in his voice, and so he decided to assume his version of a Harvard accent.

"No," I answered. "It's okay, just a little, with a lot of water."

He raised his glass to me. "Cheers," he said.

I'd never heard anyone say that before, but I smiled back, raising mine. "Cheers," I answered, feeling a little like Bette Davis in *Now Voyager.*

The first taste was as bad as I had remembered it, but like a good girl, I got it down. We sat in silence. I was uncomfortable, trying to think of something to fill the space. Dan had gone into the kitchen. Where the hell is he? I thought, and to my relief, he came in with some cheese and crackers. They began discussing a mutual friend.

Sipping my drink and watching Norman, thoughts raced through my head. So, this is the famous writer. God, I'm embarrassed, I never read his book. He's so skinny, but look at that hair, it has a life of its own, like Samson and maybe I'm his Delilah. I think he's shy because he never really looks at me. He probably doesn't think I'm attractive. I should have dressed up more, or maybe I should have worn my dungarees. I like the way he grins and scratches behind his ear. Yes, he is good looking. Sensitive and strong at the same time. I'll bet he's put away half that bottle of Scotch. Still, he doesn't seem drunk, not like Dan, who's plastered.

We were a little shy of each other, testing the air for danger. If we'd been two dogs, we would have sniffed each other's rears and immediately figured it out. I was amused at the thought. I was definitely beginning to feel relaxed and high. "Boy, it must be the Scotch," I thought.

"How long are you going to be in New York?" I asked.

"I don't know, it depends," he looked into his drink, scratching behind his ear.

"On what?" I asked. I knew it was a sly question, relating to the breakup.

He shrugged, "On a lot of things."

His answer was vague, I guess it was none of my business, so I let it go. "What did you do in Vermont?"

He laughed, "Well, I became a father of a little girl, did a lot of skiing, and finished a new novel, not necessarily in that order."

Dan refilled my glass. I took a healthy swallow. By now the Scotch didn't have such a bad taste. "What's the title?" I asked, "And what's it about?"

"It's called *Barbary Shore.* It's a political novel, and the background is a rooming house in Brooklyn Heights."

"When is it going to be published?"

"In a couple of months. Would you like a copy?"

"Thanks, Norman, I'd like that very much. You know, I went to camp in Vermont once, when I was a kid. It's the most beautiful landscape I've ever seen. Aren't you going to miss it?"

"Christ no, I like New York, but I will miss the skiing. We lived near Stowe."

"What about your little girl?" I asked. He looked troubled, and I was sorry I brought it up.

"Yeah, I'll miss Susie," he said gloomily. He took a deep swallow of Scotch and changed the subject. He talked rhapsodically about skiing for a long time. I had never skied, but his description was so vivid, I could almost hear the soft whoosh of his skis in the powdered snow and hear that white stillness at the top of the long, steep downhill slope. He talked about skiing as if it were one of the secret keys to happiness.

"It sounds wonderful," I said. "You make me want to try it."

"You should, there's nothing like it."

I looked at him, and I wasn't thinking about skiing anymore, instead I thought about his mouth and what kissing him would be like. He reached for his pack of cigarettes. It was empty, so he went into the bedroom for another. I leaned my head back against the sofa, enjoying my warm, high feelings, so different from the last time I got drunk on Scotch, that was almost a year ago. He came back with a new pack and a drink.

"Dan tells me you're a good painter."

Dan laughed, "She's very good, if you can figure the work out."

"You're not supposed to figure out an abstraction," I answered. "You're supposed to feel it."

"Touché," said Dan and we laughed.

Norman joined in. "Dan, you're not alone. I'm a philistine when it comes to abstract expressionism," and he looked at me with those eyes that would have melted the Ice Queen. "But I'd like to see your pictures," and I could tell he really meant it.

I was feeling a real contact with him, as if somebody had turned on a switch releasing the current between us. I'd never known anyone with such charisma, even Kerouac. I still felt a little shy despite the Scotch in me, but when I did share in the conversation, he listened without being condescending or phony. He made me feel important.

The performer in him charmed this small audience. He told us stories about Hollywood, the army, New York and the people he'd met there. He spoke of so many things, and we laughed often.

Such a mind to dazzle the likes of me. I mostly listened, but I talked to him with my heart, in my eyes, and he answered without moving his lips, and I knew I was falling in love.

There was good medicine in the Scotch, which I decided I loved after all. We drank and drank a shortcut through shyness and fear. Dan, stumbling, passed out in the bedroom, and we were alone. No more talk, so quiet, only the tinkling of ice cubes. My heart beating, I leaned forward and kissed him. A kiss into closeness and sweet lust. A roller coaster going up and up and then the breathless, down and down. We held on, like it would never be again, and then a last kiss, sweet with the taste of each other, loving murmurs against a background of tomorrow's light, leaving me a tender guest on the living room couch to sleep the last few hours of the night.

An early morning awakening and a moment of bewilderment, not knowing where I was. There was an impulse to flee, but then I remembered how much there was in him, an incredible explosion as if he had been bottled up for a long time. I yawned and stretched, feeling my body slide against the sheets Norman had brought out for the couch. A kaleidoscope of sensual images floating through my head, wishing he was beside me, wanting this half-stranger all over again, his sweet-smelling body and his beautiful cock inside me. But again, my fragile woman's heart whispered, go away and leave him with a memory untouched by my morning reality.

I composed a cool note in my head, the kind of note Bette Davis would write in *Dark Victory* after she sees her prognosis.

Darling,
Had to fly, loved it, will be in touch.
Temporarily yours,
Adelita

I looked for my clothes. My blouse and skirt were in a heap on the floor, but where were my garter belt, bra, and panties? I found them wedged behind a cushion. What bullshit, I thought, you know you want to stay, take a chance for Christ's sake, don't run away.

I made a dash for the bathroom. I had to fix myself before he got up. I had no toothbrush, so I squeezed some toothpaste on my finger, then I remembered I had left my makeup in my bag in the parlor. The room was dim, so I raised the shades. The day was beautiful, the sun shining, and it was all for me. There was still no sound from the bedroom, so I decided to dress and then put on some makeup. I got as far as my bra, panties, and stockings, when I heard the bedroom door opening. Slipping under the sheets, I pretended to be asleep.

I heard Dan's voice. "Adele, are you awake?"

I yawned, "What time is it?"

"About ten thirty."

If he was surprised to see me, he didn't show it. He looked tired and crumpled. Evidently he had slept in his clothes.

"Are you all right, Dan?"

"Christ, no, I have a lousy hangover. What about you?"

"I have a bit of a headache, but I feel wonderful. Is Norman awake?"

He sat on the edge of the couch. "No, he's still asleep. I'm sorry I passed out, kid. I feel awful about leaving you alone."

"Dan, it's okay, really. It just got so late, I decided to stay over."

He sat beside me, neither of us talking, and then he looked at me, and we started to laugh. I hugged him. "Oh Dan, life is so strange sometimes, don't you think?"

Norman came out of the bedroom, blinking at the sight of the real world made up of this dingy New York apartment. Here was a girl he had met just a few hours ago, with whom he had made passionate love, and a close friend sitting with his arms around the very same girl.

I wondered if Norman woke up the way I did, his thoughts making him erect, ready for me again. I hoped so, but he seemed remote. I sighed. Are we going to be strangers again? I was suddenly depressed. Maybe I should have followed my instinct and left, maybe it was just another drunken fuck. But then he gave me a long look and smiled, and my heart knew better.

"Hi, Norman," and I smiled back. "Did you sleep okay?"

"Yeah," he said, "better than I have in a long time."

I knew by the sound of his voice that we were strangers no more. "Me, too. It's a very comfortable couch."

He looked at Dan. "We really killed that bottle of Scotch."

"Yeah, and I'm hung over."

"Cheer up, so am I."

"It doesn't show," I said.

His eyes were still that clear blue, and in spite of the bacchanal the night before, the three of us were young enough to withstand the cold light of day.

He picked up the glasses and put them in the sink, came back into the parlor, and lit a cigarette.

"Adele, why don't you get dressed, and we'll get something to eat. I'm starving. There's a great bacon-and-eggs place in the neighborhood."

Dan groaned. "Don't mention food," and he disappeared into the bathroom.

Norman sat down on the bed and kissed me. "You smell good, and you're beautiful when you wake up."

Yes, I thought. He is the same man he was last night. But then he frowned.

"Listen, what the hell's going on between you and Dan?"

I was surprised at his question. "Nothing," I said. "Why are you asking?"

"Jesus, I get up, and the first thing I see is Dan with his arms around you. Did you fuck him, too?"

I laughed. "Of course not," but I realized he was serious and now I was angry. Did he want to spoil last night? "How could you think something like that? He happens to be one of my dearest friends and also yours, remember?"

"Listen," he said, framing my face in his hands, "I want you just for me, understand?"

His words excited me. I kissed him, the taste of his mouth was familiar, not just from last night or this morning, but as if I'd known it all my life. He nuzzled the tips of my breasts, and I wanted him again.

"I wish we were alone," I said.

"Mmm," he said, "so do I," taking my hand and pressing it against his hard cock.

"That will be for later, now get dressed. I get cranky when I'm hungry."

We went out to breakfast, my dear friend and my new lover. No one-night stand, this. What I gave and took was not to be discarded with last night's drinks. He was happy, I could see it in his face, and so was I, the past pain washed away by one strong wave. I knew there would be more, more of his charm, his wit, and more lovemaking. They talked just a little about Norman's wife, Bea. I could tell Dan liked her, she sounded so bright. She was a linguist and had been a music major at Boston University. I was getting depressed, forgetting how good a painter I was and that I, too, had an education.

Norman noticed how quiet I'd become. He pressed his knee

against mine, sending a silent kiss across the table. I smiled back into his eyes, reading his thought. "What I had with you last night was something I have not had with anyone, for a very long time." And I was happy again.

My darling wanted to know more about me. So far I had listened and had been rather quiet about myself, and so I talked about the things that were meaningful to me. He was an important writer, a celebrity who had traveled and lived a glamorous life. But with all that, he had humility, an ability to listen to another person without being condescending, no matter what their point of view.

I talked about my job, explaining just what it was I did. Because it was creative and I enjoyed it, I made it sound interesting. I was one of the few papier-mâché artists who had learned to develop this medium to a higher level, not just the crude forms most people think of as papier-mâché. I'm sure there are people who remember the Lord and Taylor, B. Altman, Saks Fifth Avenue, and Macy's Christmas displays in the 1940s and fifties, magical windows in which figures dressed in period costumes and fairy tale characters were displayed against fanciful backgrounds all made of papier-mâché. I had made some of those figures.

I talked to Norman about Hans Hoffman's abstract painting class and some of the painters I worked with. I mimicked the master to Norman's amusement, asking him to come to meet Hoffman at one of his open-class critiques.

I even talked about my family. I told him about my father being a printer and a linotype operator at the *Daily News*, also that he had been a professional fighter and was now teaching boxing at a Brooklyn YMCA. Norman wanted to meet him. Dan and I laughed at the idea of the two of them together.

Norman smiled. "Why is that so funny?"

I laughed again. "You'll find out when he gives you a few boxing lessons."

Norman looked interested. "I'd like that."

Norman told us a few more Hollywood stories. Norman was a frustrated actor, and what made the stories so wonderful was the way he acted out all the parts so each character came alive. We laughed so much that people stared, the last of our hangovers vanishing over coffee. The three of us were so close, I felt cared for and beautiful, happy with my two men, and I couldn't wait to be alone with my lover.

Chapter 9

Norman went back to Vermont for a few days to get some of his things and to see his daughter. He called every day to say that he was thinking about me a lot, missing me in all sorts of delightful ways. Every time he called, I half expected him to say that he and Bea were going to try again. But each time he sounded so unhappy that I knew it was finished on his part, and I was glad. He said he had to clear his head, to get some perspective on what was happening in his life, and I also think he was worried about how his mother was going to react.

He was in my thoughts a lot, and I missed him. We'd had fireworks at the beginning, but there was so much up in the air. What I didn't yet know about him was that whatever Norman wanted, he took and to hell with the consequences. But whatever was going to happen with us, I still had to get on with my life. My job, Hoffman's school, and a sculpting class at the Art Students League helped make the time pass more quickly.

After Norman came back to the city, we saw each other almost every night, spending a lot of time in bed, tuned into each other's bodies, even without the Scotch. I was in love, and because he was so responsive, he aroused my passions as they'd never been aroused before.

"Talk dirty to me, darling," I would whisper in the throes, and I would hear pornographic prose, dirty enough for my lust and literary enough for my finer senses. Sometimes we would stay at my apartment. I had always been a noisy one in bed, and the walls were like paper. My apartment was next to the staircase, so people going up and down got an earful. For all I knew, someone was selling tickets.

Norman told me he was able to hold off his orgasm by thinking of a beautiful country landscape, green meadows, trees, and a blue sky. I thought that was odd, since I'd never heard such a thing from any man I'd ever been with. It never occurred to me that a man might be thinking of yesterday's business deal, a baseball game, or God knows what. Besides, I was too absorbed in my own pleasure to care much about how he kept it up.

Norman loved my looks, intrigued by glimpses of the Indian in my face. He told me about a girl on his block he was crazy about when he was thirteen. Her name was Bunny, and she had the same beautiful Indian look. The crush was not returned. Instead, Bunny made fun of Norman's big ears.

"Oh look," she would say to the other kids, "here comes Red Sails in the Sunset." The name stuck and broke his thirteen-year-old heart.

I soon got over the feeling that I had to entertain him, that we had to be chatting constantly. I was more comfortable with him in our quiet times together, beginning to understand how preoccupied he was with thoughts of his new book. I realized I couldn't have his attention every minute. He was getting more nervous as the publication of *Barbary Shore* got closer, worried about the reception it might have. He also had the pending divorce on his mind.

He talked to me about Bea, about that last winter in the Vermont farmhouse. He had been depressed and angry, sick with one cold after another. He was bitter about his marriage to a woman he felt wasn't very feminine or receptive anymore. The lovemaking had gone sour, and he felt she had become a ballbreaker.

"Something, my darling, you're not," he said. Though I didn't say it at the time, I thought that part of the reason he wanted his freedom from Bea was out of sheer boredom. He wanted to enjoy the fruits of his new fame, and that didn't mean being stuck in a Vermont farmhouse with a small child and a cool wife.

It's not impossible that the seeds of later violence were nourished that very winter. He told me about something he had done, playing with a kitten and some string. The kitten had entangled the string around its neck. He pulled it tighter and tighter until it started to choke. The more frantic its struggle became, the tighter Norman pulled, stopping just short of strangulation. I thought it awful, and I was a little shocked.

I was staying at his place almost every night now, because his bed was bigger and we liked sleeping together. Besides, his apartment walls were thicker.

We saw a lot of Dan, and again as it was with Ed, I enjoyed the fact that the three of us were good friends. We sometimes double-dated with Dan and his current girlfriend. Norman drank during our evenings, but there wasn't the marked change in his personality that occurred much later in his life. He would get high, but I don't remember, at that period, any meanness or violence. He would just become a bit detached. I *did* notice that he would often lapse into a Southern accent. But that was amusing. There goes Norman the actor, I thought.

One summer night, Dan, Norman, and I went to Coney Island. Norman had been there the year before, and in his inimitable style, he talked up the Cyclone, the roller coaster, the same way he talked up skiing. He created a mystique about it, making it seem as if it were an original learning experience instead of just another macho test. Well, I rode that damn thing in the front car with Norman five or six times, terrified all that time, sure I would die on one of those hellish drops. But I wanted his admiration enough to swallow my fear, and I succeeded, a significant beginning for us.

Norman was very close to his family, and he always talked about them in a loving way. "There's a picture of my mother," he said one time, "holding me when I was a few months old. There's something about you that reminds me of her. Actually, you don't really look at all like her, but there's a soft expression, a love and a tenderness in her face and her eyes, in the way she's holding me, just the way you're looking at me right now."

From the way he described her, she seemed to be a typical Jewish mother, though I don't think he meant it that way, and I never heard him refer to her like that. Fanny Mailer was fiercely protective of her family and what was hers. No one outside the family fortress mattered.

Norman described his father, Barney, as a polite, dapper little man, a South African Jew. An accountant by profession, he was as secretive as his wife was blunt and outgoing. With Fanny, what you saw was what you got. Then there was Norman's adored younger sister, Barbara, a Radcliffe graduate and the darling of her father.

Norman's maternal grandfather was to me the most interesting of them all. He was a rabbi from Long Branch, New Jersey, where Norman was born. One picture I saw showed a handsome man wearing a long black coat and wide-brimmed hat. He reminded me so much of Norman, with a similar expression and the same eyes. He owned a butcher shop, also part of a grocery. Fanny ran the store with the help of her three sisters. She was sixteen at the time and worked like a slave. She could use a meat cleaver with the best of them to trim, cut, and chop slabs of meat, and she made the deliveries herself. Norman said that she had been the object of some anti-Semitic remarks, and it had not been easy for them to live in a town where there were no other Jews.

The rabbi was a brilliant scholar, but no businessman. Kind and generous, a pushover for a sob story, he was always extending credit, much to the frustration of Fanny, already a tough businesswoman.

When I met him, Norman had his grandfather's sweetness and spirituality. I responded to it and loved him for it. I think he's spent a lifetime trying to kill those qualities, which he mistook as a sign of weakness, of being just a nice Jewish boy.

Oddly enough, Norman said very little about his grandmother. Something terrible had happened to her, an accident while crossing a railroad yard. I don't recall the exact circumstances, but evidently she had fallen in front of a moving train and lost an arm. At least that's what I remember of the story.

Norman was nine when the family moved from Long Branch to Crown Heights, so that we were both growing up in Brooklyn at about the same time. My neighborhood was mostly Italian, with a small Spanish colony, and his mostly Jewish.

He was sixteen when he went to Harvard. "How could you afford it?" I asked, and he told me that his rich Uncle Dave paid most of his tuition.

"It was exciting for me," he said, "but God, I felt out of place, with all those older, sophisticated rich guys. I didn't have the right clothes, the right anything. All I had was my brains and talent. I felt lonely a lot of the time, and scared, especially at the beginning."

By now, Norman's mother was working day and night in an oil business owned by his Uncle Dave. Tired as she was, Fanny would take the train to Boston regularly to visit Norman at Harvard. She came loaded with shopping bags filled with Norman's favorite foods. Instead of tollhouse cookies, there was matzo-ball soup, herring in sour cream, chopped liver, and pot roast. He would take her directly to his room. Norman told me that he introduced her to very few people because he was ashamed of her and then, of course, was guilty about those feelings. I remember so well because I knew exactly what went on inside him; I felt the same way about my own parents.

For the rest of his life, Norman had a thing about carrying shopping bags or being seen with anyone who did. When he and Bea were staying at the Ritz in London, following his big success, she had shown up in the lobby carrying a shopping bag in each hand. Norman was furious and embarrassed. He would never carry a shopping bag for me or anyone else.

We had had a few intense days together, so we both decided to take some time off. Late one afternoon, I was coming home to my flat from my art class, carrying a heavy wooden drawing board and wearing dungarees and my dirty smock. I had just gotten to my front stoop when a cab pulled up, and I heard my name called. The door opened, and it was Norman. It wasn't our night to see each other so I was surprised and happy. He was on his way to an appointment with his publisher, he said, but he just had to see me, to tell me how much he missed me, and "what luck," he said, "you came along just at the right time."

"I love you, sweet monkey. See you tomorrow," he said and kissed me.

As the cab sped off, he waved to me from the back window. I stood there, dazed with happiness. Then I ran upstairs, to lie down on my bed, thoughts of him washing over me, warming my heart and body. Oh Norman, I love you so much. I wanted to weep.

Sometimes I try to connect the stranger I know today with the memory of that afternoon in 1951, when a slim young man, with clear blue eyes, looked at me with so much love.

Chapter 10

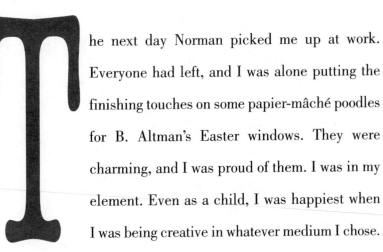

he next day Norman picked me up at work. Everyone had left, and I was alone putting the finishing touches on some papier-mâché poodles for B. Altman's Easter windows. They were charming, and I was proud of them. I was in my element. Even as a child, I was happiest when I was being creative in whatever medium I chose.

I spent much of my free time in museums, especially the Modern, hanging out with my friends in the garden or sitting for hours in the penthouse cafeteria. Norman often went with me. He had instinctive good taste, not skimming through the rooms, but really looking at the work, and we talked about what we saw. One of his favorite painters was George Tooker, of the strange silent grey-faced isolated figures. I had gone by one small Tooker painting in the permanent collection often enough and never really thought about it until Norman pointed it out as something quite special. Since I liked the surrealists, I liked that one, too.

Mondrian was another favorite painter of mine. We stood in front of one canvas, "Broadway Boogie Woogie," and I tried to explain a little about his use of color to create rhythm and movement. This time Norman just didn't get it.

Norman talked about Mark Rothko, a painter he had met at one of Zero Mostel's parties. He said he would like to bring me up to Rothko's apartment to see some amazing paintings. He called Mark, and we visited when I had some time off one afternoon.

Rothko was a stocky, dark, somber-looking man with glasses, wearing a navy-blue business suit. This was the first unrumpled painter I'd ever met. We sat, and he chatted cordially, in a dark wood-paneled living room. I was impatient, anxious to see the paintings. Finally he opened two huge sliding doors into an enormous, two-story studio. We looked at a huge canvas dominating the end of the long room. It was a painting of two rectangles of luminous color, vibrating against each other, so simple and so beautiful I wanted to cry.

I'd never seen painting like that, and for me, it was an almost spiritual moment. I've always remembered it and that Norman was there to share it with me.

Our affair had begun about four months before *Barbary Shore* was published. Norman had been a little nervous about the reviews, knowing the critics might be out to get him. This new one had better be a work of genius. As it turned out, there were more bad reviews than good ones. I remember only one; *Time* said it was "tasteless, paceless, and graceless."

Norman seemed to take the reviews well, but there was an underlying anger and depression. He assured me I wasn't the cause of his bad moods. And of course, there was plenty of diversion, mainly parties, one after another. I had very few party clothes, so my wardrobe needed a complete overhaul. Norman was generous and gave me money to buy some pretty things.

I bought a lot of black velvet. He liked that. And with the black velvet, and the parties, came the cocktails I was developing a taste for. My world was changing, everything was new; my clothes, people, situations—but not the dumps we both lived in. One of the first parties I remember, my debut, was at Viveca Lindfors's big house in the Nineties. We had made love right before we got there, and I was glowing from my beauty treatment.

When we arrived, he introduced me to Viveca and George Tabori, her husband. She was all over Norman, ignoring me. I felt shy and awkward, getting a small taste of what Bea must have felt and what was yet to come. But I wasn't really drinking, so I took it quietly and did not get aggressive. I was not bothered, of course, by men who made him the center of attraction—it was the women who flirted with him, boldly, as if I wasn't there.

A much more pleasant memory of that time was another party, in the East Sixties. I don't remember who gave it, but I do remember the dazzling characters I met. John Huston and his ballerina wife, Ricky Soma, were there. A very tall Clifford Odets, with his wild, curly hair, made an entrance with a few toots on the clarinet he happened to have with him. Stella Adler, who must have been born a grande dame, and Luther, her brother arrived. She looked down at Norman from her queenly height, flirting outrageously with him, paying little attention to me. But she was such a flamboyant character that I wasn't threatened, knowing they couldn't possibly wake up together.

But the grandest moment was when I met Charlie Chaplin. He was gallant, telling me I was beautiful, kissing my hand, and I was speechless. That party had a dreamlike quality for me, and I wondered if it was really happening. As Charlie chatted with me and Norman, I wanted to see glimpses of the little tramp, a tiny gesture here and there. I never did.

Chapter 11

In the spring of 1952, Norman was thinking of writing a novel about Hollywood. He decided to visit Los Angeles for three weeks to do some research, refresh the scene in his mind, and get some ideas. He asked me to go with him, but it was our busy season, and I couldn't leave my job. He wrote me almost every day, funny, warm, sexy letters. The first one, though, jarred me terribly—and I've never forgotten it nor really understood his casual confession of infidelity.

All the lovely things in that letter were destroyed by one sentence, which said, "I've taken two women to bed."

I wept with jealousy and rage. I thought of calling him in L.A., telling him not to come back to me, that it was over between us. But I didn't, and something happened that distracted me.

I had been invited to dinner at a married couple's loft, both were painter friends from my early days in the Village. They also invited Norman, whom they had met briefly at another loft party. I explained that he was in L.A., but that I would love to come. The wife was a great cook, and afterward, the three of us sat around drinking. A joint was passed around, and I smoked pot for the first time.

I hadn't been really drunk for a long while, since that hysterical night at Dan's apartment when I had broken up with Ed Fancher. Since then, even at the parties in my lover's social circle, I never drank enough to get so much as a light buzz. I could stop at one cocktail, not because I had to, but because I wasn't interested in drinking. I hadn't discovered alcohol's power yet, so booze did not dominate my life, as it did later on.

Norman drank a lot, but he did not become obnoxious, combative, and wanting to fuck every woman in the room. Not yet . . .

But tonight, I felt different. I was angry and hurting. My sweet love had been unfaithful, not once, but twice. I didn't care about the rest of the letter, that confession was the only thing that mattered.

With the grass and booze at work, all three of us were stoned. My host and hostess began to make love. I was shocked and embarrassed. I'd never been in this weird kind of situation before. Then they asked me to join them.

Fuck it, I thought, why not? I needed my revenge, even though I felt inhibited and awkward and more than a little self-conscious.

I certainly was no seasoned orgiast. Nobody I knew around the Village had ever been in a threesome, and if they had been, they would have kept it quiet. I had seen pornographic pictures in Ed's collection, but that was it. What innocents we all really were.

Norman had told me about the two hookers he'd been with in Paris during the time he was married to Bea. He told the story charmingly with more detail than I can remember. The whore had a good friend, and she'd asked Norman if he would mind if she joined them. Norman, being a rich, successful novelist, had enough money for both of them. Anyway, it was his first for this sort of thing, and he was quite inventive, much to the women's amusement and delight.

Now, here I was, doing it myself. At least I was fond of this couple. They were talented painters, and I liked their style and their beautiful loft. In my mind, I wasn't really being unfaithful. After all, I rationalized, it was a couple, not one guy. That would have been different.

The next morning, I talked about Norman a lot. I told them how involved we were, how much I loved him and that he was away for a few weeks and that I missed him terribly. At that moment, hurt and angry as I was, I ached for his body, his smell, his voice, his laughter, and his arms holding me, protecting me from myself.

I decided to write him, and since he had been so honest with me, it was only fair that I should be the same.

orman wired saying he was coming in from L.A. and that I should meet him at the Sixty-fourth Street apartment. I was surprised, since I had not expected to see him for another week. After an endless day at work, I rushed home to change. I wanted to look especially beautiful, so I picked out a lovely chartreuse silk dress from my new wardrobe and my high-heeled black pumps. I was so happy; I couldn't think

of anything else but him, shutting out of my mind his letter and that crazy night with my friends.

But as I climbed the stairs to his place, I began to feel guilty and anxious, remembering my own letter. I decided not to ring and opened the door with my key.

He did not come to the door to greet me; instead he sat in the enormous, shabby chair, which dominated the room like a throne. He had a drink in his hand. I was so happy to see him.

I said, "Darling, I'm so glad you're back."

The words were hardly out when he spit at me. He was so angry I thought for a moment he was going to hit me. I looked at the wet spot on the front of my dress, and my eyes filled with tears.

"Why did you do that?"

"You bitch, you couldn't wait until I got home, could you? One guy wasn't enough, you had to have a circus. How many times were you with them?"

I could feel my face flush, my guilt followed by my own anger. "And what about those women you fucked? It's okay for you to do it, but not for me? I'm supposed to be a stick of wood?" I started to cry.

He looked at me, his face still angry. Lesson number one in our affair—Norman was totally unresponsive to a woman's tears. "I'm leaving," and I started for the door.

"Goddamn it, come here!"

I turned and we stared at each other for a moment, and angry as I was, I knew I wasn't really leaving.

"Come here, baby," he said again.

I hesitated, my mind not quite made up, thinking of those faceless women and my wounded pride.

"I love you, darling," he said, and I let him put his arms around me, still resisting a bittersweet capture.

"Why did you do it?" I said. "What more were you looking for?"

"I could say the same for you," he answered.

"It's not the same, I told you how it was when I wrote you. It was nothing with them, they were friends."

"Some friends."

"He didn't even fuck me, we just fooled around, like kids. I was stupid and I got drunk, but I was so lonely for you and when I got your letter, I went out of my mind with jealousy."

He stopped my words with kisses and more kisses until all thought was gone and there was only desire.

Later, when we were lying in bed, he told me he had walked around for so many years feeling dead inside, feeling nothing, but I had changed that, he had opened to me, allowing himself to feel alive, with love and pain, and above all, pleasure.

Chapter 13

few weeks later, Dan told me there was an apartment available next to his. We would have to share the same pull-chain toilet that connected the two apartments. It was a duplicate of his place, with a bathtub in the kitchen, a separate little bedroom, one tiny closet, and a front room slightly bigger than the one I had now. It was in a dilapidated tenement, six flights up on First Avenue and Second Street. The rear windows looked out on an old Jewish cemetery, shaded by three huge elms, some of the branches so long they almost touched the windows. The rent was seventeen dollars a month. The low rent, the view, and the fact that I'd be next door to my friend all helped me decide to take the place. I needed a change, anyway. Dan had told Ed I was moving. Since he still had the truck and I didn't have much stuff, he offered to move me. I thought that was sweet.

"Sure," I said and laughed, "why not keep it in the family?"

I painted the walls white, and because the bedroom had no door, I put up a lovely wood-beaded curtain I had found in a junk shop. I liked the click and the swishing sound of the beads when I passed through. I covered the naked light bulb in the bedroom ceiling with a red Chinese lantern, bathing the little room in a fiery glow that shone through the curtain.

There, in that place, I could be Sadie Thompson, or I could be sitting in Rick's café in Casablanca. Norman loved the effect, and one night he asked me to make believe I was Sadie standing naked behind the beaded curtain waiting for Reverend Mailer to come and save her soul. We had a lot of fun with that one.

That winter, Norman wanted to share his love of skiing with me. I wasn't exactly a sportswoman. I hadn't inherited any of my father's athletic prowess. Daddy had taught me to ride a bike and ice skate, and I could do a great bellywhopper on my little sled. But none of the kids on my block went skiing; that was only in the movies and only for rich people. But Norman assured me that I would love it, and it was to be our first weekend away together.

He bought me the latest ski equipment at the Norse House, and we drove to Stowe, in Vermont. He was right, it was wonderful. It seemed I was a natural, instinctively doing clumsy stem christies before I even learned a beginner's snowplow. He was delighted at my enthusiasm, proud that I took to it so quickly. We had a wonderful time, skiing in beautiful country, deliciously hungry from the cold and the exercise, eating good food, and making love in the warmth of our little room. If we could have been on one endless ski trip during our marriage, we might still be together. But alas, life is no ski trip.

Chapter 14

Befor I met Norman, I'd always eaten in cheap Village places, but all that changed now. We both loved to eat, so he delighted in taking his Village bohemian to different restaurants. I remember the Petipas, a romantic little place on West Twenty-ninth Street, a favorite of Norman's and a meeting place for ballet dancers. It was my first French restaurant. Norman spoke French to the waiter, hamming it up and trying to imitate Jean Gabin's

Marseilles accent. I could tell it wasn't good French because I'd been watching French films at the Thalia since I was sixteen. Even though I didn't speak French, my ear was attuned to it. But Norman was such an actor, it was fun just listening to him, especially since I had a crush on Gabin, a sexy French teddy bear, a quality shared by my less burly lover. Norman ordered an expensive wine, toasting me in his growling French. "To my truth and your beauty."

There was Nicholson's, a chic bistro, in the East Fifties, where we dined in a landscaped garden decorated with white Grecian statues and two small willow trees. The place was known for its chocolate mousse, another first for me. When I ordered one, Norman gently corrected me. "Mousse, not moussay, darling." It was the start of my finishing-school education.

Norman had to give up his sublet because the owner was coming back to New York, so he found an even crummier place on Pitt Street, down on the lower East Side. He was there for about two months when, luckily, there was a vacancy in the front apartment on my floor, and he moved in. It was easy since he had little or no furniture, only cartons of books. It was perfect for me, with Dan's apartment on one side and Norman's on the other. Since he was in my place most of the time, Norman thought of tearing down the wall between our two apartments to create a floor-through railroad flat. We'd have lots of space, with two kitchen sinks, two toilets, one at each end, and best of all, a studio for me. Norman didn't need work space since he had rented a small room in Brooklyn Heights, near his mother's apartment, where he had lunch every day.

There were more surprises from my lover. Not only could he tear down walls, but he was also a talented plumber and carpenter. To my delight, he moved the bathtub from the living room into the kitchen, built a partition around it, redid the antiquated plumbing, and even installed a hot water heater. It was beautiful, a kind of Rube Goldberg creation. We loved our thirty-seven dollar, floor-through apartment and our back view of the cemetery. We scraped the floors, painted the walls white, and hung all of my pictures. On Sundays, we would knock on Dan's door, and the three of us would walk around the pushcart section looking for bargains, ending up at Katz's deli for hot dogs and pastrami sandwiches. With all the fancy places we moved to later on, I don't think Norman was ever happier than he was in that cold-water flat.

A few months after we'd set up the apartment, I quit my job. Norman said there was no need for me to work, and he opened a checking account for me. It was my first ever. I had no debts and no savings account. I'd been paying all my living expenses directly, so that a checking account was a big thrill. There would be more time for me to paint and more time to play house.

So far as I was concerned, there wasn't much to keeping house. I disliked housework anyway and kept it to a minimum. I would make the bed, sweep, and wash a few dishes, and since we ate out most of the time, that was no problem. Later on in our relationship, in other places, there were always maids. Norman was sweet, offering to have one now, but the idea of a maid climbing six flights to our dump was ludicrous.

We had a busy social life, and I was still going to Hans Hoffman's classes. Norman had offered to pay for that from the time we met. It was generous of him, and I loved him for it, but I refused. Instead, I asked Mr. Hoffman for a scholarship, explaining how difficult it was for me to pay for lessons. In return, I suggested I could be the class monitor, putting everything in order after class, booking models, and doing other chores. I was proud when Hoffman agreed, since it meant that he really liked my work.

Now, I had money in the bank and my new checking account, but I decided not to give up my scholarship—perhaps because it was the last vestige of my former independence.

I was having fewer sessions with Dr. Booth, eventually floating into his office to say I didn't need to come anymore, because I had found myself in Norman, whom I adored and would some-day marry. He looked at me with his weary hound's face.

"Has he asked you to marry him?"

"No, but he will. After all we're just getting to know each other."

He let me talk, occasionally nodding. When my hour was up, I shook his hand and thanked him, confident in my new happiness. Of course, he gave no indication of disapproval, but I sensed it.

"Keep in touch," he said, but I didn't.

Although Norman had never criticized me for going to a shrink, I knew how opposed he was to psychoanalysis, and I'm sure his attitude had influenced my decision. In retrospect, that was not the best time to have left my therapist; but again, is there ever a best time? My relationship with Norman was more com-plicated than the one I'd had with Ed Fancher. It was a rela-tionship that needed further scrutiny, looking beyond the excitement of new love, ego, glamour, and sex, demanding objec-tivity about his drinking and my growing interest in the same, his narcissistic controlling nature and my childish dependencies. But my blinders were intact, and I had neither the awareness nor the desire to remove them. After all, we were in love, and for me, this was the answer to everything.

There might have been another reason Norman wanted me out of therapy, along with his antipathy toward psychoanalysis. He had an intense need to play Pygmalion. In spite of my fluctuat-

ing self-esteem, I resisted the role of Galatea. So there was a lot
of bickering between us. And bickering with women was one of
Norman's favorite indoor sports.

Then too, he would become fixed on one idea or another, and
nothing you could say or do would move him. The Lord hath spoken, and so be it.

There was the time he turned against garlic, after having eaten
it all his life. I was developing into a pretty good cook and never
happier than when cooking up a new dish from the beautiful cookbooks he bought for me. I don't think I used garlic to excess, and
it certainly did not dominate the taste of my dishes, especially
since I slavishly followed the recipes. But he was obsessed.

"It's coming through our pores, I can smell it."

"Well, I can't. You and your overdeveloped olfactory nerve.
You're like Marcel Proust, always sniffing things. Why don't you
write a book about your nose?" I was really terribly upset, only
because all my Mediterranean dishes would have to go. "What
the hell are we going to live on? Oatmeal? And what about the
fancy restaurants we eat in?"

"We'll eat at American places, like diners."

One of his favorite dishes, which he still remembers, was my
pork chops and saffron rice. How could I leave garlic out of that?

"No garlic," he repeated.

"But that's impossible. Be reasonable for Christ's sake."

In desperation, I made two separate versions of each dish I
cooked, one with garlic, one without. I stuck it out for two weeks,
but then I sneaked the garlic back in, a little at a time. He never
noticed the difference.

When we started to live together, there were two things I had
to learn in the kitchen. Norman liked the same lunch every day,

the tuna salad his mother fixed for him since he was a little boy.
I had to make it the same way. And scrambled eggs had to be a
replica of Mama Fan's.

Norman patiently gave me a lesson in making eggs, explaining that the degree of doneness was a big factor. Once they were
undercooked, and he dumped them on the floor. I looked at the
gooey mess.

"Clean it up," he said.

"Fuck you, clean it up yourself. And you can eat breakfast
at your mother's from now on."

I finally got the eggs right, so it never happened again. Tuna
fish and scrambled eggs. Those were two dishes you had to make
like Mama—or else.

Another time he handed me his copy of *Das Kapital*, an influence in his life, he said, and consequently, on his work.

"Why don't you read it? I don't think Bea ever read it through,
but if *you* finish it, you'll probably be the only woman in New York
who has."

Would that be my only claim to fame, I wondered? If I read
this monumental book, would my newfound perceptions give me
the confidence to share in all those hot political discussions with
Norman's writer friends?

I flipped the pages. "Jesus, he's gotta be kidding." It was like
those five roller-coaster rides. After two chapters, I got a headache. That was it for Karl Marx and me.

Norman was a constant reader, even during meals. I read, too,
so that I wouldn't feel lonely. For me, the bathroom was the place
to do your thing and get out, but for him, it was the Brooklyn Public Library.

Although we went out most nights, I really enjoyed staying
home. We might go out for a quick bite, then return to the apart-

ment. I was happy watching him, content with the moment when he could be kind and loving. Occasionally he would read a passage out loud to me, and I would share his pleasure in the writing. He was always so restless, so I would cherish those rare evenings when we could just be with each other without drinking, without pressure.

Chapter 15

One day we decided to have a housewarming.

"Which celebrity would you like to invite, darling? You can have anyone you want."

"Marlon Brando, of course." Norman knew him, and he was in town.

I brought a lot of food from Katz's and just put it on the table. And of course, there was plenty of liquor. I think we even hired a bartender, which was funny—a professional bartender in this run-down tenement apartment. Only Norman Mailer could get away with giving a party in a place like that. Of course, the guests looked upon it as one of his whims.

Marlon showed up with Rita Moreno. He was obviously shy and sat in a corner with Rita on his lap, neither of them moving the whole time they were there. She looked sullen, clinging to her property. Clearly, it was hands off. She needn't have bothered, since people tended to be cool about approaching him even if they were dying to, especially the women. I was so busy being hostess that I hardly spoke to him and was disappointed when he left early.

We loved having parties, and this was the first of many in that place. But for me, there would never be one like it. It was wonderful, a mingling of personalities, painters, beat poets, writers, actors, critics, a lot of brains, sex appeal, beautiful women, and extra men, good talk against a background of laughter, the clinking of ice cubes in glasses and jazz on the radio.

It was a softer Norman, then, who drank, not yet becoming the mean, drunken stranger, driving us down the road to hell. Nor was I yet his willing passenger, possessed by my own alcoholic insanity. But now, on this night, at this time, we were a couple in love, excited by this party and life and by each other.

Some of our guests lived in town houses and had never set foot in a tenement, but none acted as if they were slumming. After all, they were invited to the castle of a young prince. Lillian Hellman came, climbing six flights, with each landing offering its delights—screaming Puerto Rican families and an old man in his shorts using the bathroom down the hall. A few cockroaches, the odor of beans and rice cooking mingling with the smell of wine from the homemade press in a store on the ground floor, and a puddle of piss along the way. Lillian didn't approve of our bohemian life style, but she shared our pride in Norman's plumbing, toasting us with a martini. "To Adele and to Norman, whose plumbing I respect as much as *The Naked and the Dead*." We all laughed.

Norman was moody. *Barbary Shore's* sales had been so-so, and he was trying to get into his new book. Unfortunately my moods hinged on his. When he was up, I was happy, when he was depressed, I was sure I was the cause. I needed a lot of reassurance, which added to his other pressures. Yes, I was supportive of him, but I also needed emotional nurturing. Sometimes more than any one person could give me.

This was especially true before my period, when I suffered from anxiety and depression. Then it wasn't called PMS. It was just "the curse," and for a week you were a pain in the ass. If there was any medication, I didn't know about it and wouldn't have taken it. Norman didn't approve of pills for anything.

"When you get depressed, you give off a black ink that's impenetrable," my lover would say. So the only thing for me to do was to sit in a lean-to out in the desert with a sack over my head until I was my own jolly self again.

We hadn't had a really bad quarrel since the Hollywood fight. (I don't count our histrionics over his mother's scrambled eggs.) One night we were coming out of the Captain's Table, a Village seafood house, when we ran into a guy I'd been dating about the time I was seeing Jack Kerouac. I introduced Norman to Bill, who was a Texan. Bill had been born with a leer on his face. It was his natural expression, and he looked at me as if I were a strawberry ice cream soda.

We exchanged the usual small talk, and Norman and I headed for home. I was in a good mood, it was a lovely night, and we were both full of good food. I noticed how quiet Norman was.

"What's the matter, darling. You look upset."

"Damn right," he growled. "Who the hell was that guy? I wanted to punch him in the mouth for the way his eyes were sliding all over you."

"He was just someone I went out with after I broke up with Ed, and it was just for a short time. It was nothing."

He frowned. "It didn't look that way to me. It must have been pretty hot, the way he was undressing you. How many other guys in the Village are we going to run into?"

"Honey, he looks at everyone like that. He can't help it, it doesn't mean a thing. Bill was born with that smirk." I was both pleased and a little angry at his jealousy. "Goddamnit, Norman, you weren't the only man in my life, and neither have I been the only woman in yours. Remember?"

We walked two blocks in angry silence, then Norman took out the small notebook he always carried. I knew what that meant, and it drove me crazy. He put it down on a car hood and began to write.

"You and that fucking notebook, you weren't really angry about that guy Bill. You were just watching yourself be angry, taking notes on your emotional condition. You might at least have waited till you were alone."

"You're wrong, baby. I was ready to wipe that fucking leer off his face because I was so jealous." He continued to scribble while he spoke.

"Then stop writing."

"In a minute."

"Now, goddamnit!" I grabbed the notebook from his hand and threw it on the sidewalk. "You don't really love me," I shouted and walked away.

He caught up, saying he was sorry, but that he never knew when he would get an idea or a sentence, a plot, anything. He had to write it down before he forgot—it had nothing to do with this moment. I wanted to demand that he show it to me, but I knew from past experience, he would refuse, so I didn't bother. I sulked all the way home. Our quarrels seldom carried over to the next day, and that night we made up in the best way we knew how—in bed. The Bill incident brought us closer, and Norman's jealousy ignited us both.

The only bohemian aspect of our life was the crummy walk-up we lived in. Otherwise we were a nice, middle-class couple, with Norman and his navy Brooks Brothers suit and me in one of my many black velvet dresses, charged to my new Lord and Taylor account. I had to dress up a lot since we got all kinds of invitations, none of which Norman could refuse. It didn't matter where the party was or who gave it. He had to go.

We ran the gamut from uptown celebrity town-house soirees to the seamy downtown parties of the beats and the druggies. Sandwiched in between were the loft parties of my painter friends, and a few literary luminaries in the Village, who lived well, but modestly.

Norman's energy was awesome, and mine almost matched his. But I would have liked a few more evenings at home for a little introspective activity.

"Why do we have to go out every night?" I complained as we were dressing for another roistering evening, my head still filled with the superficialities of the last party.

"Because, my sweet, I write alone, holed up in a room, for seven hours every day."

My expanding social circle and my role as the mistress of a literary star was exciting, but I didn't realize how much I was beginning to depend on booze to dull any anxiety or doubt about my own identity. I loved the taste of whiskey sours, tequila sours, daiquiris, all those sweet, lethal cocktails, that made me feel a queen to Norman's king—or sometimes, a cop to his juvenile delinquent.

With all this social whirling, Norman had his home base. It was not our apartment, but his parents' place in Brooklyn Heights, where we were expected for dinner every Friday night, and it was there he could feast on his mother's love food, usually pot roast and potato pancakes, comforting to his psyche and my stomach.

When I met him, he'd rhapsodized over Mama Fan's matzoball soup, the balls so light they'd bob to the surface in their golden broth. "And wait till you taste her pot roast and apple pie." Apple pie was never my favorite, and the only thing I knew about Jewish cooking was what I ate at Katz's delicatessen.

I remember the Mailers' apartment as so spotless, it was somewhat stiff. Fan had little or no visual aesthetic sense, so the decor was unimaginative, but solid and respectable. There was a cabinet in one corner filled with her best china, some porcelain figurines, and other "chachkes." The couch and chairs were slipcovered in a floral pattern, and there was wall-to-wall dark green carpeting on the floor. A large picture of Norman was hung opposite the couch. It was all very conventional, but homey, and one had the sense of the presence of a woman whose home and children had always been the center of her life and to whom chaos was unendurable.

Shortly after I met his parents, Norman asked me to do something I thought was strange. His parents were away for the weekend, and he asked me to meet him there because he wanted to make love in his mother's bed. The idea was repellent to me, so I refused. But he was so excited by the idea that I finally agreed.

We did it on top of the candlewick bedspread, because if we used the sheets, we would have had to change the linen, and she would have noticed. Then we did it on the living room floor. I was a little inhibited at first, but I forgot where we were, once we got into it. After all, it wasn't my father and mother. We showered together, then cleaned up every trace of our presence. Norman's eyes gleamed with admiration at my daring.

Chapter 16

I wanted to show him off to my family, and since I had made my peace with them, they invited us to dinner.

One of the things I loved about Norman was that he never looked down on anybody. I was much more of a snob than he was and more judgmental. He was also a good listener, which I was not, so I knew my darling would be at his most charming. Besides, the writer was curious about this new set of characters. My family knew that we were living together and that he was Jewish. But he was a famous writer, so that would get me through the pearly gates. They even promised to read some of *The Naked and the Dead* in anticipation of our visit.

It had been a long time since I'd been home, so I was nervous, going over the bridge to Brooklyn. Norman knew more or less what to expect, for God knows I had tried to describe them as accurately as I could. Since I'd seen them, they had moved to a small basement apartment on Shore Road and Ninety-fourth Street. I pressed the bell, thinking, why do they have to live in a basement, for God's sake? They can afford better. Oh well, at least it's in a nice building, in a beautiful area.

Norman sensed my nervousness and gave me a hug. Daddy opened the door with Mama and my sister Joanie beside him.

"Hi, everybody, we're here," I said. Norman watched the flurry of hugs and kisses, then the moment of truth.

"Norman, this is my mother, my dad and of course, my sister Joanie." She looked like a young Dolores Del Rio, and Norman stared. Daddy looked handsome in his dark blue suit and natty bow tie. Norman nodded. "How are you folks?"

Daddy put out his hand, giving one of his painful bone-crushing handshakes.

"Pleased ta meetcha, Norman." My knight grinned and squeezed back with all his strength.

"Same here, Mr. Morales." That's the way my father tested my boyfriends. At the slightest look of pain, surprise, or a hint of a wince, he would laugh. "C'mon, can't you take it, kid?"

Norman had passed the test. Daddy's Humphrey Bogart sneer had been replaced by a smile that lit up his handsome face.

"Well, we're finally gettin' together, and I gotta tell ya, it's a real honor meetin' a famous writer like yourself."

"Thanks, Mr. Morales."

"Ahhh, forget that mister stuff. Call me Al."

"Well, Al, I've been looking forward to this visit. Adele talks about you a lot."

My mother snickered, waving her martini glass in my direction. "I'll bet she does."

I eyed the glass, wondering how many she'd had, and then I thought of Norman's little notebook nestled in his pocket.

Mama looked pretty in her leopard print, but she'd forgotten to take off her food-stained apron. Today her hair was a dirty blonde; the last time I saw her it was black, and before that she had been a redhead.

"Yeah, Norman, it's nice ya could come." She reached up, the bells on her charm bracelet tinkling, and patted his head. "Ooh, that hair, is it naturally curly?"

"That's my ma," I said, and Norman laughed.

I hugged my sister. "You look so grown up. I'll bet every guy in Bay Ridge High is chasing you."

She was pleased. "Not now, because I've got a boyfriend. I'll show you his picture later."

A delicious smell of saffron rice came from the kitchen where my mother's specialty, paella a la Valenciana, simmered in my grandmother's brown earthenware pot.

"Oh Ma, you made my favorite, paella, you're gonna love it Norman. It's the real thing, not like those Spanish restaurants in the Village."

"Yeah," she said, "they're just cheap imitations. Sit down, Norman, take a load off your feet. I hope you're hungry."

"Yeah, Ma, we're starving," I said.

"Good, good," said Daddy, "but how about a little libation, Norman? What'll it be?"

My lover asked for a Scotch on the rocks.

Mama came out of the kitchen with a plate of antipasto and a loaf of Italian bread.

"Rocks, rocks? Is that what they call it in your part of town? We call them ice cubes." My father hadn't asked me what I wanted.

"Ma, I'll have a whiskey sour. You got any lemons? I'll make it myself."

"Whoo, whoo, whoo, get her," she said to Norman. "My little girl wants a whiskey sour. We certainly learned a lot since we been away." Taking a drag on her cigarette, she exhaled the next sentence. "How about a club soda? It's less fattening. Besides, there's no lemons."

I was annoyed, nothing had changed. My little squirt of a mother could still press my buttons, embarrassing me in front of my famous boyfriend.

Norman grinned. "C'mon, Mae, she's as sophisticated as you are."

Mama didn't answer that one. I don't think she knew the expression "touché," if she did she would have used it.

"Gee whiz, Ma, I'm not a child. I'm in my twenties, for God's sakes."

I couldn't believe the whine in my voice, as I felt that old anger again. In one minute, we'd be screaming at each other. But this visit was supposed to be perfect, so I decided to let it go. I'd sneak a drink in later. So for now, I'd have that club soda.

Their place wasn't a dungeon like most basement apartments. Three windows on the sidewalk let in a lot of light. There were the familiar pieces of furniture, some left over from my childhood. We were sitting on the same sagging couch, the gay flowered-chintz slipcovers hiding the cigarette burns. The secretary with the set of Dickens on the bookshelves and the gate-legged table whose color had changed half a dozen times and now was a grass green. The baby grand piano was taking up a quarter of the living room with Mama's sheet music open on the stand. The fake Persian carpet covered the floor, and on the wall were two awful landscape oils my mother had painted when I was in grammar school.

Mama was addicted to flea markets, auctions, and garage sales, always buying secondhand stuff that she was going to rejuvenate. I inherited this trait, my closet packed with interesting pieces of junk waiting for my creative hands to bring them to life, some still waiting.

Daddy was a pack rat, and one of the things he saved were rubber bands for those hundred-and-one uses. Dozens of them hanging on every doorknob. When Mama found one, she'd put it on her wrist for safekeeping.

I went into the bathroom. Mama's chin strap hung on the door, and there were jars everywhere. Cleansing cream, neck cream, eye cream, body cream, and patches for her frown lines. I dabbed some Tabu, her favorite perfume, behind my ears. I was taking a chance because Norman didn't want me to wear perfume. When I walked back into the room, he was talking.

"Adele tells me you're a typesetter and a printer for the *Daily News*, Mr. Morales. It's a well-written reactionary paper."

Daddy ignored the reactionary. "I told you to call me Al. Hell, I'm not that much older than you. I'm forty-nine. How old are you?"

"Twenty-eight."

"Ahhh, you're just a kid. Now what the hell were we talking about? I lost my train of thought. Oh yeah, the *News*. You're right, Norman, it is a good paper, the best, and it's been my meal ticket for twenty-six years. But ya wanna know what the most important thing is, the typographical union, that's what, the Big Six. We gotta make sure those palookas up there stay in line."

Daddy poured himself another shot of whiskey. That's the way he always drank it because ice cubes were for sissies. He was in heaven because Norman was listening to him. None of us ever listened to him, least of all me, except when he got mad. His idea of parenting, besides being a good provider, was to lecture and nag the shit out of me, with predictions of gloom and doom for all of us and for the world.

"Nag, nag, nag, you're always picking on me," I'd say.

"Don't get fresh. It's for your own good." Then I'd get the "when I was a boy, I didn't have this or that" routine.

And Mama handling him with her usual tact would say, "Oh Christ, there he goes about his union again, him and his goddamn union meetings."

But tonight he had Norman's ear, and he was happy. "You know, I do a little writin' myself. Not like you, of course, just a few union speeches and reports. I'm runnin' for chairman, ya know."

Mama made a face. "Yeah, Al, and you've been runnin' for seven years. Maybe someday you'll get elected. You know, Norman, the man's stubborn, he don't take no for an answer."

"Ahh, keep quiet Mae, never mind alla that." There was an awkward silence. I tinkled the ice in my glass, and Norman studied his drink. My father jumped up. "I hear ya like boxin'," and he threw a few punches in Norman's direction. Then he went to the closet and took out two sets of boxing gloves.

"C'mon, Norman, how about it?"

It was all too familiar. "Daddy, please, not now, we're going to eat soon, right Ma?"

She rolled her eyes. "Who knows? Don't ask me."

Norman got up slowly, and he and Al went into a boxing crouch. They danced around, Norman throwing a right and then a left. My father moved fast so none of them landed. Norman was enjoying himself, and my father was ecstatic, it was his turn on stage. It was a small, cluttered room, and Daddy knocked over a lamp.

"Albert, for Christ's sake, look what you did, you and your boxing. Leave the man alone."

A few more punches and they went into a clinch. "Albert, will you stop it."

"Whadya yellin' about, Mae? The man can take care of himself." Norman laughed, so did my father.

"Hey, Paisan, ya gotta pretty good left. Been punchin' the bag a little?"

Norman scratched behind his ear. "Yeah, I work out now and then. But you're a pro." He sat down and took a swig of his drink. "How did you get started, Al?"

Norman was really interested. They shared the same passion, and there seemed to be a mutual respect. Daddy showed Norman a framed, autographed photo of him and Jack Dempsey sparring, and another of Max Schmeling with his arm around my father.

"Yeah," he said to Norman, "I did a good bit of boxing in my time. I started foolin' around with the gloves when I was a kid in Hell's Kitchen. Of course, I didn't know much at first, just usin' my fists." He jabbed the air. "Pow, pow, pow, it was a tough neighborhood, and you had to fight to get anything. I started hanging around Stillman's gym, some of the big guys took a shine to me. I kept my eyes open, and I picked up a few pointers. They said I was good. Later on things got rough, it was the Depression, and there wasn't much dough, so I did a lotta club fights. Let's see if I can remember, yeah, I won twenty-five amateur fights, and I lost twenty-five, all by knockouts. Jesus, it's no wonder I'm not a little punchy. Anyway, I figured I'd go professional, and I came out with ten winners and ten losers, believe it or not, all the same way."

I chimed in. "Daddy, when I was six, I can remember you coming home with your face all bloody and your eyes swollen shut, me and Mama used to cry."

My mother sighed. "Yeah, I remember all right. Ya know, Norman, that's the way he is. He didn't know when to stop. He still doesn't. His nose was startin' to look like a pig's snout. It scared the hell out of the kids and me."

Daddy shrugged. "Ahh, ya know how women are. I just wasn't ready to throw in the towel, but she said it was the ring or her, so I quit. How about another drink?" and he went to get more ice.

"Honey," I said to Norman, "aren't you getting hungry?"

"It's okay. I'm enjoying myself. I like them."

Daddy came back with Norman's Scotch. "How did *Barbary Coast* do, Norman?"

"It's *Barbary Shore*, Al."

"Oh yeah, gee, I'm sorry."

"It's okay, I get that a lot. Well, it got mixed reviews, and it's not doing too well in the stores."

"That's too bad. Say, listen, Ed Sullivan is a friend of mine at the *Daily News*. He likes me. I drop into his office once in a while to chew the fat. Maybe he could give you a plug."

"Thanks a lot, Al. I appreciate the thought, but I don't think he'd be interested. It's not his kind of book."

"Well, anytime, Norman, anytime. Me and Mae are reading *The Naked and the Dead*. You're one helluva writer. You were there, so ya didn't have to make it up. It's good stuff. I was in the First World War, but not for long. I enlisted when I was seventeen, I lied about my age. The whole thing was lousy. I hated it because I wanted to see some action. The bastards stuck me in the kitchen with another Peruvian kid, washing dishes and peel-ing potatoes, woman's work. We were scrubbing pots one day, and we just got fed up and walked out. We hid for a couple of days, but that was that, they never came looking for us."

"Just like that, Al?"

"Yeah, just like that." Daddy laughed and clinked his glass against Norman's. "Here's to the army."

"L'chaim."

"You speak Yiddish?"

"Yeah, sure. I picked it up when I lived on the lower East Side. I speak Italian, too."

Mama came in from the kitchen. She always cooked with wine, more going into herself than into the paella. She sat down next to the guest of honor.

"Say, Norm, can I be frank?"

"Sure, Mae, be my guest."

I cringed when Mama said that. It was dangerous, the family had experienced her frankness, usually when she was under the influence. Oh God, I thought, everything was going so well, and now she's going to spoil everything with her big mouth.

"Ma, please, is supper almost ready?"

She dismissed me with a wave of her wineglass. "No, not yet. As I was saying, Norm, honesty is the best policy. That's always been my motto."

"Mae, the man is hungry. Will ya put the supper on the table, it's gettin' late."

"Have another drink, Al, it'll make ya more mellow. Now, let's see, where was I before I was so rudely corrupted, ha ha. But seri-ously, I thought you was taller, you know, from the way you wrote about all those sexy peccadilloes and my God how do you put all those words together. You know, I probably shouldn't mention this, especially to you, but I write a little, too. It's nothing really, mostly poems. Believe it or not, I happen to have one right here. Just a little ditty dotty about Albert."

"Sure, Mae, let's hear it."

"Ma," I said, "I think the paella is getting overcooked. Could you read it later?"

"So, go stir it up."

She took a big sip of her drink. "The name of this poem is 'My Pal Al.'"

I cringed while she read, the two drinks I'd sneaked weren't making me feel any better about the way I thought the dinner should be going.

By the time we sat down to supper, it was really late. Norman was wonderful. I knew how surly he could be when he was hungry. He actually got hunger pains if he had to wait too long.

But it was worth the wait. Mama surpassed herself, ending the meal with flan, a rich Spanish caramel custard. All we were missing was some background Flamenco music. The meal ended with a toast from my father.

"I'd like to propose a toast to a great guy, a great writer, and my future son-in-law, *or else*. Haw haw, Norman, I'm just kiddin', just kiddin'."

When we finally said our goodnights, Daddy threw a light left at Norman's arm. "I'll take you to the fights sometimes, in the Brooklyn Arena in Bay Ridge, introduce you to my buddies still in the ring."

"Sure, I'd like to, Champ," Norman said. "I'll call you," and he meant it.

We took a cab over the bridge. I had looked at that harbor view so many times in my young life. Times of hope and times of despair, but tonight it seemed especially beautiful because I was happy.

It's true, my mother had annoyed me, but generally speaking, both she and my father had behaved themselves, and it had been a good visit. Mama was a skillful sniper, and you had to be alert. But in spite of her resistance, Norman had charmed her, parrying her potshots with wit. Whatever went on that evening, I don't think these characters bored him. He could have ripped them apart, but unlike me, he was almost never mean spirited.

He had paid some attention to my sister, who was shy and had not said a word the entire evening. He complimented her by suggesting the possibility of looking into a modeling career. Joanie beamed, saying it had never occurred to her. And no wonder, I thought, coming from a background where women were second-class citizens, meant to serve their lord and master.

"I'm still in high school," she said.

"If I were you, " Norman said, "I would think about it. If you need some good pictures, I'll give you the name of a friend of mine, a good fashion photographer."

Sure, I thought, but first she'd have to get away from my parents. "That's a great idea, Joanie," and even as I said it, I felt a twinge of jealousy because he had never suggested a modeling career for me.

Though the evening went well, I must have been more tense than I realized because I was exhausted and went straight to bed. Norman stayed up reading, his usual nightcap in his hand. I was half asleep when he came to bed, my body curved to his.

"Sweet monkey, now I understand you a little more than I did."

"Is that good or bad?" I murmured.

He laughed. "A little of both, and I love you, darling, even more for it. They're a strong family, and they don't let go easily. So I understand how much courage it took to stand on your own."

orman had been in love with Provincetown ever since he went there with Bea in the mid-forties. "I want to share it with you, darling," he told me, "because I know you'll love it. It's a Portuguese fishing town with a beautiful harbor and a pure north light that's perfect for painters."

So, in 1951 we spent the first of many Provincetown summers in a small apartment on the harbor side. It was a good idea to get away from New York for a while. Norman was still recovering from the *Barbary Shore* reviews. He didn't show it in public, but I know how disappointed and depressed he was; and though he never talked about it, I sensed he was running scared. We both believed in the healing powers of the sea. So we hoped Provincetown would be good to us. He thought he might work well up there. *The Deer Park* was starting to take form in his head, and he'd been making some notes.

Over the years, we rented many places, from small apartments to big houses, but living on the bay side was the most desirable. As far as I was concerned, it wasn't worth being there unless you could stay on the water.

Sitting on the deck was a theatrical experience for me, watching the light change in the sky and on the water throughout the day, the colors always different. The only other place I've seen that kind of pure light is the Greek islands, a reflection of light from the white houses of the village to the blue of the water and back again.

Those first summers in Provincetown were an important part of my life with Norman, that special light illuminating a bit of happiness against the dark background of his shifting moods. The same light that darkened and flickered out during that last psychotic summer of 1961, the year a part of me died.

Many of my friends from Hoffman's New York school came to his summer sessions at his home in Provincetown. Since I was not one to lie on the beach all day, the school was perfect for me. The sessions went from nine to three, four days a week. While I painted, Norman worked on his book.

When we arrived in June, the town was always fairly quiet, before the July and August frenzy of cocktail parties. So there wasn't much to do in the evenings. There was one movie house, a few galleries, and dinner in one or another of the really good seafood restaurants. If you really got restless, there was the Old Colony, a popular year-round watering hole on Commercial Street. Norman was a bar and party boozer, and he didn't do too badly at home, but I was primarily a party drinker. However, I did enjoy the Old Colony's atmosphere, the sawdust floor and the feeling of being in the hold of an old boat. It was crowded, even in June, the customers a mixture of Portuguese fishermen, writers, actors, painters, beatniks, tourists, beach bums, and anybody who wanted to be where the action was or just wanted somebody to talk to.

When July came round, the invitations began coming, and we were out almost every night. There was always something going on, a party, a gallery opening, someone's act to catch or a jazz combo at a nightclub, or dinner at a friend's house. To me, it was a perfect combination, painting during the day and partying at night. Our invitations were not limited to Provincetown. There were the more literary parties in Truro and Wellfleet, with people like Dwight and Gloria Macdonald, Edmund Wilson, and Mary McCarthy.

When Norman told me about the Macdonald party, our first in Wellfleet, I was lukewarm.

"God, Norman, I hate swimming in squishy-bottomed ponds, and it'll be buggy. Why couldn't they have it on the beach?"

"Well, it isn't, so stop bitching. You've never been out to the Wellfleet ponds, they're beautiful. Cheer up, nobody dresses up, and they all swim in the nude."

"Oh goody, an orgy with Edmund Wilson and Dwight Macdonald, how exciting. Gloria would love to see your charms. She's been rolling her little blue eyes since I've known her, flirting with you in that fey little-girl manner of hers. You've probably fucked her, too, and God know who else you've had in that snooty Wellfleet crowd."

Norman grinned devilishly. "You'll never know, will you, baby? If you don't want to go, I'll go by myself."

"Like hell you will, I can't let you out of my sight. What about us, I hope we don't have to stand around bare-assed."

"I don't know, we'll find out when we get there."

Dwight was one of my favorite people of all that literary crowd in New York. Unlike some of those types, I was comfortable with him because he was real and I was able to talk to him. He was always sweet to me, and I sensed he found me attractive. Besides, he was bright and funny, and it was always interesting to hear him sparring intellectually with Norman.

When we got there, Dwight greeted us warmly, wearing nothing but his rimless glasses. He was a funny sight, with his white goatee, a long string bean of a body, and his cute little pot belly. I'd never visited a nudist colony, so I was unprepared for the sight of these paunchy, aging bodies, sipping martinis, engaged in conversation as if they were fully dressed. We chatted with Dwight, drinks in hand.

"Why don't you two go for a swim?"

"Is it cold?" I asked, hoping he'd say yes.

"No," he smiled, "it's wonderful."

Norman and I exchanged looks, and I shrugged, "Sure, why not," and I stripped, folding my clothes neatly. Norman watched me, then he took off everything but his shorts. I was surprised, but since Dwight was standing there, I made no comment. I'd get Norman for that later. After all, I didn't leave on my panties.

The water looked murky, so I was reluctant to plunge in. I stood there, feeling self-conscious. Dwight was in the water, and Norman was chatting with a lady of Rubenesque proportions. He waved to me to come join them. She wasn't pretty, so I didn't rush over.

Guzzling my drink, I watched all those naked intellectuals, talking animatedly. God, I thought, I need to get high to get through this. I remembered the few pimples I had on my rear end that I'd forgotten to cover with my pancake makeup and the tummy I was beginning to develop. (Norman didn't care how fat I got!) There were some blankets on the grass and a picnic spread, but I was more interested in another drink. Then I would have to circulate.

I stared at a red-haired woman with bright red pubic hair. I wondered if that was Mary McCarthy. Then I counted the phony blondes. No one was paying attention to me, but I still felt conspicuous. The liquor was on a picnic table nearby. I helped myself to a large drink. I was not quite ready to stroll about as if I were fully clothed. That would take at least two more gin and tonics. Meanwhile I sat down on the nearest blanket, keeping my knees together. I introduced myself to a woman sitting nearby. She had a cherubic face, huge pendulous breasts, and more hair below than above.

"My name is Joan," she said between bites of her hot dog. Like me, she was an artist, so we chatted about how difficult it was to paint waves, neither of us glancing below the chin. However, I became distracted by a blob of mustard that plopped on her left breast, slowly sliding down to her large pink nipple. She went on talking, seemingly oblivious, and I stifled an impulse to lick it off.

With dusk and the mosquitoes coming, we said our goodbyes to the Macdonalds. In spite of our alcoholic haze, we didn't have the usual quarrel. Instead we ended up on a deserted road near Provincetown making love standing up against the hood of the car.

Norman wanted as much variety in our summer social life as we had in New York. Besides the Wellfleet and Truro literary clique, there was the Hoffman school clique and the subterranean group of beatniks, drunks, and junkies. Norman was one of the very few stars in town, so he had easy access to any circle, our mobility assisted by drinking and pot.

Provincetown in the fifties was afloat on a spongy marijuana foundation. We could get it anywhere, anytime, and cheap. Norman liked the sleazy parties in the local underworld, the rooms filled with dropouts, boring drunks, and potheads, some with police records. Every once in a while, there would be a police bust, but luckily, it was always the one party we missed. I was bored, but a few drinks would fix that, and I was driven to keep up with him. Making the scene, any scene, was part of it. If I fell back, I was afraid I would lose him.

Chapter 18

I t was 1953, and we were still in love and very much a couple, sometimes at odds with each other, but nonetheless, it was Norman and Adele to us and to our friends. My feelings about Ed Fancher were long buried, along with the pain of that ending. I almost never thought about him, but it seems true that a part of those people we loved so passionately remains inside of us, for always. I was becoming less clear about who I was, and for whatever reason, I seemed to have had a stronger sense of self in my other life with Ed. With Norman, most people were extensions of that all-encompassing ego.

I always felt he was incapable, in any way, of putting himself in another person's place to try to experience what others were feeling. There were no colors in Norman's spectrum, only black and white. But because he was so bright, he could mix them into a myriad of convincing greys.

Norman needed to create and impose a persona for everyone he knew. You were this or that, however he wished to paint you with no relation to what was real in your personality. I was emotionally immature, with deep vulnerabilities and deep strengths and a need to express the actress in me before I ever thought of becoming one. I tried to take on the roles that Norman, the director, had assigned to me. But then my independence would surface, and I would tell him to knock it off. There was always that back and forth between us, and my self-esteem was on a roller coaster. I was confused because, in spite of myself, my identity was slowly being absorbed into his.

I knew I was talented, and I was certainly productive, though the crazier our life got, and the more I drank, the less I painted. I was trying to juggle everything—mistress of a famous writer, painter, perfect party hostess, and later on, his stunt partner. Because I loved him, I handed everything over, my heart, my body, and my talent.

In spite of my childishness, my lack of discipline, and my slovenly housekeeping, I tried to please him in every way I could, and it was getting harder the closer we got, the more we were together. I was up against a perfectionist, a relentless critic, especially of people closest to him, with an ego that devoured everything and everybody. He was tougher now, and the bickering between us accelerated. There never seemed to be an in-between.

One minute I was his little tigress, his beautiful Pasionaria with the grace and beauty of Spanish women. I would smile and bask in his compliments. But then with my occasional lapses from an adored goddess into someone who went to the bathroom every day, or worse, held her fork the wrong way, he could obliterate me verbally. He was a sadistic master, with a rapier tongue that slashed me until I bled. His anger was exacerbated by whiskey.

"Stupid bitch," he would say, "you can't learn anything. You're stuck in your background. You're a piece of meat."

How I hated him at those moments, and I fought back in the only way I knew how, by yelling, my voice echoing the snarls and whines of my mother raging at my father.

"Shut up, you son of a bitch, you and your fucking, fancy, ass-kissing friends. You think they're better than me, you superior bastard, with your phony Harvard accent. You fucking Mama's boy."

When I was thirteen, my mother took me to see *Carmen* at the Brooklyn Academy of Music. It was my first opera, and I loved it. I decided I was going to be that beautiful temptress who ate men alive, flossed her teeth, and spit out the bones, wearing an endless supply of costumes by Fredricks of Hollywood. I never dreamed I would find my Escamillo in the guise of a nice Jewish boy. To me, a relationship was like that opera. You lived from crisis to crisis, sang love duets, and had screaming fights. I was acting out the drama of my life with a willing actor, albeit a ham, whose need for drama equaled my own.

My life now totally revolved around him. I had to keep up with his obsessive need for parties, so we were out almost every night. I could sleep late, but Norman would go to his studio every day, no matter how depressed or hungover he was. Hangovers were no problem with me until later on in my life, when I would get so sick I felt like being hospitalized. However, with all this night life, I still kept up my art classes. I was beginning to paint less and less on my own, however.

One night we gave a rather sedate party, unlike one of our big splashy gatherings. We invited a few editors from *Commentary* magazine, a literary critic, and a couple of novelists, and our permanent guest, Dan Wolf. I was busy serving some party food and making drinks. And I was also in the process of getting high, my usual way of coping with whatever I had to be for that evening, bright and charming, beautiful and a perfect hostess—the opposite of all the things I really felt about myself. At one point in the evening, I watched Norman drunkenly holding forth about another of his obsessive themes, the psychology of the orgy. The party seemed stiff, not like our usual lively scene, and I was tired of being part of the ring of admirers listening to the guru. I can't think what possessed me to do what I did next, maybe the devil made me do it because he knew I was fed up with Norman's constantly talking about the orgiastic experience. I was going to call his bluff, aided, of course, by the four drinks I'd had.

I heard myself shout in a voice that seemed to come from someone else. "Okay, Norman, you want an orgy with these squares. Well, you'll get one," and I took off all my clothes, angrily throwing each piece at him. That shut him up, and he lost his audience. There was a hush as I stood there calmly finishing my drink, smiling at those smug faces. Look at all those uptight superior bastards, I thought, they don't know what to do. Vance Bourjaily, the novelist, with whom I'd been talking, had never liked me, so he had a big happy grin on his face.

Dan laughed, and all he said was, "Oh, Adele," as if he were admonishing a naughty child. It was a cool crowd, after all this was New York, so following immediate shock and a few titters, they resumed their conversation, drinks in hands, talking to me about everything else but my act of defiance, never allowing their eyes to leave my face. I'd had my moment, and I knew it was time to put my clothes back on.

Any other man whose woman had done something like that would have been furious, but not my Norman. He enjoyed every minute of it, his eyes sparkling with admiration, because I was his tiger again.

I had mixed feelings about his approval. I felt betrayed and hurt, because I wanted him to be angry, because I was his woman, and in spite of what I had done, I was not up for grabs.

Chapter 19

I was gradually drifting away from the friends I'd had from the past. They were replaced by Norman's entourage—barflies, freeloaders, ex-pugs, and a token priest who wore a red-striped T-shirt and had a rich vocabulary of four-letter words. The first time he said "fuck," I went into shock, but at the same time, it was exciting. After all, I'd received my Holy Communion at Saint Rosalie's in Bay Ridge. When we went out to dinner, there was always somebody trailing along. I wasn't shy about

complaining. "Goddamn it, Norman, out of all the interesting people we know, we always end up with these losers who never pick
up the check. Don't you realize how far beneath you they are?
They're all refugees from the No Name bar in the Village. Let's
call up Marlon and go out with him, or are you afraid of the competition?"

Once in a while, we would do something without his entourage,
just the two of us, movies and dinner out.

He would order two whiskey sours for himself at the same time
to make sure of an immediate backup before dinner and then a
Scotch during the meal. I drank more when we were out with other
people. I would have my predinner whiskey sour, and that would
be pretty much it.

If Norman was in a bad mood, the booze could make him
vicious, and with no provocation, he would sit there and rip me
apart, pick on me for petty things till I would leave the table in
tears.

His anger and depression were coming from some other place.
I think it had to do with his feelings about himself, feelings of
omnipotence clashing with the self-doubt that he was a failed
writer, his rage over the *Barbary Shore* reviews, his tension and
worry over his work on the new book, *The Deer Park*, and a lot
of other stuff I couldn't understand at the time.

The truth was, and this was just a part of it, and neither of us
could face it—we couldn't deal with our drinking. I was totally
unaware of my own personality change when I drank, but I could
see his. It was a real Dr. Jekyll and Mr. Hyde switch from a fairly
reasonable, charming guy to a sadistic little bully. His blue eyes
would develop a mean squint, the corner of his mouth would turn
down in a sneer, and he would speak with his put-on tough Texas

hombre drawl. When he was drinking, there was a lack of joy and spontaneity, a kind of desperate grimness in everything he did.

Sometimes I could be intolerant. I was not as accepting as Norman. I did not have a suspicious nature, but what I did have was a built-in bullshit detector, if need be about myself and equally about others, smelling it even before the person opened his mouth. Norman knew this, and occasionally he would ask my opinion. But in the end, he did what he wanted.

"You're small minded," he would say. "You don't like anyone."

He didn't remember what he had said to me, in a moment of closeness when we first met.

"After the success of *Naked*, I was never sure about whether I was liked for myself or my fame, and that bothered me a lot."

In the summer of 1953, we decided to drive down to Mexico. Norman had been there once before to see Susie, who was living with Bea in Mexico City. Aside from wanting to see his daughter, he also wanted to share his enthusiasm for that country with me. I was thrilled at the idea of going.

Bea was living with Steve Sanchez, a Mexican and one of my past lovers. I wasn't surprised when I found out they were together, since the Village was so incestuous, with everyone connected in one way or another. But it was ironic to think that both Bea and Norman ended up with Latin lovers—for better or for worse.

Bea had met Steve through Dan Wolf when she was on a visit to New York. It was just about the time Norman and I had moved into the First Avenue cold-water flat together. She and Steve obviously felt strongly about each other, strongly enough for her to go off with him to Mexico. I had met her once or twice by then. She was glacial, but interestingly enough, she never attacked me verbally—at least not to my face. She was angry and hurt, of course, because she had been dumped. But let's face it—the marriage was in trouble long before I met Norman.

I was not thrilled about seeing them again, but I wasn't going to worry about it till it happened.

Two days before we left New York, I got into one of my panics. It was silly, but I worried about being shut in the car with no one but the two of us for days at a time. I didn't drive, so Norman had to do it all. How would I entertain him, when I was not a brilliant conversationalist, a stand-up comedian, or philosopher?

But we got along, leaving the city's tension behind. I was relaxed, happy to be with him, excited about seeing Mexico together.

Norman wanted to stop in Marshall, Illinois, to see his friend, James Jones, who was living in a writer's colony founded by Lowney Handy. That meant a long detour. I wasn't happy about the idea because I was anxious to see Mexico City and have some great Mexican food.

When we met Jones in New York, there was a mutual admiration for each other's work and genuine liking between them. But I sensed a certain competitiveness between Jimmy and me for Norman's attention. When Jones got drunk, he looked like an angry dog, straining at his chain, dying to get at you. With that thick neck set on a powerful torso, and muscular arms, one would think twice before challenging him.

Though he treated me politely enough, I felt he didn't really like me; and I basically didn't like him. I wasn't jealous of the camaraderie between him and Norman. It was his display of macho bullshit that annoyed me, and now, I knew I was in for a lot of it.

The heat had been bad throughout the trip, and it was unbearable the day we arrived. I assumed they would have air conditioning, but I turned out to be wrong.

Jimmy was really happy to see Norman. He welcomed him with a bear hug and was cordial to me. He introduced us to Lowney, a woman in her fifties, with a horsy face and a good ol' girl manner that barely concealed her toughness and smarts. She loved writers and had been Jimmy's mentor for a long time.

Lowney was polite enough to me, but, like a lot of women I met in New York, I could tell she was what they call a "star fucker," so Norman got all of her attention. She had a famous writer of her own, but I could see her mind clicking away as soon as she met Norman, and it pissed me off. During the three days we were there, no one paid much attention to me. But that was partly my fault; my shyness and insecurity got in my way. Drinking helped me get rid of those feelings, but I was being careful because I was getting along well with Norman and didn't want to spoil it.

Jimmy showed me around the colony, which included his big wooden house and smaller barracks-type cottages for the others. The atmosphere was monastic, with a few shirtless young writers silently raking the pebbled walks, tending the lawn, weeding the vegetable garden. It was still hot, and I wore as little as possible, a tiny bra and a pair of brief shorts. I don't think Lowney was too pleased by my seminakedness tempting her monks. They were an attractive bunch of guys, but oddly enough, they never looked at me nor did Jones introduce us. I thought that perhaps they were scared of Lowney. There were strict rules for the boys, she told us. No drinking, no staying out late, no getting laid, at least not on the premises.

Discipline and clean living will a writer make. Hell, it didn't work like that for Norman and Jimmy, who were drunk every night, the whole time we were there. One night he and Norman got down on the floor to see who could do the most push-ups. Jimmy, the bull, was in better shape than Norman, who was putting on weight. Lowney went to bed, but I stayed up and counted. Jimmy won. Along with the push-ups, there was arm wrestling, which I found more boring. Why didn't they just compare cocks and be done with it?

Most of the time, the macho competitiveness, the compulsive cursing, the showing off was ridiculous. But it was interesting when they just sat and relaxed without slugging booze, really talking to each other about writing and their lives before and after their success.

I thought *From Here to Eternity* was a good novel, and it certainly held me. But I didn't agree with Norman, who thought *Eternity* was in certain ways superior to *The Naked and the Dead.*

One thing I did envy Jones was his gorgeous collection of Navajo turquoise jewelry. He would deck himself out, his shirt opened down to his navel, with two or three silver turquoise necklaces nestled on his hairy chest and his wrists circled by turquoise bracelets.

When we left Jim and Lowney in Illinois, our next stop was North Conway, Arkansas, for a very forgettable visit with Norman's old army buddy, Frances Gwaltney, known as Fig, and his wife, Ecey. Then it was on to New Orleans, which I was looking forward to after the paralyzing heat and boredom of Arkansas.

After we got settled in at our hotel in New Orleans, we looked up the local bohemian bookshop. When we met the owner, a fat, bespectacled young man with a bad complexion and a long ponytail, I'd never seen anyone so visibly excited about meeting Norman. He almost did a spastic jig, like he had just won the lottery.

"My God, are you the guy, are you really Norman Mailer? I don't believe it, not here in my little shop, it can't be!" There was nothing blasé about this guy; his enthusiasm was refreshing. He finally calmed down and invited us to a party in the French Quarter to meet the local literati, which we did.

Unlike the bookshop owner, their response to Norman's celebrity was friendly, but cool. We were told that this was a peyote party.

"What's that?" I asked.

I was told that peyote was made from cactus juice and used by some Indian tribes during their religious ceremonies.

I looked around the room. No one seemed to be acting crazy, so I ambled into the kitchen where a girl was stirring a huge pot filled with the mysterious cactus brew. For some reason, she was wearing a nurse's uniform. Was this part of the ritual? I wondered.

She offered me some, and feeling adventurous, I took it. I gagged on the taste and was handed an orange from the pile beside the vat.

"Suck on it, that will cut the bitterness."

Norman wasn't around, so I supposed he'd already done it. He could have waited for me, I thought. I leaned against the refrigerator. The coolness felt good. I closed my eyes, waiting for it to hit; but I felt I was going to be sick.

"It takes awhile," I heard someone say.

I opened my eyes. There was a black guy, eating a sandwich, watching me.

"Are you okay?"

"I don't feel anything yet, but if you wave that sandwich under my nose, I'm gonna throw up."

He laughed. "No you won't. Try not to fix on it. You won't feel sick in a little while. Just hang in."

"Why?" I asked, gagging even as he spoke.

The guy's name was Ray. I don't know why I remember it,

except maybe because he seemed to take over as my private coach.

"Because you'll have the greatest experience of your life, you may discover secrets beyond your imagination, and you'll never be afraid of death. That is, if you don't throw up."

Even through my haze, I was impressed. "I guess you're an old hand at this."

"Yeah, and it gets better every time."

I wandered back into the living room, thinking longingly about the bathroom, trying to distract myself by talking to some of these characters, and since I was not stepping over puddles of vomit, I was encouraged. If they could do it, so could I. I saw Norman, and I wondered if my complexion was as green as his. We spoke to each other with tight mouths.

Where were the promised secrets? When would it happen? Someone suggested we go to a famous jazz joint to hear Max Roach and Charlie Parker.

"Let's go, Norman. I like listening to music when I'm high, and maybe by then, we'll be feeling better. This place is giving me the creeps."

I invited Ray to come with us. After all, he was my coach. Norman drove, since he wasn't high yet, just sick. Ray was as cheerful as we were glum.

"You guys are going to have a ball, I can tell. Just don't throw up. It'll get better."

By the time we got to the club, my nausea had subsided. When we left the car, I felt as if I were moving in slow motion. It was the same sensation I'd had in a recurring nightmare in which I was pursued by a monster. The faster I tried to run, the more leaden my legs became. Now I moved slowly because I felt no danger. I was relaxed, totally involved in my experience, not interested in my lover or what he was feeling. The club was crowded, the music blasting the room.

I had the sensation of distance from myself, of watching a film of everything I was saying and doing at the moment it was happening. It seemed to take forever to form a thought, and when I did have one, I would seem to see it printed out on film. I followed the waiter to our table, still in slow motion, looking down at my feet. They seemed far away from the rest of me, as if I were looking through the reverse end of a telescope. I'd suddenly gotten much taller. Giggling, I said to Norman, "I'm Alice, and I've had a nibble from the left side of the mushroom." He was silent, and, like myself, he was on his solo flight.

My black-suede high heels had a life of their own. They were on my feet, but then again I saw them walking by themselves, the sound of heels tapping on the floor. How funny, I thought and wondered if anyone else had noticed.

We sat down, and Norman ordered drinks. I laughed at something Ray was saying. "Man," I answered, "my nausea is gone. I feel great."

Our table was next to the bandstand. Closing my eyes, my every pore filled with sound, and I saw one beautiful color after another. That made me happy, and I laughed. "Ya boom," I said, like a delighted child. Ray grinned back. "You know it, baby."

Ya boom, the music ripped into my open mouth, down my throat through my stomach to my groin pressing against the silken crotch of my panties, pressing against the fabric of my dress, and against the chair seat. I felt like the cat, I thought, who nibbled the cheese that was on the plate that lay on the table that was in the house that Norman built. I was overwhelmed by the profun-

dity and the variety of my thoughts, which were suddenly interrupted by a wave of nausea so strong that the bile rose in my
throat. "Ray," I said, in a strangled voice, "it's over, this is it."

"Don't do it, just hold on, it'll pass. Man, I could tell you were
on a beautiful trip."

"Who cares, you fucking sadist."

I made it to the ladies' room, for the best puke I ever had.
But by now I had absorbed more than enough in my bloodstream
so that, like it or not, I was stuck with it. Norman had managed
to keep it down. It was easier for him since he could never throw
up, no matter how nauseous he felt, no matter how many fingers
he stuck down his throat.

As for me, I was a Roman who could barf anytime, anywhere.
I floated from the bathroom on the endless journey back to our
table. Norman had been unusually quiet since the start of our
adventure, no doubt nausea reducing some of that ego. He sat
there with his eyes closed, involved in the music and whatever
sensations he was experiencing, the peyote enabling him to tune
into his usually tin ear. I preferred this Norman to the one in his
cups, who indulged his public image with stunts like arm-
wrestling bouts and fistfights. I began to hallucinate about Max
Roach again, who played on, unaware he was fucking me pub-
licly and in the presence of my famous lover.

I had no sense of time. It could have been ten, two, or eight,
now, or tomorrow. My fantasy had changed. I was finished with
Roach, and now I wanted to go home with Norman. I got up from
the table slowly, since if I moved too quickly, I would leave my
legs there, and I needed them.

We said goodbye to Ray, who talked very fast, "You got it,
baby, you puked, but you got it, go with it."

I was surprised that Norman was coordinated enough to pay the check. We walked out together, smiled, and waved at Roach. "Thank you," I said.

"You're welcome," he replied.

No one would have known how stoned we were even if we were moving in slow motion. We were going back to the hotel. Norman drove through the dark streets, weaving back and forth, cursing his lack of control and the nausea that was still with him. "Fuck it!" he said and came to a stop. We left the car in the middle of the street. I had no idea where we were, and through some miracle, we found our way back to the hotel.

A red neon sign spelling the hotel's name blinked on and off outside our window, and even with the drawn shades, the room was intermittently flooded with red light. I felt as if we had died and gone to hell.

"I'm going to bed, I'm sick of it, I want it to go away."

When I closed my eyes, the hallucinations began. We lay in bed, not touching, two lonely figures in prison, with our burning images. I saw women with huge pregnant bellies that exploded into a kaleidoscope of exquisitely colored flowers. I sat up and the pictures stopped. Every time I tried to sleep, they would begin again. Norman lay there, his eyes closed.

"Do you see anything?" I asked.

He described an Aztec sacrifice. Little Indians in ceremonial dress chanting and climbing a pyramid with knives in their hands, stabbing at something or somebody on a slab at the top of the pyramid. Then he said the scene changed to banal, Walt Disney cartoons.

I took a shower, drank hot coffee, and paced up and down the room to keep awake. I was afraid to lie down. As exhausted as we were, we got dressed and went out for the rest of the night and part of the next day till the effects of the peyote wore off.

I don't know about Norman, but it was a frightening experience, and I would never do it again. There must be less painful ways to expand one's consciousness.

Besides our psychedelic trip, we did touristy things like dinner at Antoine's and a little historic sightseeing of some antebellum architecture.

It was nice being alone with my lover again, doing normal things. And I was looking forward to our destination, Mexico City.

Chapter 20

When we arrived in Mexico City, we found a lovely furnished house in the suburbs with a walled patio and a flower garden shaded by a giant tree. We unpacked and the next day called Bea and Steve. They lived in an apartment in the city, spacious but falling apart. Bea was distant, barely cordial. She didn't smile at me as much as bared her teeth, gums and all. For all the weeks we were there, she never lost her smug expression. She really hated me, with good reason, I guess, but for her daughter's sake, she kept her resentment in check. She knew I might be taking care of Susie in New York when she came to stay with Norman.

Steve was nice, but also very reserved. Susie herself seemed a little bewildered by it all, and I felt sorry for her. After all, she had been shunted around after the breakup of the marriage, spending a long time with Norman's mother in the States. Now here she was in a strange city.

Bea was a show-off, especially when she got drunk. But I was not threatened by her intellectual posturing, especially since I knew it was really dead between her and Norman. For Steve and me as well, it was as if nothing had ever happened between us. At the beginning, our visits were a little awkward, but gradually, the atmosphere was more relaxed. We were not that dependent on them for our social life, but Steve was very hospitable, showing us a Mexico City tourists didn't see and introducing us to some wonderful Mexican friends of theirs.

As soon as we settled in, Norman called a few people, and we had an instant social life. Of course, he was a big celebrity among all the expatriates living in Mexico. I loved the house and the garden, and we found a wonderful maid named Flora who was a great cook.

My mouth still waters at the memory of her *huevos rancheros* and the best chicken mole (chicken with chocolate sauce) I have ever eaten. Poor Norman lost out, since he was having trouble with his liver and had to go on a bland diet. While I was enjoying Flora's gourmet cooking, he was eating boiled, unspiced drearys on tortillas, the only Mexican food he was allowed. And, of course, no booze. On top of all that, his writing was not going well. To put it mildly, he was not in the best of moods.

But in spite of that, we both found Mexico exciting. I loved the colors, and for me it was a painter's paradise. I went happily to work and set up a still life in the garden. It was truly one of the pleasantest places I have ever painted in, with its profusion of flowers, shaded by that huge, 150-year-old tree.

Norman's liver got better, and as soon as it did, he started drinking again. I was right beside him. Those two-dollar quarts of tequila made a lot of margaritas, and I could mix a mean one.

Norman had had insomnia for a year, and he'd gotten hooked on Seconal. A doctor in the States supplied him with unlimited prescriptions. I would watch Norman open a capsule and empty it into a glass of Scotch so it would work more quickly. Sleep had never been a problem for me, but for some reason, I let Norman talk me into trying the pills for a few nights.

"You'll never have the kind of sleep you'll get on those," he said.

"But darling, I'm not like you. I sleep very well, I don't need pills."

"Just try it," he insisted, and I did, for two nights. I ended up feeling like a dead person lying next to another corpse, and I was woozy all the next day, needing three cups of morning coffee to wake me from my torpor.

Two Seconals were not working for Norman anymore, so when he got up to three, I was really alarmed. But you could never tell him anything. He knew it all. There was a rationale for everything, including his own self-destructive behavior.

We settled into a routine. I painted every day while he worked on his novel. At night, we were off to the city. Steve obligingly showed us around, taking us to one of his haunts to hear the best mariachi music in town. Sometimes Bea would be busy at home, so there would be just the three of us. I was comfortable with

Steve, we liked each other, but when Bea was around, there was always an edge. She was competitive, not just with me, but in general. However, I was not threatened because there was nothing left between her and Norman. Except for Susie, it was as if they had never been married.

We did the usual touristy things, but what really fascinated us was the bullfight, the *corrida*. Steve took us the first time, the first time for Norman, not me. I had seen Manolete in Lima when I was sixteen. Before we left New York, we had read Hemingway's *Death in the Afternoon* as a preparation for this beautiful ritual.

Every Sunday, I would wake up with a sense of excitement and anticipation, the same feeling I had as a child before going to the circus.

I thought of Flora's tasty Sunday breakfast, those *huevos rancheros*, the sauce so hot it made my eyes water, dousing the fire with a big glass of freshly squeezed orange juice. I would eat in the garden, the aroma of her coffee blending with the fragrance of the flowers, and at one o'clock, we would drive to the Plaza de Toros.

The corrida led us to other connections. We called Lewis Allen, a New York friend who has since become a successful Hollywood and Broadway producer. Lewis had been in Mexico City for a couple of months, staying with David Ford, a film actor, and his wife, Betty Ford, a model turned lady bullfighter. She had proven herself fighting bulls in small arenas outside Mexico City. Lewis promptly invited us over for a drink that evening. It was good to see Lewis, who greeted us warmly, and it looked to us as if he, the lady bullfighter, and her spouse had been partying much of the day. They were all more than a little drunk. David and Betty were in the middle of some kind of childish game, the hi-fi was blasting, and they were dancing around under a serape bedspread, with only their feet visible.

There was much shrill laughter from the invisible lady matador as she admonished her giggling husband. "David," she screamed, "will you stop it."

Lewis was laughing as we exchanged introductions with this blanketed mass. Norman thought it funny, but I did not. I disliked Betty immediately for all this actressy bullshit, all done, of course, for Norman's benefit.

"C'mon guys," Lewis said, "come on out wherever you are."

Throwing off the blanket, Betty said, "Jesus, it's hot under there. I need another drink." They were fully dressed, and I saw a woman a year or two younger than me. David was attractive, I thought, reminding me of Ralph Bellamy, the forties movie star.

Betty was the cutesy Hollywood starlet type, with curly hair, turned-up nose, and greenish eyes, a typical American girl. Lewis seemed enthralled by her. Who could have guessed she was a bullfighter?

I took a big swallow of my drink, watching her operate on Norman, wiggling her ass in his face.

"C'mon Betty," Lewis said, "show them your technique." Of course, she needed no urging, showing off her cape work with David playing the bull. Norman was eating it up. What a challenge it would be for my lover to fuck a woman who had more balls than he did.

At this point, I felt completely pushed into the background. Greedy little Norman wanted a Waspy *shiksa* who fought bulls. How could I beat that one?

Occasionally, we went with Lewis and the Fords to the bullfight. Needless to say, I wasn't too keen about being around Betty. Again I felt pushed into the background because Mexican men love Waspy blonde women and practically threw their bodies in front of her, muttering extravagant compliments. I just looked like another Latina, albeit a pretty one, but no novelty. I had to wait for a trip to Sweden or Germany for that kind of attention.

Once in awhile, we would see a beautiful fight where everything was perfect, a brave bull and a classy matador, but alas, there were mostly *novelleros* (rookies) who made sickeningly sloppy kills or even worse, were gored.

At one point, we were invited to visit a bull-breeding farm owned by a widely known but not yet famous matador. Presumably we were just there as sightseers, but Norman was invited to work with a small bull. Not small enough, as far as I was concerned, but he would give it a shot since he had been practicing a few passes he had learned from *Death in the Afternoon* and Betty Ford. With a cape and a wooden sword, he would play matador at parties, and I would play the bull.

But this was for real, and unfortunately my once-slim lover had put on a little weight. He was not going to be fast enough for that little bull with those not-so-little horns. I could already picture Norman with his stomach ripped open. I got hysterical, begging him not to do it, and to my surprise, he agreed.

Besides the corrida, there were other diversions, like the one Forest Waldman offered us. Forest was a gay painter friend of ours from New York who was living in Guanajuato. When he called us to say he was coming to Mexico City, we invited him to stay with us for a few days.

Forest, a world traveler, was always sniffing around places way off the beaten track. He told us about a live sex show he knew of in a little town outside Mexico City. We'd never seen that sort of thing, so we told him we'd like to go. The day before our excursion, Forest asked if he could invite a woman friend of his, another expatriate, who was a big fan of Norman's.

Of course, Norman said yes. I expected to meet the usual celebrity fucker, but this time I needn't have worried. Eleanora was a six-foot-two lesbian, wearing knee socks on legs as thick as tree trunks. She had a long nose on a rather plain but nice face. Her mousy brown hair hung straight on her shoulders, and her bangs blended into her black shades, which she kept on through her entire visit. She said something about being an archaeology student, and after a few introductory remarks, she hardly said a word. I couldn't imagine why Forest would have wanted her along on our decadent adventure.

We drove for an hour and arrived in front of a small and simple adobe hut.

"Is this it?" I asked. "It looks like nothing." I think Forest had been there before because he asked us to wait in the car while he made the arrangements.

When we got inside, the only person we met was the madam. She called herself Señora Alvarez and asked us what combination we would like—two men and one girl, or one girl and two men. "Two women and a man," Norman said. "Is that okay with you, honey?"

I was not enthused. "Sure," I said. "Why not?" I looked at Forest. "Maybe they can throw in a couple of mules." Forest laughed, but Norman glared at me.

"She can understand English, you idiot." I looked at her face and knew she hadn't heard me.

We had to order tequila because that's all they had, and it was sold by the bottle. We'll need more than one, I thought, before this is over.

Señora Alvarez took us into a tiny room painted white, furnished with a bed that took up almost the entire space. There were no decorations except for a large crucifix on one wall.

We sat on four chairs at the foot of the bed and sipped our drinks, speaking in hushed tones as if we were attending a lecture. I felt terribly uncomfortable, not from a moral point of view, but that here we were, fat cats, for amusement about to watch the peasants copulate. On the other hand, the voyeur in me was beginning to be excited. I glanced at Norman, who looked distracted and a little bored, and I wondered if he had brought his notebook.

There was a curtained opening to the left of the room leading into another cubicle where the performers were waiting. The stage was set, ready to be lit by the three players whose names were Arabellita, Concepción, and Ramón. The white-sheeted bed, the only prop in the room, was given another dimension, by the large wooden crucifix. It's an omen, I thought, we're going to be punished for this, so I tried not to look at Christ's anguished expression.

We heard giggling and whispers behind the partition, as Ramón, a good-looking young Indian, padded into the room. Wearing only white cotton pants, he bowed, flashing a toothy smile. "Buenos tardes, señores y señoritas. We are so happy to see you."

We nodded and smiled back. Enter Arabellita, a pretty teenager wearing thick makeup and a frightened smile, which made me wonder if we were her first gringo audience. She had hair down to her hips, unbraided and a dark reddish-brown, her body, chunky and rather square, with small breasts. Seeming shy and uncertain of what to do next, she looked at Ramón for her cue.

Putting his arms around Arabellita and fondling her breast, he gave her loud smacking kisses, at the same time helping her to remove her dress. As he pulled it over her head, her long hair got caught in the fastening. The more Ramón struggled to free her, the more entangled she became, her headless, nude body flopping frantically about like a fish caught on a hook.

Ramón swore under his breath. He said in Spanish, "Will you hold still so I can get it off." Frustrated, he gave a yank, and the girl gave a muffled yelp. It was an awkward moment, one in which I could have helped. But I preferred neutrality. "Perdona," Ramón mumbled, finally untwisting a long strand of hair from the inconvenient hook.

Arabellita's head emerged, her face sullen, her lipstick smudged, and her hair a mess. As Ramón slipped off his pants, his cock popped up like a jack-in-the-box. Arabellita pushed her breasts in his face, inviting him to suck on her brown nipples, turning her head away from us in a paroxysm of nervous giggling. Glancing at the poker faces of my companions, I stifled an impulse to do the same, but of course giggling does not lend itself to erotica. Fucking was serious business, especially when you were paying for it.

Arabellita knelt and began to suck Ramón's cock, like a dog attacking a bone. I wondered if she would growl if I reached forward to touch it. Either she read my mind or her mouth got tired, because she suddenly grabbed his cock, sliding her hand up and down it like a piston. Christ, I thought, if she doesn't stop, the show will be over before the other girl comes in.

Arabellita, proud of herself, plopped on the bed, spreading her legs. Ramón, with a leer, waggled his cock in our direction. "What would the señores like us to do next?"

Jesus, I thought, that was pretty quick. Was that his idea of sex-show foreplay? I tried to think of something exotic, but I felt self-conscious, or maybe I wasn't drunk enough. But no one else, including my writer boyfriend, had any suggestions.

I shrugged. "Anything you want, Ramón." The tequila was giving me a headache, and the slight buzz I had seemed to be fading. The waiter appeared with another bottle of lousy tequila we didn't want but had to take. I was getting impatient to see the other girl. Did she have stage fright? Why weren't all three of them on the stage from the beginning? As if my thoughts were audible, Concepción appeared, wearing what looked like a pink nightgown.

The two girls, ignoring Ramón, embraced self-consciously, chattering as if they were meeting in the marketplace. Andale, I felt like saying, let's get the show going. Concepción, tittering, tweaked Ramón's splendid hard-on. Oh, swell, I thought, we now have a titterer and a giggler. Ramón, not wanting to play favorites, administered to Concepción in the same way, helping her to undress, revealing her dimpled, plump parts, shaking as she moved. She wasn't as pretty as Arabellita, and a black mustache didn't help. She lay down with Ramón, thus cozily sandwiched between the two girls with his cock, rising above the moundy rounds of flesh. Ramón was happy at his work with a wealth of asses, tits, and cunts to prong and play with.

They were like kids in a candy store, titty tasters, cock suckers , nibblers, and lickers of clits and cherry-lime lollipop tongues. Ramón mounted Arabellita first, giving us a thrusting, jiggling, brown-balled rear view. What a closeup, I thought. If we could ever see ourselves doing it from this angle, we'd never fuck again.

Concepción was passively waiting for her turn. It looked as if she was about to fall asleep. Ramón, grinding away in Arabellita, whispered something in her ear. We couldn't hear it, but judging from the speed of her recovery, he must have said something like, "You little cunt, you better pull your weight, or you'll be out of a job." She immediately got to work, sucking on Arabellita's nipples, moving her toward her phony orgasm. I was almost beginning to feel Ramón's thrusts, but the bench we sat on was backless and hard, not conducive to empathic sexual stimulation.

The room seemed crowded with bodies, and I was aware of legs filling the tiny space—Eleanora's great tree trunks ending in army boots; Forest's bony knees and huge feet in thong sandals; my long, unshaven legs; and Norman's baggy pants covering his slightly bowed calves, his socks falling down over the tops of his scuffed black shoes.

It was a boiling hot day, with no ventilation in that cell of a room, so the bouquet of exposed orifices mingled with the odor of our perspiring flesh. Poor Norman's sensitive nose must have been on fire.

There was more moaning and thrashing about, punctuated by Arabellita's accelerating shrieks of ecstasy. Ramón's murmuring of obscenities in Arabellita's ear was accompanied by Concepción's wailing "aye aye chihuahua" as she frantically fingered her clitoris. The juicy slapping of Ramón's cock in and out of Arabellita's open flesh played a duet with the squeaking of ancient bedsprings.

Finally, with Arabellita's last attenuated shriek, our stud withdrew his stiff cock, glistening angry red, to service Concepción in the same missionary position. Climbing over Arabellita's supine body, Ramón drove into Concepción, with Arabellita sluggishly licking and fondling only what she could conveniently reach.

The novelty and the small fire in my own private innards was beginning to wear out. I was getting bored with looking at Ramón's gyrating, pimply rear. "Excuse me," I said. At the sound of my voice, Ramón paused. I continued, the tequila loosening my tongue. "Would you mind lying across the bed, not the way you are, so we can see more of your beautiful bodies?" I couldn't seem to make myself understood in Spanish, and I stammered, trying to explain with gestures. Three pairs of brown eyes stared blankly at me, smiles pasted on their faces. They took the interruption as a sign of my displeasure. "Is the señora not pleased with us?"

"Sí, sí," I said. "Me gusto muchíssimo, just turn around, ARRAVUELTA." They still didn't get it, and I almost threw myself on the bed to demonstrate.

Norman was annoyed at the fuss. "What's the difference? Let it go. It's too abstract. It's normal to sleep on a bed vertical, not lying across it. It's too fucking narrow."

But I was obsessed. "Well, I don't like foreshortening. Forest, for Christ's sake, explain it to them."

Forest spoke the best Spanish although he had an atrocious American accent. "Ah sí, sí, señorita, we understand," the kids replied, shifting around with Ramón still buried in Concepción.

"Gracias," I said, "es mejor, much better." But their legs dangled awkwardly over the edge of the mattress. Ramón looked discouraged, gave a few half-hearted thrusts and withdrew from Concepción. He lay between the girls like a stale filling in the enchilada.

"Would the señores like some other positions?"

"No," we chorused, "you're all very good, and we are enjoying it very much."

For the finale, they formed a daisy chain, but there was still another interruption from Ramón. "Would the señora like to join us?" I politely declined. The last orgasm rippled through the chain, and we applauded. The bill, including the tequila and a generous tip, came to about fifty dollars.

Chapter 21

When we left for the States, we took Susie back with us to visit her grandmother and, of course, to spend time with us. She was fine, though it was a long drive for a little girl. We managed to keep her amused while she wasn't napping, acting out all the characters in her favorite fairy tales. After driving for twelve hours, we stopped for the night at Ciudad Victoria. Susie had slept for most of the way, so now she was wide awake. She was only five at the time, and we made the mistake of putting her in a room by herself.

Norman was a wreck, and so was I. We were dying to get into bed. He, of course, had his sleeping pills just in case. I tucked Susie in, telling her about ten bedtime stories. "I want to go for a walk," she said, and then, of course, she wanted to sleep with us. It was a definite "no" to both requests.

Norman decided to give Susie a quarter of a Seconal sleeping pill. I thought it was a terrible idea, but as usual, he ignored my objections. "It's so little, it can't hurt her," he said. Of course, it worked immediately. Come morning, I went to wake her up. I shook her, but she didn't move. "Oh God," I thought, "maybe she's dead." But I could see her chest rise and fall.

I ran back to our room. "Come quick, Norman. I can't wake Susie up."

He felt her pulse, and it was okay. "Susie, Susie, wake up," he said, shaking her, lifting her, and walking her on the bed. She was still asleep. Norman's face paled, and I knew he was as frightened as I was.

"She's got to wake up, Norman. If she doesn't, what are we going to do? We'd better call a doctor." At that moment, she opened her eyes. The whole thing lasted just a few minutes, but it seemed like an eternity. Holding her in my arms, I cried with relief. When I look back, I cannot imagine what possessed Norman to do such an insane thing. I knew it was wrong at the time, but he seemed so sure that the minute bit we gave her was safe. Thank God she was all right.

We finally made it to New York, with no major crises; but it was not the kind of trip I'd ever want to make again.

The following year, we went back to Mexico. Since Susie was with her mother, we stayed at the Turf Club, outside Mexico City, where we rented a modern, two-floor, glassed-in house with a sleeping balcony.

There were new faces, new parties, new sycophants, and our undiminished fascination for the bullfight. And again, our drinking accelerated, as always accompanied by more quarrels. Norman was working on *The Deer Park,* and the writing was not going well. He was in a rotten mood, so I got a lot of the flack.

Forest was still living in Mexico, and again we saw a good deal of him. He knew a lot of people, and we were new in this part of town. He invited us to a party one night in Lomas, a wealthy suburb. The hosts were Boris Lattimore, a rich American, and his wife, Rhea. Forest, always the gossip, filled us in. It seemed the Lattimores' main diversion, besides being wealthy, was having sex with as many people as possible and at the same time. Norman's eyes lit up. More stuff for his notebook, I supposed.

The house was an impressive English Tudor, and the grounds were magnificent. A butler answered the bell, and we were shown into a great hall, greeted by the Lattimores and two gigantic Great Danes. Boris was tall and slender, with a black goatee. Kind of like the typical image of the devil—but no pitchfork and tail. His wife, Rhea, was a thin, stringy blonde with a cold manner and an affected British accent, somewhat like a forties movie star. Her dress was elegant, an intricately beaded vintage sheath, and must have weighed in at about twenty-five pounds. Even her hair was worn in the tightly shingled bob of the twenties. The party, as I remember it, was rather dull, despite the thirty or so people there. After a few drinks, we left.

Driving home, we discussed the Lattimores. "He looked like Mephistopheles with that beard, but she was too tight-assed and snotty to be into balling," I said.

Norman's grin was devilish. "C'mon baby, you know you're interested in them."

I giggled. "Speak for yourself, he's not my type. Is he yours?"

"No. Is she yours?"

"Fuck you, Norman. She's not your type, either, but on the other hand, who isn't your type?"

He didn't answer, and then I burst out laughing. "Thirty people in one long Daisy chain. Their living room isn't big enough. What a sight, it would certainly be interesting to paint, but the one on the end would be cheated."

Norman laughed. "My little Roman libertine would like that, wouldn't she, but most likely narrowed down to four."

I kissed him. "Just four, how boring."

"You should know," he said.

That was a crack about that Easter Sunday with my married friends, my only transgression so far. But I let it go, and we drove in silence, both of us into our own thoughts.

"Well," I said, "I don't like them. They're creepy. But he at least showed some charm." I waited for Norman's comment, but there was none. "He said I was beautiful, and when was the last time you told me that?"

"I tell you when it counts."

"He paid a lot of attention to me. He talked to me for a long time, mostly about himself."

"So I noticed."

"Rhea the Ramrod hardly noticed me."

Our conversation was a tease turning us on, giving our love-making that night an extra edge. Norman obviously had a plan in mind. Moving inside of me, his eyes on my face, Norman breathed the words of his script against my mouth between kisses, describing the way all those Lattimore tentacles would wrap around me, touching and exploring all those lovely secret little places only he knew about. Despite myself, I was being sucked into his fantasy with the ghostly pair. But in the end, reality won out. Digging my nails into his back, I cried out, "I love you so much, I don't want them, only you, my darling, love me, yes, now, yes . . . " and I was off and away.

Afterward, drowsy and content, I giggled about them, imitating her British accent. And all the while, happy in my arms, loving me, he still pressed me about what a session with the two of them would be like.

"But I don't really want anyone else. It was so good just now. Aren't you happy with me? We don't need them."

Still, I was ambivalent about the whole idea. It excited my imagination, even though I didn't even like these strangers. She seemed so haughty and unsensual, and there was something sadistic about him. I didn't tell my lover, but I was afraid of it, and it hurt because he seemed to want it so much. The sex was still so good between us, so why should he want to share me? That wasn't it, he said, and in his dishonesty, he went into all kinds of rationalizations. Finally I got angry.

"What is it, just wife swapping, or are you going to do something with him, too? What if he makes a grab for you, though I doubt he will. I'll tell you right now, he was really coming on to me, so I'm probably the main attraction. Two men together does absolutely nothing to me. It's just depressing, and the idea of you and Boris really upsets me."

Norman laughed. "That part doesn't interest me."

"But God knows what will happen, so why should we do it?"

"For the same reason you want it."

"But I don't really."

"Yes you do."

The next day, he kept pressing, cajoling me into a half-yes, until I finally said, "Okay, call them and invite them for a drink."

I was scared. It was like all those tests he put me through. But at least she wasn't attractive. If she had been really gorgeous, I would have been crazy to say yes. I wouldn't have taken a chance on letting Norman get really involved in all this.

"By the way," I said, "tell them to leave the twin mastiffs at home."

Norman asked the couple for cocktails at seven on a Saturday. That way if it wasn't going well, we could say we had a late dinner engagement. Of course, they snapped at an invitation from Norman Mailer. Norman was especially attentive to me before they came, saying how much he loved me and how beautiful I looked. But I was feeling a lot of anxiety and trying to quiet it by telling myself I was Norman Mailer's woman, and I could do anything I wanted. And of course, with enough liquor in me, I could.

When they arrived, Mephistopheles kissed my hand. There weren't many hand-kissers around, not in this country anyway, so the few times it happened, I always felt like Bette Davis being hand-kissed by Paul Henreid, only this was not Paul, and it wasn't *Now Voyager.*

"My dear, you're as beautiful as ever," he said. As his beard tickled my hand, I wondered what else it would tickle. "Isn't she charming, Rhea?" Rhea nodded as her eyes brushed over me, and with a stiff smile, she said in her phony British accent, "Of course, my dear, so nice to see you again." She put her hand out, and I took it. It felt like I was shaking a dead fish. She looked around. "How nice of you to ask us, and what a charming place. And isn't the architecture quaint?"

She looked down her nose at my substantial cleavage as I answered, "Yes, it is unique, isn't it?" And I knew that they knew that we knew why they were there.

For a long time, it was so terribly polite. Norman, inflated by Scotch, served the drinks, and I brought out some canapés. He, of course, was the center of attention, discoursing brilliantly, throwing around some of his cockamamie ideas about Mexican politics, the Aztecs, Diego Rivera, and other topics, the Lattimores hanging on every word. Rhea must have had a few before she arrived, but she probably was one of those people who can drink and drink and not show it, till at one point, the alcohol just takes a poke, and the drunk falls over. She seemed stiff as ever, holding that long cigarette holder in her crimson-painted talons. Looking at me, her eyes glassy, she gently blew a puff of smoke in my direction. "You know, my dear, you're terribly, touchingly attractive, and I'm dying to suck your pussy."

I stared into those cold blue eyes. "Thank you," I said, like a nice little girl, and I almost curtsied. Jesus, I thought, is this supposed to be a warmup? This is crazy, what are these characters doing here? It's unreal. God, I need another drink! But, then again, did I really give a shit? What little King Norman wants, little King Norman gets. Who was going to make the first real move? Maybe we should play spin the bottle? I knew I was getting drunk because I laughed out loud at the idea. "Do we have a milk bottle, darling?"

"No, but I've got some great stuff," he said, bringing out the big guns, a couple of beautifully rolled joints he had fixed for the occasion. Rhea abandoned her cigarette holder, sucking the smoke greedily into her throat. After a few tokes, I was ready for the takeoff into the wild blue. "Hey everybody, including you, Lady Windemere, let's dance," and I put on some music.

We'd brought very few of our records, so I couldn't find anything but Dave Brubeck and a couple of Miles Davis's mournful tunes. Where was Ravel's *Bolero* when I needed it?

Well, Brubeck or Miles Davis, what the hell was the differ-ence? Maybe this was going to be fun after all. Mephistopheles couldn't wait to grab me for a dance. His nice body in that fancy suit, along with his black beard, was turning me on.

He was a smooth dancer, and I was enjoying that. Norman had a lousy sense of rhythm, except where it counted—in his writing and in bed—so dancing was never part of our curriculum. But sometimes I missed it; it must have been in my blood.

Someone turned off all the lights, but there was a ray of moon-light shining through the big window. That's all the illuminating I want, I thought.

Dipping and swaying to the music, Boris kissed me, paying me lavish compliments, slowly undressing me, describing the delights that awaited me. He was breathing hard, and his goatee seemed to get more pointed with each breath. His tongue was down my throat when I heard a faint click. Did he have false teeth? I tried not to think about it, though I was so stoned it's a wonder I could think at all.

All that booze and pot went directly from my brain to my pussy, and there was no retreat. Boris was putting everything into it, keeping me busy, but not too busy to check out Norman and Rhea, who were only at the grope-and-kiss stage. But when I looked over at them again, they were nude.

Boris was pretty thorough. His quicksilver, purplish tongue had found my belly button. At first it tickled, but then I discov-ered a new sensation, a well of pleasure. If that snaky tongue could do that to me, I had a lot to look forward to. He went down on his knees, his goatee blending into my black triangle. I opened my eyes and saw Norman and Rhea in the far corner of the room.

She was kneeling at his feet, her head bobbing while he sipped his drink. Her pale body so thin, her shoulder blades stuck out like stumps of wings. For a moment, my bleary eyes met his. He had a funny look on his face. Poor Norman, I thought, but why should I care? He wanted it, so, it's his funeral.

Then my lover took off, leaving me to the pleasure of strange mouths, feathery tickling, sucking, ding-dong bells pealing for the whore queen.

We went on from there, three of us in twisting paroxysms of pure, unadulterated lust.

Finally, Boris joined me in a last whimpering spasm, releasing the dead weight of his body on mine, pressing me down into an early grave. Then a long heavy silence was broken by my sudden claustrophobic panic.

"Get off of me, I can't breathe, get out of here. Leave me alone, don't touch me." Bewildered, haggard, Rhea's mask rubbed away, frightened by my anger.

"Boris, whatever is wrong with her? What did we do?"

"I don't know, too much to drink, I guess. She's wild. Where's Mailer gone? We'd better fetch him. She's a mess."

"Never mind about Norman, just get out, both of you! Now! Or I'll kill you," I screamed.

My rage sent them scurrying into their clothes, slamming the door on the famous writer and his crazy woman. The sound of their car faded, leaving me in an unbearable silence. I looked around at the mess of spilled drinks, scattered cushions on the floor, and a marijuana roach smoldering in the rug. In his haste, Boris forgot his expensive tie and Rhea her cigarette holder.

I giggled at how fast they beat it. I needed another drink and was desperate for a shower. I took my drink into the bathroom, turned on the hot water, and scrubbed until my skin was red. Then I went upstairs, praying he was there.

He was, pretending to be asleep. The bedroom was just an open area on the balcony, so there was no way he could have slept through my hysterics or anything else. I was dizzy, my flesh felt sick, and I was shivering. I needed his warmth desperately to put me together again. But he was like stone, his back to me.

I looked around the bedroom, feeling like a frightened little girl in a place I didn't know, far away from home, with someone I knew once, a stranger now, who didn't love me, who had thrown me to the dogs like a piece of meat.

I pressed my trembling body against his back. "Norman, please talk to me." He turned around, his face pale and drained, his mouth tight with anger.

"Get away from me, you slut." He shoved me so violently, I almost fell from the bed. There was such hatred in his voice that it crushed whatever person there was left in me. He smelled blood, and that always excited him.

"That was quite a show you put on." He mimicked me. "Oh, Boris, I love sucking your cock."

"I didn't say that."

"Whose cock don't you love to suck? Dogs? Pigs? Anybody's?"

"I didn't really enjoy it." I knew I'd gone too far because I thought he was going to hit me. "Well, maybe just a little, but I wished it was you, and then you left and I was alone with them, and they just kept going. They wouldn't leave me alone, and God, I'm still so drunk."

"I'll just bet you thought of me, with all that moaning and bleating. I heard it all up here. You disgust me." I couldn't believe he said that, and rage replaced my vulnerability.

"I disgust you? Why you son of a bitch. You wanted this even more than I did. You could have thrown them out, it's your fucking house," I screamed. "I'm your fucking woman, remember. Just because it wasn't going little Normie's way, you couldn't take it, so you didn't wanna play. You couldn't get it up, could you? What were you afraid of? She was no bargain, but you've had worse dogs. Or maybe you were jealous because I was having a ball, and you weren't the big cheese. You were so tough, getting your orgiastic experience as a writer, of course." I mimicked him. "'A writer must experience everything.' Well you didn't, you ran. You couldn't stand another man making love to me, or another woman, for that matter." I started to cry. "Oh, Norman, we're two souls in purgatory, but I love you. You wanted this, and maybe I wanted it, too, and I thought it would please you and make you love me more. Oh God, I'm so mixed up,"

He turned his back to me, not touching me, unmoved by my soft weeping in the darkness. Finally we slept, worn out with rage and pain.

I was awakened by his kisses in the middle of the night. Half asleep, his mouth on my breasts, we made love—not angry love, but soft, hot love.

"You're right," he said. "I couldn't take anyone else making love to you. You little bitch, don't you understand, I love you."

"Yes," I murmured, "this is what we really are now, because no one else matters, just you inside me now. Darling, I love you so much."

I slept late, and when I opened my eyes, I was alone, aware of the pain in my head and the furry inside of my mouth. My system was dehydrated, and I had to go to the bathroom. When I stood up, I still felt drunk. It was the worst hangover I'd had in a long time.

What had it all really been about? Was I testing him, pushing him to the limit to find out how much he valued me? He had copped out of last night's game, leaving me to fend for myself.

It was all so complicated, I got dizzy trying to figure it out, but then I had an odd, painful thought. Perhaps he hates me because he loves me. Jesus, what a complex man Norman was. There were so many layers, would I ever understand him? But what I knew, and didn't want to face, was how costly that night would be for us, the beginning of the slow disintegration of our relationship.

There was so much of my father in me. Like Daddy, I could go round after bloody round in the ring, never knowing when to quit, a questionable virtue, one that would someday almost cost me my life.

It was late, but I was still so sick, I had to sleep off the rest of my hangover. When I woke, I went downstairs to make some coffee and put something easy into my stomach. I was beginning to revive, so I tried to paint, but nothing would come. My thoughts were scattered, and I was unable to concentrate. I was still feeling vulnerable, wounded, and in need of tender treatment. But Norman's mood shifted so quickly, who knew what it would be like when he came home? I hoped he had a good day's work because that would help.

When I saw him that evening, he seemed preoccupied, creating a distance between us, in spite of our closeness the night before. It was not exactly coldness, but a cautious distance with neither of us wanting to talk about the Lattimore debacle.

We never ran into them again, and gradually the pain of that night passed. The wounds of the young heal more quickly, and soon we were back on the familiar merry-go-round.

Chapter 22

By the end of 1954, we'd been living together for three years, and I began to think seriously about marriage. Why not? I was pushing thirty, and I was also beginning to think about having a baby.

In spite of the emotional storms created by our mutual insanities, we did care for each other and even managed to be happy in between fights. I didn't exactly nag Norman about getting married, but I would introduce the subject at every opportunity. He was evasive, never really saying whether he did or didn't want it.

Once, when I was complaining, he made one of his clumsy sadistic remarks that hurt and angered me. "We could try it, baby, but if it doesn't work out we could get a divorce. At least I would have given you my name."

"What do you think I am, a suit of clothes you buy in the store, and if you decide you don't like it, back it goes? You can take your stinking name and shove it!"

In the next breath, I contradicted myself. "I'll tell you another thing, I'm fed up with being introduced as Adele Morales. What *am* I to you anyway? A girlfriend? A roommate? Your whore? How about the word wife, W-I-F-E? You'd better think about it because I think about it every time some woman climbs all over you, as if I wasn't there. People would have more respect for me if we were married. I can just hear those snotty friends of yours, putting me down."

I fought not to cry because Norman was a stone when it came to women's tears, his callousness made me angrier. "Is marrying too bourgeois for our bohemian writer?" I asked sarcastically. "Well, I want to be bourgeois and with all the trimmings." By now my rage was spent, and in spite of my efforts, the tears began and I wailed, "And I want that piece of paper."

I let him put his arms around me, my body still tense, not trusting him. To my surprise, he was tender.

"Yeah, baby, you really are my wife. It's just that I feel like I've always been married. I was so damn young when I met Bea. I never had a chance to be out there."

"Well, you've more than made up for it with me around. You love me, honey, you know you do. God knows you've told me often enough."

"Yes, I do," he sighed. He shook his head at me and smiled. "You know, you're a terrible housekeeper, but you're right, monkey, you are my wife, for better or for worse. You know, I've given you as much of myself as I've ever given any woman. So cheer up, if it means that much to you, you'll have that piece of paper."

I looked at him, thinking he could be so terrible, making me hate him so much, but then there was the other side, the sweet charmer, making me love him all over again.

"I love you, Norman," I sniffled, wiping my tears, "and I'll try to be neater about the apartment, I promise."

It was not exactly my idea of a marriage proposal, but I was happy anyway. We made a date for April 19 at City Hall. It wasn't romantic, but at this point, what difference did it make? We'd been through enough emotional ups and downs in this relationship to total ten marriages.

Whatever it was that kept us together, pain or pleasure, or both, at least it wasn't boring, not for me anyway.

We decided to be casual. Flowers and fussy festivities, that was for squares. Just treat it like another day, that sort of thing.

Of course, his parents were to be our two witnesses. My mother would have hated our doing it this way. I could hear her sniff, "My God, with all his money, they could have done it up with pink and blue ribbons."

Still, when it came down to it, they'd be relieved. My parents wouldn't have cared if we were married by a Buddhist priest.

Once we were man and wife, my father could go around the *Daily News* talking about his famous son-in-law. "He's a nice guy. I'm teaching him how to box, showing him a few moves."

Norman's mother offered to buy my wedding outfit. I wanted a beautiful floral print. Instead, I let her talk me into buying an awful suburban matron's brown suit with jet buttons from Bergdorf

Goodman. Given my reverse snobbery, this was a store I wouldn't have been caught dead in.

Norman picked up a thirteen-dollar wedding ring for the ceremony, promising to replace it with a diamond. He never got around to the diamond, but I couldn't have cared less. I rarely wore rings, and I disliked diamonds. I really preferred jade or turquoise costume jewelry instead. Eventually he did buy me a simple gold band, and I wore it throughout our marriage.

For the few weeks before the wedding date, Norman had been feeling draggy, in a funk. He was having trouble again with his liver and was depressed after finishing a draft of *The Deer Park*. He felt depleted and anxious about the book's future. The night before the wedding, he'd taken his usual sleeping pill. As always, I slept well, but in the morning I had to shake him from a dead sleep.

"Come on, honey," I said cheerily, "wake up. It's getting late. Today is our wedding day." I giggled, looking at his inert body. "Till death do us part, right?"

"Yeah, yeah, what time is it?" he asked, talking through a yawn.

"Nine thirty, and it's raining out. It would, on one of the most important days of my life."

He burrowed into his pillow. "Yeah, well, maybe we can do it on another day."

I had the feeling he was half-serious.

"No, dammit, you promised, and we already took the blood test." He propped himself up on his elbow and reached for a cigarette. "Okay, okay baby, cool it. I was only teasing."

I was annoyed, but I didn't want a quarrel, not today of all days.

Sipping my coffee, I was suddenly depressed as my own thoughts turned gloomy. Maybe it was just another day, like all the others. What was I so excited about? Was that little piece of paper going to make that much of a difference?

There was no partition between the kitchen and the bedroom, and while I buttered my toast, I could see my future mate, sitting naked on the edge of the bed, staring into space, hung over from last night's party. I was hung over, too, but aided by coffee, aspirin, and the excitement of finally getting my heart's desire, the ache in my head was subsiding. Norman frowned, his lips moving silently between drags on his cigarette. Oh, oh, I thought, he's going to start writing in his notebook. We'll be late for sure.

I was used to him going off like that. It could happen in the middle of a conversation. His voice would trail off, his eyes would glaze over, and I knew his pet notebook needed to be fed again.

"Norman, you haven't heard a word I've been saying."

"I'm listening," he would say, getting out his notebook. "But I've got to get this idea down before I forget it." As he wrote, a little smile would curl around the corners of his lips, and I knew he was pleased with his thought.

I was curious. "Norman, what's so funny? Can you read it to me?"

"Not now, monkey. I just want to put this down. It's just some notes that wouldn't mean anything to you."

"Am I in it? Was it something I said?"

"No, darling, it's nothing to do with you."

I would try not to be annoyed; after all, I was in love with a great writer, and living with a genius had its price.

Norman wouldn't show me his notes, but he shared his writing with me and read passages of *The Deer Park* aloud as he worked on it. He really valued my opinion and was attentive to my comments.

"You're like my mother. She sees things with the same honesty, the same perceptive editorial instincts. You'd make a good editor, darling." I was annoyed at sharing the compliment with Fanny. However, I thought it high praise from so critical a person.

I took a shower, sitting in the tub using the little hose Norman had rigged up. When I was done, he was still sitting there writing. "Darling, will you please hurry up and get dressed. I'm almost ready. You'll wear your navy blue suit, won't you?" I picked out a tie, one of many I had bought for him. "Here, this one is just right. The colors are beautiful with that suit."

We were meeting his parents at the marriage bureau. They were in the anteroom with two other couples, so we had to wait our turn.

Fanny was dutifully cheerful, and Barney was cordial, but in his mind, the prince should have made him father-in-law to Jackie Kennedy or Marilyn Monroe; for Barney, a prospect of endless possibilities. Well, too bad. Like it or not, I was going to be part of the family. Barney had already started his celebration at home and in a dignified glow, winked conspiratorially at me and pinched my cheek.

Afterward they took us for a pleasant lunch at Tavern on the Green, and then it was back to the reality of our cold-water flat. Norman was going to his studio after he took me home, and I was going to art class, wearing my ring. He was laughing as he carried me over the threshold.

"Well, Mrs. Mailer, it's the beginning of a new chapter." What he should have said was, "Fasten your seat belt, my darling, because it's going to be a bumpy ride."

We may have downplayed the wedding, but I was pleased that a few friends didn't. Norman's sister planned a small wedding party, and so did Tobias Schneebaum, a gay painter friend of ours. He said he would give the party and take care of all the details, but since his place was too small, would we care if he gave it in our apartment? Of course, we agreed, giving him our lengthy guest list. The next day he showed us this clever invitation he had whipped up. It was a drawing of a circumcised penis, and when you opened the card, it continued on, the length of the penis, that is. Come and celebrate the Mailers' wedding, it said. We all thought it amusing, but I'm not sure if some of our guests, like Lillian Hellman, Harvey Breit, the literary critic, and Diana and Lionel Trilling shared our raunchy humor. But what did it matter as long as they came?

It was a terrific party, but then we had a talent for throwing good parties. True to his word, Tobias did all the work, the Middle Eastern food wasn't greasy, and the liquor was plentiful, served by a bartender. The heart of the party was our guest list, a clutch of writers, painters, actors, poets, a few of the lesser-known drama critics, and to tie it all together, our token psychiatrist. (Norman was not yet cultivating rich society types. That began with the wife after me, Lady Jean Campbell, the daughter of the Duke and Duchess of Argyll and the granddaughter of Lord Beaverbrook.)

Jimmy Baldwin came with his brother, David, and some Harlem friends, carrying a pair of bongo drums, an interesting background beat for New York party repartee.

It was a noisy gathering, not boisterous, but with a nice rhythm and energy, everybody flirting, talking, the fragrance of perfumed beautiful women blending with the sweetish cloying smell of a stick of marijuana that was being passed around. As I circulated, I heard bits of interesting conversation, from politics to boxing, mixed with laughter and the clink of ice cubes. A lot of liquor poured down the gullets of our varied guests.

James Jones was there with his current girlfriend, actress Faith Dane. Faith was an attractive brunette with strong features, a wild, curly black mane of hair framing her large expressive licorice-black eyes. She had a New York street-smart manner, but she was warm and funny, and I liked her a lot.

(A few years later, she played a stripper in the hit musical *Gypsy*. She was very good, playing a trumpet and bumping and grinding her way through a number called "You Gotta Have a Gimmick," belting out the words "If you're gonna bump it, bump it with your trumpet.")

Jones got blasted and disappeared at the height of the party. When he didn't return, we were worried. He was too drunk to be wandering around the lower East Side at night. Besides that, he was wearing about three thousand dollars worth of Navajo silver and turquoise jewelry.

Faith, who was as bombed as the rest of us, was dancing with an attractive guy. She didn't seem concerned. "Yeah, he does that sometimes, but he'll be back. Hell, you'd have to be suicidal to mug him."

Dan got the idea that he might have wandered into his apartment next door. Dan couldn't find his keys, so we crossed over the fire escape, climbing through the window. The place stank of gas, and there was Jonesy, sitting on a chair with his head in the oven. He seemed very much alive, so I don't think his head had been in there more than a couple of minutes.

Dan laughed, turning off the jets. "What the hell are you doing, Jonesy? Are you crazy? You're gonna blow the place up."

"Leave me alone. I wanna die," he bellowed. "Nothin' is any fuckin' good anymore, and Scott Fitzgerald is a better writer than I am."

So is Norman, I was tempted to say, but I was not one to kick a man when he was down. It was all so ludicrous that I started to laugh. He took his head out. The wild-eyed boar glared at me. "What the fuck are you laughing at?"

"C'mon Jonesy, we all miss you, especially Norman. You can't kill yourself because it'll ruin my fuckin' party, and I'll never forgive you."

He was going home, he said, but we cajoled him into staying. When we came back into the party, Tobias was having a bath in our kitchen tub. "I'm a warm martini, and I'm much too dry," he sang. One of the guests obliged, pouring a bottle of vermouth into the tub while someone else emptied three jars of my cocktail onions over Tobias's head.

"I'm still too warm," he complained. So we cooled him off with the contents of an ice bucket. I was as high as everyone else, but it was a fun drunk, unlike the angry drinking I so often got into where I would lash out at people around me.

Tonight was for me, and I was happy cutting the first slice of my wedding cake with Tobias's machete. I looked at my handsome husband, entertaining his circle of admirers, and I was happy because he was obviously in a good mood. There was a sparkle, a liveness about this scene, and that made me happy, too. But most of all I was happy because I was Mrs. Norman Mailer. A pretty girl in Norman's orbit, her head close to his, was laughing at something he was saying. I didn't know who she was, but she seemed a little too intense. I decided to join the conversation.

"Hey baby," he said, putting his arm around me, glancing about the room. "It's a good party, isn't it?" He turned to the girl, who looked annoyed at the interruption. "Sonya, have you met my wife, Adele?"

I loved hearing him say "my wife," the two words I naively thought would change my life. They did, but not in the way I expected.

Chapter 23

There was no settling down into married life for us since we had already had three years of dubious domestic bliss. Furthermore, the words "settle down" imply acceptance and order and perhaps some tranquility. But given my maverick of a husband's driven, megalomaniacal nature and my fathomless need for love and approval, we were incapable of any kind of spiritual or emotional peace.

Through the years, I never let go of my painting, but I was undisciplined, compelled to keep up with Norman's frantic public life and at the same time wanting to be successful as an artist. There were endless party invitations, with an occasional picture of me in *Women's Wear Daily*—usually awful pictures of a woman who had had too much to drink.

Many of these parties were literary affairs, including the prestigious Pen Club soirees. At one of these, I was seated next to a besotted John Cheever. I'd never met him before and was shocked to see him so terribly drunk. We chatted, as much as one can with someone who is scarcely coherent. I admired his work, and though I'd just met him, I liked him and felt sorry for the desperate man I sensed beneath the red face and messy facade. By the end of the meal, he had slumped over on the table with his face almost in his plate. I remember how everyone there, including his wife, went on talking, ignoring Cheever's loud snores.

I remember a dinner party at Lillian Hellman's where I met Dashiell Hammett, her lover. He was even more quiet that night than I, so I hardly remember much more than our handshake. Lillian had always been nice to me, and because I was rather shy in the presence of this imposing woman, she'd made a genuine effort to draw me out, asking me about my painting and mentioning how much she had liked a charcoal nude she had seen at our flat.

As much as I liked Lillian, I admit that I was irritated by her incessant flirting with Norman—who could never resist flirting back. Especially with a famous woman playwright. Underneath that confident manner, she must have been terribly insecure about her attractiveness. She was, without a doubt, a very homely woman, with almost masculine features. But Norman had never been discouraged by the lack of attractive physical attributes in a woman. What turned him on was their hungry availability.

That night I was looking forward to a gourmet dinner, perhaps some exotic dish from New Orleans, Lillian's birthplace. Instead the main course was beef stew served on exquisite china. There were also an appetizer and a salad, which meant three or four different forks at each place setting. I was seated at the opposite end of the table from Norman, and as the meal began, I picked up what I thought was the proper fork for the appetizer. I became aware of Norman fixedly staring at me, trying to catch my eye. He was holding a larger fork than the one I had picked up. Frowning, he was waving it ever so slightly at me to let me know that I had the wrong fork. No one noticed his gesture, but I was furious and told him so later.

Emily Post's book on etiquette was one of the many how-to books on my mother's shelf. One of the rules I remembered was that one always started with the outside utensil, working in towards one's plate with each course served. I can still hear my mother yelling about my manners, quoting from Emily Post.

Norman may have been concerned about the right fork, but at home I'd watch him shovel in his food, eating the way he talked at the speed of machine-gun fire, his eyes glued to an open book.

Even with his overly critical nature, I was never made to feel like an appendage. On the contrary, he enjoyed walking into a room full of people with his beautiful wife. Nor did he mind my shyness during heavyweight intellectual discussions. If I did get up the courage to ask a question, it wasn't a stupid one.

When Norman wanted to, he could be considerate, always careful to include me in the conversation, pressing my hand, smiling at me in a special way. I never felt pushed into the background because I was essentially not competitive with him. If anything, I was proud of my darling when he was at his sober, intelligent, funny, best in public.

Yes, I enjoyed my status, but this did not quiet the demons that still plagued me while hiding behind Mrs. Norman Mailer's décolletage and well made-up face. The one thing I could depend on were my cocktails, magic equalizers stilling that nagging voice in my head that whispered, "You're an impostor. You're not this cool, beautiful wife of a famous writer. What you really are adds up to nothing." Drinking also released the actress in me, permitting me to play any role to Norman's liquor-induced personalities. At different times, I had to deal with God, Svengali, Ivan the Terrible, Rocky Marciano, Jesse James, Miles Davis the Cool, and Scott Fitzgerald the Drunk.

Norman enjoyed provoking me by flirting outrageously at parties. One night, at Gloria Vanderbilt's, I saw him writing down a beautiful girl's phone number, not even bothering to be discreet. I dealt with it by getting stinking drunk. I thought of doing my Carmen act, stamping out her party flamenco dance of rage on the top of Gloria's priceless antique coffee table. Instead I wailed a sobbing song of obscene curses at my husband and in the same breath threatened to kill that society bitch who had been coming on to him from the moment we arrived. I wanted to obliterate that snotty, beautiful face, smirking at me from a safe distance.

James Jones was there, and I remember how kind he was, holding me, trying to calm me down. I was surprised because he was really Norman's friend not mine. But he was sweet and didn't gloat, perhaps because he knew what it was like to be out of control. The hostess looked at me as if I were insane, and maybe I was at that moment. A drunken Norman picked me up, kicking and crying hysterically, and took me home.

He didn't always take care of me. There were times when he would take off, leaving me to look out for myself while he was out

Adele
Morales
and her
mother.
A happy
sunny day.

Adele Morales and Ed Fancher, late forties.

Adele and
Norman Mailer,
already a celebrity,
at the Copacabana.

Adele in Connecticut, pregnant
with her and Norman's second child,
Betsy.

Adele—a formal pose.

The beloved black poodle, Tibo, and Norman, on the deck in Provincetown.

Norman, with Howard Fertig, trying out one of Norman's wooden creations.

Norman and Adele on the verge of separation and divorce.
COURTESY BETTMANN ARCHIVES

The literary
giant being
carted away
in a paddy
wagon.
COURTESY
BETTMANN
ARCHIVES

Arrested
while visiting
Adele at
the hospital,
Norman
being taken
into police
custody.
COURTESY
BETTMANN
ARCHIVES

G. Maillard Kesslère—1948

THE NAKED AND THE DEAD

"The only war novel of any distinction to appear hitherto."
—GEORGE ORWELL

BARBARY SHORE

"The most interesting American novelist to appear since the war."
—V. S. PRITCHETT

THE DEER PARK

"The serious and reckless book we have been waiting for since Scott Fitzgerald's *The Last Tycoon*."
—MALCOM COWLEY

Robert Frank—1951

Judy Scheftel—1955

THE WHITE NEGRO

"A revolutionary literary and social

Mailer in Connecticut.
A moment of peace and
contentment.

Norman Mailer—
a literary history
in author photos.

Adele's sister Joan and her second
husband, Mickey Knox, on the set
of Marco Polo.

Another formal pose,
this from the 1970s.

Mailer in full cry, the political campaigner with running mate Jimmy Breslin.

Adele Morales Mailer, nine months after the stabbing.

in the night, creating his own sloppy messes. Needless to say, we were never invited to Gloria Vanderbilt's again.

Norman, in his cups, could at times be rational, charming, and fun, but I never knew when it would turn or in which direction. The behavior of the drunk Norman and the sober one was becoming delineated more finely, as it was for me. I could change from a rather pleasant, reasonable person into an unrecognizable, mean broad, imitating my husband at his worst, sometimes following, sometimes leading his destructive antics. All that anger I suppressed since I was a child, the anger I was never able to deal with, even in therapy, was released, and off I would go, riding my broomstick, striking out at anyone I thought was in my way. Ultimately I did more damage to myself than anyone else, which is more than I could say for Norman, who, in his time, has inflicted more injuries and wounds than he has sustained.

Norman was obsessed with the party scene, incapable of refusing a single invitation. During the holidays, they never stopped. Boring or not, and some were, he was always the last to leave. I would stick it out for as long as I could, not daring to leave him alone. My solution to boredom was to have a few drinks, but some of those affairs were so tedious that even getting high didn't help. So I would go home, leaving Norman to do God knows what.

I could never understand why he stayed so late at parties. What was it he hoped would happen? Was it another meaningless, drunken fuck with a stranger? Another fistfight? Would he find the love of his life? (I thought he had one—me.) Was he looking for material for his book? What demons of the evening were riding him? What revelations awaited him in that dense dreary drunken remnants of a party?

I would swear in exasperation, "Jesus Christ, why are you always the last to leave, when even the host or hostess is dying to go to bed?" The only answer I got was some quote from Gatsby, something about parties that changed people's lives.

Norman never checked with the hostess about bringing extra guests, and we would arrive with as many as six. The hostess never objected, at least not to his face. She may have resented his cavalier attitude toward invitations, but at the same time, she was happy about landing her big fish. Before we left our apartment for a party, we would have a few drinks. Norman would bring along his Jack Daniel's, and we would slug it in the cab, ensuring Mrs. Mailer a relaxed comfortable entrance into a roomful of strangers.

New Year's Eve was a special madness for us. Norman kept score on party invitations, so we weren't happy unless we got at least eight. It was marathon night for the Mailers as we covered them all, never staying long enough to enjoy anything or anyone. Whether we would go out with a whimper or a bang at the end was anybody's guess.

Besides the drinking, those parties meant competition with women. If we were introduced to an especially beautiful girl, Norman would look at me with a spiteful gloating expression on his face as if to say, "I know you're feeling insecure. Here's someone really gorgeous to rock your boat, another one you'll have to look out for."

I began finding names and telephone numbers on the inside of his matchbooks. Young ones, old ones, beautiful ones, and plain ones. Selectivity be damned, all they had to be was hungry and tenacious, with visions of unseating me from my throne.

It wasn't as if we didn't have good sex. With everything that happened, I still loved my husband, and I still wanted him. He was the only man in my life. I had no desire to be unfaithful—

not yet. He had so many meaningless screws. Why would he have to prove over and over again that he was attractive to women? Christ, would he never believe it?

One night he was having dinner with an old friend he'd known when he was married to Bea. I'd met the lady before, a plain, dowdy, ex-Communist who was nice enough, but no competition as far as I was concerned. I didn't mind him seeing her alone. He came home early, and I was happy he did. It had been a pleasant dinner, he said, but added that there was some tension between him and his old friend. My antenna went up. "Oh, yeah, what kind?"

It seemed that the lady had had the hots for Norman ever since she'd met him, but he'd never responded because she was not sexually attractive to him. So he said, at least.

"That hasn't stopped you before."

He ignored my remark. "You've met her, you saw how plain she is."

"I'll say."

I had a feeling he was leading up to something, and I wasn't going to like it. But in all our shared insanities, I wasn't prepared for what came next.

"She's so fucking lonely, and she's a good woman. She just has a problem getting laid. God, baby, you don't know how much she wanted to fuck me. She came on so strong, it was embarrassing."

"Oh, you poor thing, she tried to rape you, and you fought her off."

"No, I told her that I loved you, and I was being faithful."

"How gallant of you."

He sighed. "Darling, you know there isn't a woman who gets what I give you."

I laughed. "Like Lord and Taylor and Bonwit's charge plates?"

"C'mon baby, look at all you have in your life. She has nothing. So why don't you let me run back to her place and fuck her. You can afford to be generous. You'd be doing her a big favor. And I'd adore you for it."

He was so persuasive, so sure of his logic, so reassuring, talking, talking, talking, saying things like fucking her meant nothing to him and that he wouldn't even enjoy it.

There's something unreal about this conversation, I thought. I was feeling disconnected from the sound of my voice as I heard myself agree to his suggestion.

What was I doing? This isn't right. It stinks! But I put a lid on my doubts, telling myself it was harmless. After all, I was his wife. I could afford to throw her a bone.

Norman was combative, and in general, we argued a lot. When I thought he was wrong, I let him know it, but what I still didn't understand in myself was the power he had over me, the insidious way he was sucking me into more and more of his craziness. Now he was tender, taking me in his arms, telling me what a beautiful, gorgeous person I was and how much he adored me.

"Sweet baby, I'll be back in a short while."

"You better make it real short," I snapped.

Blowing a kiss, he was out the door as happy as a little boy who had permission from his mommy to go out to play.

How his subconscious could have made me, Adele Morales, into his mother Fanny, I'll never know. But maybe that was what it was really about.

When he returned, he said he'd told his friend how I'd given my permission and how grateful she was. Those words made me feel nothing but contempt for this woman who was willing to accept my leavings.

I was angry at him and even more so at myself for going along with his bullshit. On top of it, he tried to make love to me that night, but I was repelled. There was a foulness about him, and I wouldn't let him touch me. All I wanted was sleep so I could blot it all out.

Chapter 24

In ten years, we were to live in six different places. Neither of us felt we had roots, so I suppose that was part of our restlessness. In 1955, we had been in our second flat since 1951. Then Norman found a loft rental on Monroe Street near the East River waterfront. He was enthusiastic, but from his description, the only thing to recommend it was lots of cheap space. It was enormous, he said, and I couldn't wait to see it. We'd still be on the lower East Side, but a loft that size had its compensations.

First Avenue and Second Street was Park Avenue compared to Monroe, the meanest of all the streets in that area. Garbage-littered and gang-ridden, it was shadowed by the Manhattan Bridge, which added to its dark grimy look. Norman had not exaggerated the size of the loft. It was big enough to ride a bike from one end to the other. Though it had nineteen windows, there was really only one through which there was a glimpse of the East River.

There was no kitchen to speak of and a minimal bathroom. But no matter, all that could be fixed, and at $150 a month, we had to take it. We'd be living there without a permit, since this was before lofts became fashionable and therefore zoned for residence. But there was a way to get around it, we were told by a fashion photographer who had the floor above us and by a painter who lived below. Like Norman, I was excited by all that space, thinking of the great studio I would have where I could work on big canvasses. And the parties we could give!

We ignored the fact that we would be living in a neighborhood where my husband would have to walk me home from the subway carrying an iron bar in a rolled-up newspaper. We wanted that place, and with our customary lack of foresight, we jumped in.

The few sticks of furniture we brought with us looked lost in that cavernous area, but I was already decorating it in my imagination, with all the beautiful furniture we would buy. The low rent meant we could afford major renovations—and I do mean major. But first we decided to give a painting party, inviting ten people. It would take twenty gallons of white paint to cover the wall space, plus ten wide brushes for the guests. I bought some deli from Katz's and a lot of booze.

Monty Clift came dressed in a work shirt and dungarees. He loved the idea, but, not surprisingly, he ended up very drunk along with the rest of our crew. Monty entertained us with some Hollywood stories, and there was an interesting political discussion while Sergeant Mailer barked out orders with no one paying much attention. But paint they did, getting more on each other than on the walls.

We could have hired professional painters, and had I insisted, Norman would have. But this was an interesting excuse for a party. Predictably the walls were sloppily streaky, especially Monty's section, and, of course, we hadn't thought of washing down the walls, so there were streaks of grease coming through. But everyone nicely offered to finish it with a second coat the next day, and of course, we accepted.

Later on we gave a housewarming with a variety of guests. Kevin McCarthy, the actor, was there along with John Aldridge, author of *After the Lost Generation.* Lillian Hellman came, by now quite used to the crazy places we lived in. Norman invited some uptown society types, acquaintances, who came wearing dinner jackets.

Brando came, he didn't talk to anybody. Clift came and didn't talk to Brando. But at least Monty was more sociable, not quite as shy as Marlon.

As usual, the party had a nice energy, with people mixing and talking. Keeping the hi-fi supplied with some background jazz, I tried to be a relatively sober hostess, paying attention to food, making introductions, being on my best behavior.

I was at the bar, refilling a friend's glass, when I heard yelling in the far end of the loft by the door. Checking it out, I saw five vicious-looking punks from the local street gang, trying to crash the party, arguing with Jean Malaquais, the French writer and a friend of Norman's.

Jean, a little rooster, was excitedly flapping his arms about, trying to reason with these pirates in his Parisian accent. Between the music, the yelling, and the talking, I couldn't catch all the dialogue. But knowing Jean, he was probably saying things like, "Get out of here, you sociological misfits!"

They were looking for this chick, the leader said, claiming she'd insulted him, and they were not leaving until they could talk to her. I don't know who the girl was, most likely she was someone's date, but there was no way in hell we'd let these guys get past the door.

From what I could gather, the woman and her date had walked past the candy store, and one of the gang had made an obscene remark. There had been an altercation, and she had slapped him, a suicidal gesture. She got away in one piece, and that was a miracle. According to one of the tenants, there had been some incidents like rape and a couple of break-ins involving two of the members of this gang.

A tanked-up Norman swaggered to the door, wearing his mean, squinty-eyed look and using his tough Texan accent. "Hey, man, you heard my friend. The girl's not here, so get the hell out."

"Fuck you. We saw her come in here," the leader said, shoving past Norman. Simultaneously, a hammer flashed, zing, zing, zing, three hits against Norman's skull. My little bull refused to go down. He sank to one knee, but was up in a minute, anesthetized, luckily, by all the booze in his system. Before Norman could grab the hammer, the kid raised it again, slamming it on his head two more times, and then the gang was gone.

I screamed at the sight of my husband standing there with blood steaming down his face. "Oh, my God, what did he do? Somebody get a doctor before he bleeds to death."

Norman was in a daze. "I'm all right, baby," he kept saying. "Calm down, I'm okay." I don't think he realized he'd been hit. Most of the guests had been grouped at the opposite end of the loft, absorbed in the party, unaware of the drama going on. A few had been watching the confrontation, but the attack happened too quickly for anyone to stop it.

"Get the police," someone shouted. People crowded around Norman, and there was a lot of confusion.

"What happened to Norman?" "Who were those guys?" they asked.

One of the guests was a psychoanalyst with an MD and a heavy German accent. He and Norman joked around while he did some clumsy first aid.

"Yah," he said, "I haven't had so much fun playing doctor in the last twenty years. I don't think there's a concussion, but the cuts are fairly deep. You'd better go right away to an emergency ward because you might need stitches."

The doctor was right about the concussion, and the gashes did need stitching. I don't remember why Norman decided not to press charges. Since there was no major injury, he might not have wanted to take time out from his work to go through all the legalities. I hated having to pass that candy store every day with that same gang standing there. We ignored them, and they looked the other way. It seemed they all had records, and one or two were parolees. They were not in a hurry to press their luck by messing with us again.

Norman had to be with me every minute because I was scared to be alone in that loft, especially at night.

"Why don't we buy a gun?"

But my husband laughed. "You're always so dramatic." Even so, we were very tense. It was a lousy way to live.

Looking back at the histrionics of that housewarming party, I realize that in all the drunken fistfights Norman ever had, his head always took the most punishment. Which brings back the memory of something my mother used to say to my dad during their incessant quarreling. "Albert, ya got no sensitivity. It must be from all those punches you took to your head."

Chapter 25

We stuck it out for a while, but it was impossible. I'd had it with our bohemian style of living, and so had my husband. We went to the other extreme, moving to the upper East Side, where we found a duplex in an unusually narrow four-story brownstone on Fifty-fifth Street between First and Second Avenues. When we were shown the apartment, the first thing the landlord mentioned was the name of the tenant below us. It was Billy Daniels, the famous black singer of the forties and fifties whose rendition of "That Old Black Magic," sung in his own unique style, had made him famous. That meant more to me than to Norman, who knew little or nothing about pop music. In the two years we lived there, Billy kept to himself, declining our party invitations. Our acquaintance was confined to a nod whenever we met at the downstairs entrance.

I wanted a completely new beginning, so we left all our junky furniture behind. We took our clothes, a bed, and Norman's hundreds of books. With the recommendation of an architect friend, we furnished in the Danish-Modern style. Norman knew nothing about interior decorating nor was he particularly interested. Sometimes he would go with me to pick out stuff, but mostly he went along with my taste.

We always hung my paintings first when we moved into a new home. I knew they were important to Norman. Just going through that brief ritual together made me feel close to him, made me feel that there was some stability in our crazy marriage. I felt that at least we were trying to make a home together, like a real-life couple.

I had a definite flair for decorating, and I loved furnishing that Fifty-fifth Street apartment. It was a joy, spending as much as I wanted from my constantly replenished checking account.

At the same time, we got a black royal standard poodle puppy because I had wanted a dog for a long time, and Norman didn't like cats. We adored that dog so much, we got him a wife, a brown one from the same poodle breeder in Connecticut. Zsa Zsa was not in the same class as our Tibo, a Prince of Darkness, who was really a highly intelligent, sensitive person in a dog's body. Zsa Zsa had a rather cantankerous nature, and though we tried to divide our attention equally, she was jealous of Tibo, who was the handsomer of the two. In spite of their incompatibility, they produced two litters of beautiful puppies over the next four years.

Norman never really liked Zsa Zsa. She was harder to train than Tibo. One day, Zsa Zsa pooped on the rug. Norman, who had very little patience with either animals or humans, got angry, picked her up, and bodily threw her down the stairs.

"She did it on purpose, the little bitch."

I was horrified, but not surprised at what he had done. Luckily she wasn't hurt, but from then on, she was frightened by him and more neurotic than ever.

I love animals, and I hate bullies who vent their frustrations and rage on helpless animals, and I told him so. All he could say was, "She's stupid, she doesn't learn. That's the only way she understands," a comment that made me even angrier.

Norman had a mean, sadistic streak toward animals, and with the exception of Tibo, he didn't really like them. Tibo was very good and always asked to go out when he needed to. But I remember Norman's rage and the way he beat him when Tibo pooped in the living room, probably because we slept late. The poor dog couldn't hold it in, and the next morning when Norman got up, he stepped into the neat little present Tibo had left outside the bedroom door. In spite of his anger, he had to laugh at Tibo's revenge.

Norman's daughter, Susie, visited us occasionally, and I tried to be as nice to her as I could, which was easy since she was a real charmer. There was a lot of the mother in me, and I wanted a baby of my own, but Norman kept postponing the subject.

In spite of Norman's preoccupation with himself and his writing, he was good to Susie when she was with us. He gave her as much time as he could, took her to museums and the zoo, doing things that kids like to do, with me along, of course. She was with us one Christmas, and I remember the pleasure I got going to F.A.O. Schwarz to give her an unforgettable holiday. One of her gifts was an expensive dollhouse, complete with intricately made copies of antique furniture. We were delighted by Susie's reaction, her expression of wonder and delight on that Christmas morning.

One night during that same holiday, our old friend Dan Wolf came over, and the three of us planned to go out for dinner. I hadn't seen Dan for a while and was looking forward to it. When he arrived, Norman, who'd been in a foul mood all day, began to pick at me. I answered him back, setting off the usual bickering between us. I've a vague recollection of what it was about, something petty on his part, ending up with the comment that I should stay home with Susie and the babysitter.

Norman was being irrational since we had used this sitter before, and Susie was secure with her. I lost my patience and said, "Listen, Norman, I don't want to argue anymore. I've been with Susie all day, and I'm looking forward to going out tonight." I said it as a fact, not a complaint. Without warning, he backhanded me across the face. Dan was shocked, and I stood there speechless with shock and pain.

I wanted to hit him back, but he had that mean look I'd seen before, so I backed off. I began to cry, both from the pain and feeling humiliated in front of our friend.

I thought Dan should have said something, but instead he was quiet, making no effort to comfort me, by word or by touch, and I was hurt. Was he afraid of Norman? Either that or he had chosen sides.

I could have avoided what happened by catering to Norman's rotten mood, the way I sometimes did, but tonight I was damned if I would let him bully me again. I fixed up my face and went out anyway. I was furious, hating him, sulking the whole time, ignoring him, fastening all my attention on Dan. Luckily I didn't drink much, but Norman had his usual ration, acting as if nothing had happened, not apologizing for his vicious behavior.

Up to this point, his abuse had been emotional, but now he was beginning to be more free with his hands.

Chapter 26

Now that we had a civilized, even chic, apartment like some of our affluent friends, we gave more dinner parties. I'd worked at becoming a good cook. Next to painting, I loved cooking best and still do to this day. It was even more enjoyable because I didn't have to clean up afterward. There was always a maid to do that. Norman's mother now owned a domestic-help agency and provided me with an endless supply of maids.

Norman was still working on *The Deer Park*, but I was painting less and less, devoting most of my energies to entertaining and decorating the apartment, while trying to match my husband's nervous energy. We were out almost every night, drinking, smoking pot. To please Norman, I tried to be everything I wasn't and if I were sober, would never have wanted to be.

I remember one early Sunday morning, I was walking the dogs, still drunk and dressed in my evening clothes after an all-night party. As I passed the church on the corner, I paused, watching people go in, when I hadn't been to bed yet. Look at those hypocritical squares, I thought. But inside, I felt like shit, hating myself, envying those normal people, the families going to Sunday mass.

We had a guest room, and at various times, Mickey Knox, an actor friend of Norman's, would stay with us. They had met in Hollywood, right after Norman's success with *The Naked and the Dead*. There were similarities between them. Both were intelligent, both were little roosters, and both were from Brooklyn.

Mickey had left Hollywood, and a small career, to live in Rome. I don't know whether it was true or not, but the story is that he was blacklisted in Hollywood during the McCarthy witch-hunt period and was unable to work. However, he did very well in Rome and became thoroughly involved in the Italian movie scene on different levels.

I introduced Mickey to my sister Joan early in the fifties when she was sixteen. He thought she was gorgeous, but to him, she was just a kid, since he was more than thirty at the time. He didn't see her again until many years later, when he became her second husband. He had fallen in love with Joanie, who was on her way to success as a high-fashion model. She towered over him, especially in her high heels, but for Mickey, the bigger the better. He loved my sister very much, but I do think the Mailer connection was not without its special appeal. Norman and Mickey's friendship was intense, and there were times when they were so wrapped up in each other even I would feel excluded.

Mickey worshiped Norman, rarely disagreeing with him on any level, no matter how insane his behavior was. Mickey has lasted all through Norman's six marriages, his changes in fortune, and his career. Now they are sharing old age.

Gore Vidal had known Joanie and Mickey throughout their marriage. Years later, Joanie told me about a conversation she'd had with Gore around the time she and Mickey were having problems. She was complaining that her husband seemed to be more devoted to his male friends than to his wife. Naturally, Norman's name came up, and Gore, who was Norman's friend, remarked in that dry, superior tone, "My dear, Norman has always been married to Mickey. There's never been anyone else for him."

Over the years, Norman was extremely generous with Mickey, always picking up his tab in restaurants and nightclubs. Mickey rarely reciprocated. However, with all this, we did have some pleasant times together, since Mickey was attractive, bright, and a good storyteller.

Mickey collected celebrities, mostly from film. He knew a lot of people and brought us along to some fun parties. Half the time, Mickey never bothered to check with the hostess about bringing us, and in spite of the reception of *Barbary Shore*, and later on, *The Deer Park*, people were always interested to meet the author of *The Naked and the Dead*. Norman, as always, charmed people with his humor and intelligence—when he wasn't being a drunken jerk. Which was happening more often.

I'd been getting the full dose of Norman's dark side, so there had to be some pluses. Meeting movie stars was one of them. More often than not, we would spend the evening with Mickey and his girlfriend of the moment, usually an attractive actress. Leslie Caron and Eva Marie Saint dated him. So did Lois Andrews, a sometime-actress, who at fifteen made headlines by becoming the child-bride of Georgie Jessel. She was beautiful, tough, and almost six feet tall to Mickey's five foot seven. Lois had a drinking problem, and her drunken scenes with Mickey rivaled mine with Norman. The only thing I didn't do, that Lois did, was throw things at her boyfriend in public. I must confess, I liked seeing someone else screw up for a change.

Leslie Caron was pleasant, very much the way she appeared on screen. I liked Eva, who was not only beautiful, but unpretentious, as well. She lived on Grove Street in the Village, in a large top-floor studio apartment with a skylight. I think she was in the middle of filming *On the Waterfront* when we met her.

Mickey also introduced us to Christopher Plummer and Tammy Grimes, his wife at that time. Robert Ryan, a wonderful actor, was even more handsome offscreen, but socially, rather withdrawn and gloomy. In passing, we met Alain Delon, the French movie star, gorgeous and quite unassuming, and Raf Vallone, when the two stars were filming *A View from the Bridge*. I believe Mickey, who spoke fluent Italian and French, was working on the film as dialogue director.

The meeting that truly excited me was with Jean Renoir, the director. He lived on Riverside Drive, in a cavernous two-room apartment. A charming, warm person, he made me feel at home in spite of my shyness. It was a thrill to meet him not only because of his beautiful films, but because he was the son of Renoir the painter.

I've never quarreled with Mickey, but there was one unfortunate incident between us. I did something rather stupid. Like

Norman, Mickey was his mother's darling. She had just died, and Mickey had flown in from Rome and was staying at our apartment for a few weeks. Mick and I were having a few drinks while waiting for Norman to get back from his writing day at the studio. Mick was talking to me about his mother when he broke down and cried—and I laughed. I can't think why I responded in that way, since I'm not at all an unkind person. It must have been a combination of the booze and surprise at this rather guarded tough guy in tears. I apologized, and even though we talked and were friendly on the surface, I always got the feeling he never really forgave me. He was like Norman in that way. Once you got on his shit list, you were there for life.

Chapter 27

Norman finished *The Deer Park* in the mid-fifties. Rinehart and Company, publisher of *The Naked and the Dead*, was going to publish it, but at the last minute Stanley Rinehart, who was running the company, reneged. He had never really liked the book and was shocked at a particular passage, describing a starlet going down on a Hollywood mogul. Stanley was afraid there would be trouble because the scene was too explicit.

This is the way Norman wrote it, and it was hardly explicit:

> *Tentatively, she reached out a hand to finger his hair, and at that moment Herman Teppis opened his legs and let Bobby fall to the floor. At the expression of surprise on her face, he began to laugh. "Don't you worry, sweetie," he said, and down he looked at that frightened female mouth, facsimile of all those smiling lips he had seen so ready to serve at the thumb of power, and with a cough, he started to talk. "That's a good girlie, that's a good girlie, that's a good girlie," he said in a mild little voice, "you're an angel darling, and I like you, you're my darling darling, oh that's the ticket," said Teppis.*

Norman was given an ultimatum, delete the passage or no publication. Of course, he refused. I loved him for having the courage and integrity not to give in.

Norman had never been easy to live with, but now it was hellish for us both. His agent sent the novel to seven other publishing houses, and at each rejection, he would get more angry and depressed. There were times he would just sit staring at nothing, drinking Scotch, and chewing ice cubes. Sometimes in the middle of a conversation, he would seem to be distracted. It was as if he was out of his body. He would smile to himself, as if I weren't there, his lips moving soundlessly, having a dialogue with himself. I would watch him get up from his chair to fill his glass again, and then the pacing would start, back and forth, whispering to himself.

This was behavior different from his usual preoccupied manner when his writing was on his mind. These trancelike states had never happened before. Rather than being alarmed, I chose to ignore the strange episodes, leaving him alone, thinking he'd be better off working his own way out of it.

Norman was handling a lot that year. Besides the trouble with his book, he was writing a controversial column for the *Village Voice*. The *Voice* had been started around 1955 by Dan Wolf, Ed Fancher, Norman, and Jerry Tallmer. We had all been excited by the idea of a new Village newspaper. I remember sitting in on a meeting when we were trying to come up with a name for it. I'm not sure, but I think the name was Dan's idea. The paper took off, but Norman's friendship with Dan, who became the editor, ended because of Norman's egomaniacal outbursts and his insatiable need to control everything and everybody. His concept of the *Voice* was in direct conflict with the others.

At the start, Norman said he wanted to be a silent partner. That's a laugh because Norman was and never will be silent about anything. Predictably he ended up writing a column called "The Hip and the Square." Though there were some interesting ideas in the column, the writing at times was obsessive and almost incoherent, as if he were using the *Voice* as a receptacle for his bile.

I felt terrible about Norman and Dan because I loved my friend, but my loyalty was to my husband, crazy or not. During the period of Norman's fights at the *Voice*, Walter Minton of G. P. Putnam's decided to publish *The Deer Park* uncut. Thank God! Now maybe Norman would calm down. When it came time for Putnam to design a cover for the book, Norman wanted them to use a lovely small abstract gouache, one of my four paintings from a group show at a gallery on East Tenth Street. Norman had always loved that painting and had named it *Fires*, a title I liked. I was really excited about the prospect of seeing my work reproduced on the cover of what I hoped would be a bestseller. It was turned down. Too arty, they said. It didn't explain what the book was about. Norman really fought for it, especially when he saw the cover they chose. I saw it, too, and it was awful.

The worst was yet to come, when the reviews appeared. Most were vitrolic, attacking not only the book, but the author himself, calling him a psychopath, a no-talent pervert. Some of the words used were, "Unsavory junk," "dull, moronic," "the year's worst snakepit in fiction." There was a sprinkling of good reviews, but not enough to balance the bad.

There was a favorable one from the *New York Times*. "Though it is not a wholly successful novel, it is studded with brilliant and illuminating passages, by and large it is good reading. If it lacks the impact of *The Naked and the Dead*, which still stands as probably the best fictional account of the War's actual fighting, it is far better than *Barbary Shore*."

Still, the bad ones kept pouring in, not only the New York press, but the out-of-town papers, as well. Norman was in a never-ending rage. I got so upset and hurt for him that I would cry. There was fear and bewilderment in his face, but he would hold me in his arms, comforting me.

"Don't cry, darling. You just wait. I'll show those mother-fuckers," and he'd pour himself another Scotch. There might have been some compensation if the book had sold well. But the reviews killed it.

Chapter 28

Norman's pot smoking and drinking was accelerating—and he had ten times my tolerance and stamina. I'd always been a cheap drunk. Three martinis and I was gone; seven tokes from a joint and I was flying. For me, it wasn't how much I drank or smoked, it was how much trouble I got into when I did.

Norman had a bigger menu than I had. Besides booze, pills, and pot, and whatever else he was experimenting with (unbeknownst to me), he was a heavy smoker.

But as I've already mentioned, and I must say it again, no matter what state he was in, wrecked, hung over, depressed, he would get up and go to work in his Brooklyn Heights studio.

We always had an intense social life, and party-giving was important to it. Each place we had lived, we had at least one outstanding party given by the mad general and me, his aide-de-camp. I only remember a few incidents from a big bash we had at the Fifty-fifth Street apartment. One lovely memory was of a bombed Monty Clift and an equally bombed Adele necking on the white-carpeted stairs with Monty giving me wide-screen kisses. Meanwhile, Norman was stretched out on the living room floor in a room grey with pot smoke. His head was close to our glittering new hi-fi equipment with its attenuated woofers and tweeters blasting out Dave Brubeck. Norman was convinced that pot would cure his tone deafness.

A few novices were complaining that they were feeling nothing after smoking one of our neatly rolled joints. The general would put a brown paper bag over his or her head, telling them to inhale deeply and hold the smoke in as long as they could. That usually worked. When the bag came off, they were stoned enough to dig Norman's rambling, disconnected lecture on the marijuana mystique.

His behavior was getting more bizarre, out of control, and violent. He announced that he would analyze himself and that his sessions would take place on a Bongo Board. Norman would bring his to every party, where he would be in the center for hours.

The fiery prophet, seesawing back and forth, haranguing his audience.

Words, words, words. A kind of nonstop, frenetic, drunken, psychotic babbling. About what no one really knew. To him, analyzing himself meant acting out and gratifying any impulse he had, wherever and with whomever. Everyone ran for cover. Being Svengali's wife, I just had another drink. Norman never rested, never relaxed, sweating constantly, pacing up and down, drink in one hand and a joint in the other.

One night we came home late from a dinner party. Norman went out to walk the dogs, and I slipped off to bed with my book. A half-hour went by and no Norman. He should have been back because the dogs usually did their stuff in that time. Another hour went by, and I began to get anxious, calming myself with the thought that he might have gone to P. J. Clarke's for a nightcap. Another half-hour passed, and I really began to worry. I was about to go out to look for him when I heard him come in, the dogs bounding up the stairs.

When I saw him, all I could say was, "Oh my God, what happened?" His raincoat was torn and filthy, one eye was swollen shut, and he had some bloody cuts on his face and head. "Look at your face, dammit, who did this?" I wailed.

"Honey, it's all right. I'm okay."

The funny thing was that he seemed to be in a good mood, almost exhilarated. "I got into a fight with two sailors outside a bar."

"Why, for God's sake?"

"Well, I was walking by these guys, and one of them pointed to Tibo and said, 'Mister, your dog is queer.' I wasn't going to take that. So I asked the other guy to hold the dogs, and I went for the bastard who made the crack. Tibo, the coward, never came to my defense and neither did Zsa Zsa."

Poor beautiful Tibo, how did he know that his crazy master was getting beaten up for defending him? After all, he was just a pampered pompom-tailed fancy dog, not a police dog. Norman must have gotten the worst of it because that sailor was an eye gouger. It scared me to look at his eye, it was so inflamed and swollen.

I pictured my polite husband asking the other sailor to hold his two gorgeous clipped poodles so he could get his brains beaten out. I called Jack Begner, a doctor friend who lived nearby. Jack didn't like the way the eye looked, insisting Norman see a specialist. It turned out to be a detached retina, and he had to have surgery. That was the second bad fight Norman had gotten into, and both times he had taken a beating.

Another night we were awakened by an insistent ringing of our doorbell. It was three in the morning. That's always scary whether you live in a dump or a chic little apartment. We had no intercom, just a buzzer.

"Don't let him in," I said. "It's probably a drunk."

Whoever it was kept his finger on the bell and then began to pound on the door. "Fuck it," my husband said. "I'm going downstairs."

"Just ignore it. Whoever it is will go away. If not, call the cops."

"No, I want to know who the hell is making that racket."

Cowardly me stayed upstairs while Norman opened the door. "Who is it, Norman?" I shouted down the stairs.

I could hear Norman's voice speaking and a male voice answering. In a moment, I recognized the voice. It was Monty Clift, and he was dead drunk. There was more talk and then a loud crash. "Oh, shit, what's going on?" My curiosity getting the better of me, I ran downstairs.

Monty looked like a crazy man. I don't think he recognized me, and he hardly knew where he was. "Honey, are you okay? What did he do?"

"He broke a lamp and knocked down a bookcase. Go upstairs, he'll be okay."

"Oh, great," I said, "our place is going to be wrecked by a movie star." Nevertheless, I did my master's bidding and waited for the sound of more breakage. I could hear Monty cursing and then silence. Norman came back upstairs.

"Monty's in bad shape. I've seen him drunk, but never like this. He wanted to stay here, but I thought he'd be better off if he went home, so I put him in a cab."

Norman sold the film rights to *The Naked and the Dead* to Charles Laughton for $100,000, a big deal in those days, when we lived in that apartment. Laughton and Paul Gregory, who was married to Janet Gaynor, were going to produce it.

One afternoon, I was in the upstairs bedroom dressing to go out when I heard Norman call me. "Come down, baby. There's someone I'd like you to meet."

I could hear Norman talking and someone replying. There was no mistaking Charles Laughton's voice. As I came downstairs, he smiled at me, looking like he did on screen. I had never met a more charming and gracious man, and with all his fame, so real.

That same year, Norman made his first television appearance on David Susskind's show. I remember how excited we both were going to the studio that night to meet David. That was in the days when it was all live, no tapes. Norman knew enough not to go on camera drunk, and though he was nervous before going on, he had watched his intake. That night he was at his most lucid, attractive, and brilliant. It was also the night Truman Capote was a guest.

Truman was fun and extremely clever. He and Norman liked each other immediately. The conversation was stimulating, and

Truman made his famous bitchy remark about Jack Kerouac. "He doesn't write, he types," Truman said, dismissing Jack with a flip of his hand.

After the show, Truman took us to the Stork Club. He was delightful company and in his own way, not pretentious. I could tell he liked me because I felt at ease with him.

"You're a beautiful woman," he said in his high-pitched, slightly singsong voice. "You must have a dress from my friend, Balenciaga. You'd be a sensation. I'll take you there myself."

I was quite flattered, assuming it would be his treat or at least, that there would be a huge discount. "I'd love it, Truman," I answered with enthusiasm. But, of course, it never happened. It was just in the spirit of the moment.

Alberto Moravia, the famous Italian novelist, was a guest at one of our dinner parties. We had met Moravia at Chumleys, a restaurant we liked a lot in the Village. He was with Judy Sheftel, a photographer friend of ours, who later met Jules Feiffer through our introduction and became his wife.

Alberto was highly intelligent and rather withdrawn, with an air of deep gloom about him. It was a relief to see an occasional smile dispel the glumness. He had a hawk nose and thick black eyebrows overshadowing piercing black eyes.

Norman and Moravia shared a mutual respect for each other's work, and I myself had read and admired his novels even before I met my husband. On the few occasions I saw him, I began to sense his interest in me. He wasn't obvious about it, but I knew he was responding to my rather flirtatious nature. Nothing much happened at the time because I felt a streak of cruelty in him, and one sadist was enough in my life.

Then Moravia started calling me during the day on one pretext or another when Norman was at his studio. At first it was just to chat, but then he wanted to meet me for a drink. He was insistent, but I declined as tactfully as I could. Before he went back to Rome, we gave another small dinner party for him. That night Alberto was an interesting, informative guest, and he appeared to be enjoying himself.

Not wanting to cook anything Italian, I decided to serve roast beef and Yorkshire pudding. I was in the kitchen carving up the beef when Alberto came in to ask for more wine. Seeing me hacking away at the roast, he offered to help. I gladly handed him the carving knife. We made small talk as I sipped my martini and checked out the pudding rising in the oven. I could tell he'd had a lot of wine by the way he carved at the roast, cramming little pieces of meat into his mouth all the while. There was an uncomfortable silence, and I made an innocuous comment. "Men are better at carving than women."

"Is that what you think?" he asked, waving the knife at me.

His smile was wicked in that dark gloom of a face. I said nothing by way of response. Then he abruptly grabbed my arm in a tight grip and said in his heavy Italian accent, "I see that you are playing with me, and I do not like it. Do you not think of me? I think very much about you, Adeley." (I liked the way he pronounced my name.) "I want to make love to you. You must come to the hotel tomorrow. If you say no, I will kill you." He tried to kiss me, still holding the knife.

I felt like an awkward teenager pushing him away. "Please Alberto, don't fool with that knife. You surprise me. Really, I do understand your feelings, but my husband is waiting for his roast beef, and he gets so cranky when he's hungry." I finished off my martini, and being high myself, I was rather enjoying this little backstage melodrama. I liked surprises, and this grave, fiftyish, black-suited author was one of them.

But then I became really frightened because he brandished the knife again, cornering me. I decided I'd had enough of this silly drunken game. "Alberto, this is ridiculous," I said, leaving him in the kitchen. In a few minutes, he appeared with the roast beef and the wine, looking gloomier than ever, not saying much through the remainder of the evening. The next time we saw him was in Rome. Our little contretemps seemed to have been forgotten.

Chapter 29

I n the spring of 1956, we decided to take a belated three-month honeymoon trip to Europe. It was my first visit ever, and I can still remember how excited I was. We both needed a radical change, and we hoped this would be it. Norman was in and out of his depression and still taking heavy doses of Seconal for his insomnia that was worse than ever.

We sailed second class on the *United States of America*, the passenger ship famous for having broken speed records to Europe. Norman had made all that money from the film sale of *The Naked and the Dead,* so we could have gone first class. It wasn't really important, but I suppose second class represented the small-potato side of us both.

On the other hand, I was so thrilled about sailing instead of flying that I didn't care what class we were in. We could have taken any of the Italian, French, or British ships. I could never understand why Norman chose an American line. Maybe it was because his mother and sister had sailed on it to visit him and Bea when they were living in Paris in the late forties.

The ship was enormous, painted a battleship grey inside and out. Our stateroom was tiny with a double-decker bed. It wasn't terribly romantic, considering this was supposed to be the honeymoon I never had. The ship was as regimented as if it were still part of the navy. Deafening school bells, not chimes or gongs, were rung for meals and ship's activities. If one was late for breakfast, arranging for another was complicated.

Norman noticed the name of someone we knew on the first-class passenger list, but when we tried going to the upper deck to look him up, two sailors were standing guard in front of a chained, barricaded entrance. We were damned annoyed about that. After we were invited to the captain's table, we were allowed to go anywhere we pleased.

We fought a lot less on that trip. I'm sure it had to do with the fact we'd cut down on our drinking and smoking. It was good for us to be far away from the pressures of that New York world. It even seemed to lessen my desire for alcohol.

When we arrived in Paris, we checked into the Palais Royal hotel. I was dazzled by the charm and elegance of the city, never having seen anything like it. Norman enjoyed seeing this beauty again through my eyes. There was nothing blasé about me. I was like a child oohing and ahhing over Paris and the escargot we gorged ourselves on every night. But alas, the real honeymoon had been on the boat. There'd been some peace for a while, and we'd gotten close again, making tender love. But now we were on land.

Norman's drinking picked up again, and with that, his nervous restlessness. My own drinking was under control. I seemed to be sticking to wine, partly out of necessity, since I couldn't get a decent martini, or any other cocktail for that matter. At that time, the French were not big on cocktails.

The first thing we did was to look up Jean Malaquais and his then-wife, Galy, whom we had not seen since our big Monroe Street party. Norman's friendship with Jean went back to the days of his first marriage when he and Bea were living in Paris. Jean was an attractive and serious intellectual. He was extremely political, a Trotskyite. He and Norman had an instant rapport when they first met.

Jean admired Norman's work, but he was also very critical and perhaps a little jealous. He was an egotistical opportunist and a user, but in spite of such negative traits, he was likable, putting his continental charm to good use.

Galy was part French and part I don't know what, maybe Polish or Russian. She was quirky, quite filled with herself, and humorless. Not pretty, she had a kind of style, very French. I liked her paintings, which were semiabstract and quite lyrical with beautiful color. Galy spoke English with a strong French accent, but when she did, she acted as if she were doing one a favor by speaking English at all. There were times when she displayed a childlike charm, which could be unintentionally funny.

Jean had done the French translation of *The Naked and the Dead*, and he had been extremely critical of that book, as he was of everything Norman had written. Norman seemed to accept

Jean's opinion as the word of God. I suppose Jean played the part of mentor, and in that role, he had some power over Norman. I think it was partly Norman's need for a strong father figure; Jean, who was ten years his senior, seemed to serve that need.

Norman grumbled about the French all the time we were in France, saying they were arrogant, superior little bastards. It's true. They did at that time have a snotty attitude and were not particularly tolerant, especially toward foreigners who mutilated their language. Still, Norman's French wasn't bad, when he wasn't trying to outdo Jean Gabin. Mine was nonexistent.

Throughout the trip, there were brief periods when he wasn't on display and could be his nice, sweet self, truly enjoying where he was and what he was doing. But for most of the trip, he was a pain in the ass. I'm sure there were times when I got on *his* nerves. After all, we were together a great deal, but my neurotic foibles were nothing compared to the load of angst he was carrying. He had been so much more relaxed on the ship, but now we were back to reality, quite a different reality than New York, but nevertheless a reality, and things seemed to be too much for him.

Norman put up a front to the outside world, but I was the one who knew his insides. He was still reeling from *The Deer Park* disaster, and he was scared and at the same time, in a rage at everything. Whenever he felt like it, he would dump his foul mood on the first convenient person. I was there, but not always an easy target; and I don't think I ever was. In my own way, I could fling a lot of his shit right back in his face.

During the entire trip, it was up and down, and in spite of him, I had to take what I could. Norman's insomnia plagued him constantly while we were in Europe, and since he had chosen this time to try to kick the Seconal habit, withdrawal symptoms were awful.

Chapter 30

Having planned from the start to see more of Europe, we left Paris in a rented car for a leisurely tour through Germany, Spain, and Italy. Norman's mood picked up when we left Paris. Being on the move seemed to tone him down, and the drive through the French countryside was especially calming for us both. It was so beautiful. One day we came across some castle ruins where we picnicked on paté, fruit, and wine. The sun was warm, and we made love behind a high stone wall.

I still hadn't learned to drive, which was an occasional annoyance to Norman. I couldn't really blame him. Since our Mexican trip, I had made no attempt to take driving lessons in New York. I was terrified at the thought of maneuvering a car through city traffic and had a childish fear of getting lost. Obviously (though not obvious to me at the time), I was using my fear of learning to drive as an excuse for maintaining my dependency on my husband. I didn't take driving lessons until the last year of our marriage, and by that time, it was too late.

There were two reasons why Norman wanted to go to Germany, aside from the fact that he had never been there. He wanted to visit Munich to see his German publisher, Hugo Weichlein, and then go to the site of the Buchenwald concentration camp. I didn't want to go to the camp, but Norman said that as a writer and a Jew he should. When the time came, I went along even though the thought frightened me.

As we approached the German border, we got our passports ready. I remember telling Norman that I was feeling anxious and my heart was pounding. "Maybe the guards have two heads."

Norman laughed. "Baby, mine is pounding harder. I'm a Jew, you aren't."

When we got to Munich, we checked into a hotel and phoned Hugo. The Weichleins, who spoke English, were warm and hospitable, and I liked them both. They showed us through Munich and introduced us to their friends, most of them bilingual. There were only three things I can remember about that city; the bombed-out areas, something I'd only seen in newsreels; the museums, where we saw some superb Albrecht Durer drawings and paintings; and the night the Weichleins took us to Hugo's favorite restaurant and treated us to the best roast duckling I'd ever had. A banal memory, perhaps, but not surprising since I loved to eat well.

I felt much more attractive in Germany than I did in Paris. Frenchmen hadn't paid that much attention to me. But the men in Munich made much of my dark good looks. I would overhear words like "schoene mädchen" in restaurants and elevators. Norman looked pleased. "They're talking about you, baby."

Men flirted openly with me, and at the time I needed that ego boost, given Norman's up-and-down moods. I put on a lot of weight eating all that rich, heavy food. And, of course, there were those giant steins of wonderful beer, which weren't too good for Norman. My slim lover of old was already paunchy and bloated from drinking. But Norman didn't care how plump he got.

Neither of us spoke German. Norman knew some Yiddish, and with some hesitation, he used it, once even to ask for directions from a stranger. I wondered what the man's reaction would be to someone speaking Yiddish. Would he be hostile? After all, this was 1956, only a dozen years after the war. This man was friendly. With gestures and the help of a road map, he showed us the way.

We visited Buchenwald, and we saw it all, the ditches for the blood, the gallows, the gas chambers with the human claw marks on the walls, all of its horrors. The most vivid memory I have was of that crematorium with the small oven for children, for me the most graphic and the most heartbreaking.

With that visit, we left Germany, glad to be on our way to Rome.

Mickey Knox was living there, and we stayed with him at his apartment near the Spanish Steps. At the time, he was working with Dino di Laurentiis on spaghetti westerns, for the most part as a dialogue director.

Mickey was at his most charming, bustling self, telling us fascinating gossipy stories about Dino and his wife, Silvana Mangano. From our first day, he brought us to meet his very large circle of friends, mostly celebrities.

Mickey really made that visit for us since we didn't know anyone in Rome except for Moravia. Mickey knew everyone on the Via Veneto, the street where anyone who was anyone showed up sooner or later to lunch or chat over a glass of wine.

On our very first afternoon, Mickey arranged a lunch with Federico Fellini and Marcello Mastroianni. Mickey spoke fluent Italian and Fellini and Mastroianni, limited English, so Mickey was the interpreter. Mastroianni was quite like the image he projected on the screen, but I thought he was not as attractive in person. Fellini was rather shy, tall, with a leonine head. I found him the more interesting of the two.

Norman seemed to be in better spirits, which meant less bickering between us. The warmth and beauty of Rome helped a lot, and, of course, so did the food. I was in heaven. I could eat pasta three times a day and still discover dishes I'd never heard of before.

We were so busy enjoying Rome that we didn't look up Moravia until it was almost time to leave. We met for a drink, and he seemed glad to see us, especially me. He wanted to show us some little out-of-the-way places in Rome, insisting we take a horse-drawn sightseeing carriage. I remember little of that afternoon except being squeezed between Norman and Alberto, who kept pinching my bottom. That was one of my last memories of Rome. We left the next day.

One evening back in Paris, we decided to be tourists and have dinner at Maxims with Irene Fornes, an American we had traveled with. She and I got all dressed up to look our most beautiful. We had a few drinks in our room before dinner, so we were all pretty high, Norman more so than Irene and me, because he had smoked pot. Lately I had been cooling it and not smoking as much as my husband. When we got to Maxims, we had to wait, although we'd made a reservation.

It was not a long wait, but Norman was furious and wanted to leave. I talked him out of it. Finally a snobby maître d' showed us to our table. I could tell that Norman's back was up the minute we had entered the restaurant. He was into that edgy kind of drunk I knew so well. I was feeling good, on my own high, so I didn't pay much attention to what he was feeling. When the waiter came to take our order, Norman asked for a bottle of expensive champagne and two different kinds of equally expensive wine. He had the waiter uncork them all at once. The waiter looked pained, but Irene and I were amused. I assured Irene that we would drink it all. We had barely finished our first glass of champagne when the *enfant terrible* ordered still another along with some kind of liqueur, crème de menthe, I think. We now had a total of five bottles at the table, barely leaving space for our dinner plates.

I was somewhat alarmed. "Darling, who's going to drink all that?"

"We are," he said, lining the bottles up before him. He began mixing the wines together. White into red, dry into sweet. Like the mad scientist, gleefully pouring from glass to bottle and back, stirring and tasting the mixture of crème de menthe with the white and red wine. "Not bad," he said, offering us a sip.

Irene and I were in shock, not quite believing what we were seeing. All that beautiful wine was being destroyed. The waiter was even more shocked, and it was a wonder he didn't complain to the maître d' about the crazy American. But I suppose they didn't care since Norman was running up a big tab. We ate our dinner horri-

bly fascinated by this wild man who hardly touched his own. Dr.
Jekyll had been so nice these last few days, but now Mr. Hyde was
on a rampage.

I was angry at the waste and the bill we would get. "Goddamn,
Norman, will you stop mixing and leave it alone? You know how
I love champagne, and now you've ruined it. Why are you doing
this, anyway? If it's for attention, you've succeeded, because
everybody's staring. They're probably going to have us thrown
out."

"Fuck the French," he said, giving me that poisonous stare
I knew so well. "Baby," he said in his Texas accent, "if you don't
like it, you can go back to the hotel with Irene. You're too stupid
to understand what I'm doing." I knew we were on the dangerous edge of a big scene. That was the one thing I didn't want. I
shut up for the rest of the evening.

One morning I awoke feeling dizzy and nauseous. It couldn't have
been a hangover because I'd had just one glass of wine the night
before. I thought it might have been something I'd eaten. Then
it struck me. My period was three weeks overdue. "Of course, you
silly," I said out loud. "You're pregnant."

God, I was so happy. This was what I had been wanting with
all my being, and I knew that Norman, for all his inner torment,
was happy, too. When I told him the news, he said he knew exactly
when we made the baby. Our lovemaking had been especially
sweet and passionate that particular night, with Norman holding
me tenderly afterwards. No booze or pot in us, just our uncom-
plicated naked lustful souls.

And who cared that I spent our remaining days in Paris heav-
ing up all that lovely French food? I was happier than I'd been
for a very long while.

We'd been away three months, and it was time to go home with my precious gift inside me. There had been some good times on this trip, but much of it had been difficult. Norman had been a mess through most of our wanderings, and given my insecurities, I had never learned to disentangle myself from his moods, to stand off and look with some objectivity at what was going on with him.

However, with all my confusion, the one thing I was secure about and truly believed was his happiness about the baby. It was a much-needed sign that he loved me, and in my naivete, I thought it might give us the balance and clarity we needed so desperately in our life together.

We said goodbye to Irene soon after that crazy dinner at Maxims. She had been fun to be with on our travels together, and I was sorry to see her go.

We took the same ship back on which we'd come—the *United States*.

The morning sickness I'd had in Paris was even worse on board, the motion intensifying my nausea. Instead of his usual impatience with illness, Norman was really sweet, bringing me orange juice and crackers in the morning while I was in bed. Once in awhile, I could get down a soft-boiled egg. My desire for liquor disappeared. Even the smell on Norman's breath made my stomach lurch. I had the same feeling once in a while even before I was pregnant, as if I was unconsciously preparing my body for the baby. My aversion to liquor continued throughout my pregnancy and while I was nursing. God, how I wish it had stayed that way for the rest of my life.

Chapter 31

After we'd been back in the Fifty-fifth Street apartment for a couple of months, I began to think about how nice it would be to raise the baby in the country. Norman had given me the idea, and he, in turn, had gotten it from Bill Styron, the novelist, who was living in Connecticut.

We had first met Rose and Bill Styron back in '51 at a party in the Village, where the Styrons then lived.

Norman and Bill seemed to hit it off from their first meeting, each admiring the other's work. Norman thought Bill's story, "The Long March," was terrific, and I think he liked part of *Lie Down in Darkness*. Some years afterward in an essay in *Advertisements for Myself*, Norman called it one of the prettiest novels of our generation—which infuriated Styron enormously.

Bill was from Virginia, I think descended from Southern aristocracy. That good 'ol boy surface masked a petulant, envious, mean-spirited nature, and an insecurity about his masculinity, which manifested itself in an air of smug superiority. He was cordial enough, but I didn't trust him.

Norman trusted my instincts about people, and he would often ask me about anyone new he brought into our life. Obviously he enjoyed Styron, so this time I kept my opinions to myself and let him discover Styron for himself.

As for Rose Styron, she was Jewish and rich, an heiress to the Burgunder department stores in Baltimore. Of course, it all fit, our good 'ol boy would always take care of Numero Uno by fair means or foul. Once we were invited to have a drink in their apartment before going out to dinner. Rose wore one of those prissy little starched cap-sleeve dresses from Peck and Peck. But what I couldn't believe were the white gloves she put on before we went out.

She was no beauty, but she was attractive, with a face carefully trained never to show any improper emotion. Her speech was affected, the kind where one hardly moves one's lips with the voice slightly strangled in back of the throat. She was polite enough, but her manner toward me had a hint of condescension—that is, when she could tear her attention away from my husband, who was being charming.

At one point during the conversation, there was the sound of drumming on the kitchen pots. There was a kid sitting on the floor in the far corner. The light was very dim so I hadn't noticed him until he started his banging. We tried to ignore it, but he didn't let up. Bill was really annoyed.

"Jimmy, will you knock it off? We're trying to have a conversation," and then he introduced us to James Dean. I don't remember him, since he looked at the floor and mumbled into his chest. Dean was not yet the *Rebel Without a Cause* sensation, but just another talented kid who wanted to be an actor.

From that first meeting with the Styrons and all through our later association in Connecticut, the thread that ran throughout my uneasy acquaintance with Rose was that *she* was not married to a literary superstar but I was. How it must have rankled her ambitious, diminutive soul. At the time, Styron was not established as a writer of any reputation, but Norman was famous, considered one of the best writers in the country in spite of the troubled reception of *Barbary Shore* and *The Deer Park.*

Norman liked the idea of moving to Connecticut, to be part of an enclave of good writers and critics like Malcolm Cowley and Van Wyck Brooks and his wife Gladys, a charming and distinguished old man and his equally pleasant wife, who were as Waspy as their names.

In 1956, we found a lovely old house in Bridgewater, Connecticut. It was a large white saltbox with five bedrooms. We liked it immediately. When we bought it, I was thrilled.

This was yet another move in our nomadic existence—four in the six years we'd been together. I never questioned it, thinking it was perfectly normal. But looking back, what in hell was driving us? Was constant change supposed to be an antidote for my husband's psychic pain?

Was this beautiful house going to do it for us? Yes or no, the one thing I was certain of was that it was the ideal place for the baby, and I hoped a nest for a peaceful pregnancy.

It really was a perfect house, with a screened-in porch and a big wood-burning fireplace in the living room. The master bedroom had a private terrace, and every room was filled with light. There was a downstairs den for Norman, and the kitchen was a dream, large and with all the right equipment. Two giant elms shaded the house, which overlooked about 200 rolling acres of green. To my delight there was a strawberry patch and a barn that could be converted into a workshop for Norman. Besides all that, it was doggy heaven for Tibo and Zsa Zsa, who went wild the day we let them loose on the grounds.

The few pieces of furniture we had weren't enough to furnish a big, elegant house. Danish-Modern just didn't seem to fit, which meant we had to start from scratch. It would be a huge task. Another woman would have hired a professional interior decorator. Not me. That was for squares, not for artists. However, I was pregnant and had neither time, energy, nor patience for all those three-hour trips into New York City to confer with decorators and do the shopping. Predictably this elegant house ended up looking like a Danish-Modern beatnik pad for the three years we lived there.

Norman renovated the attic, making it into a spacious studio for me. He did most of the work himself, installing a picture window that filled the room with light. It was the nicest studio I ever had, with a lovely view of the hills.

Chapter 32

For a time, we had some order in our lives. After breakfast, Norman would work in the den, and I would go to my studio. We would have lunch together, but he would either be reading while he ate or thinking about his writing. I might as well have been eating alone, but by now I was used to it. Norman was working on a couple of projects, probably "The White Negro" and *Advertisements for Myself*, and he may have started the play version of *The Deer*

Park. After lunch, I would nap and then go back to work. I painted all through my pregnancy, going through long periods when it was difficult for me to finish a painting. I would start a canvas, never satisfied, changing and overworking it until the nice quality and the freshness it had was ruined. It was all part of my driven search for perfection. After all, I had to paint a picture that was no less than a Matisse or a Picasso. An artist friend suggested I work on a few canvasses at the same time, so if I got stuck, I could switch. That worked for a time until my old obsessive self took over.

Occasionally Norman would visit the studio to see what I was doing. Sometimes he would get furious because the painting he had seen the week before and liked would be gone, replaced by a completely new picture.

"Why the hell didn't you leave it alone? It was finished."

"Well, I didn't like it. There was an area that didn't work for me. You're not a painter, you don't understand. Besides I'm not painting just to please you."

Norman knew next to nothing about abstract expressionist painting. However, he had a discriminating eye, an innate sense of what made a beautiful painting.

Once he asked me if he could have one of my large blank canvasses because he wanted to try to paint á la Jackson Pollock. He said it with such confidence that I began to laugh. "Okay," I said, "I dare you to paint a Pollock." And I gave him some of my cheaper colors, diluting them with linseed oil.

"Norman, you really should use housepaint for your little experiment. I'll bet Jackson doesn't use Windsor Newton, not the way he pours it on." Norman climbed on a high stool, poised over a white canvas on the floor, a can of paint in each hand, like a fighter plane ready to drop its bombs on the target.

"Why do you need that stool?"

"My instinct tells me height will give me more control."

I was amused, watching him pour and drip black, blue, and some red.

"I'm getting into the rhythm," he said and paused.

"You're not finished, are you?" I said. "It needs another layer and more red in this area because it's not balanced. There's too much and . . . "

"All right, all right" he interrupted, annoyed by my criticism. "I can do this as well as Pollock. There's nothing to it." He started pouring again, up and around and down, then flinging the paint from a brush, trying to get a spattered pattern.

"Why don't you pee on it now?" I said. "That's what Jackson did."

He was so concentrated, he didn't hear me. I left him alone and went to work on a still life I'd been struggling with for weeks. After a half-hour of frantic activity, he said, "It's finished. Come take a look."

To my surprise, it wasn't bad. There was actually some form to the drips, and I told him so. I could see he was excited and pleased by my comment.

"Can you spare another canvas?" he said. "I'd like to try a Picasso."

My God, I thought, this is what comes of a mother who tells you what a genius you are every day of your life.

"I think I'll try a Picasso woman."

I laughed. "Should I pose for this one?"

"No, I'll do it from memory."

He finished it in ten minutes.

"Forget it, Norman. You're no competition for Pablo."

His artistic inspiration did not end there. He got the idea of making a plaster cast of his balls and cock in full erection—with my assistance. Before he even mixed the plaster of Paris, he greased himself carefully with Vaseline after which I used my persuasive skills until his penis rose in angry splendor.

Working against time, he scooped up gobs of thick plaster, packing it around his penis and balls. Since he was standing up, some fell off, but he kept slapping it on, so eventually enough of it stuck. Naturally it was difficult to keep an erection, weighed down by all that muck. I had to keep tickling and caressing him from behind, murmuring dirty little nothings in his ear.

There was plaster all over everything, including my studio floor. The result of our messy efforts was a chunk of plaster with two round indentations and a blobby-longish shape with some brown pubic hairs stuck to it.

"It's not good enough for the Smithsonian," I remarked, "but maybe you could mount it and hang it on the wall like one of Hemingway's trophies."

Norman the photographer was better than Norman the painter or sculptor. He took some lovely nudes of me, not porn stuff, but nicely lit mood pictures, probably the best I've ever taken.

Chapter 33

Arthur Miller had a small house in Roxbury, where he and Marilyn Monroe would stay. I'm sure Norman was fascinated at the prospect of living just a few miles from Marilyn. His obsession with Monroe started about the time she married Miller. When that happened, he could barely disguise his envy, and it made me furious. He would have dumped me or any wife he was with if Monroe had shown any interest. His conceit was that she didn't need a stiff like Miller. What she needed was a tough, hip genius, with a wonderful understanding and sensitivity about women. He, of all men, could understand and bring out the best in her, make her into a great actress. I have to laugh when I think of what a dance those two monsters would have had, while devouring each other in a narcissistic feast.

The Millers were pretty secluded. I don't think anyone, including the Styrons, were asked to visit. Norman was really pissed that Miller didn't call to invite us over for a neighborly drink. But then again, why should he? The two had never really liked each other, even in the forties when they were unknown and both had studios in Brooklyn Heights. Norman was writing *The Naked and the Dead* and Miller *Death of a Salesman*. When I first started going out with Norman in 1951, I met Arthur and his first wife at a party given by Norman Rosten, a poet friend of Norman's. At the time, Miller was rather cold and remote, perhaps a cover for shyness. His wife was a handsome, tall, blonde, matronly looking woman. Miller showed no animosity, just a coolness toward Norman.

Miller finally did extend an invitation. At last we would meet Marilyn Monroe. We were both pleased and excited.

Arthur came out on the porch as we drove up. But where was Marilyn? It was a modest two-story house, furnished simply. He offered us a drink, and we chatted, but not a word about Marilyn. I could sense Norman's impatience. After a boring conversation, Miller casually mentioned that Marilyn had been called to the coast. I was terribly disappointed. Too bad, I thought, we probably would have liked each other.

The visit came to a rather abrupt end. Norman was pissed at Miller all the way home. "The bastard waited till she was away to invite us over," he said.

Later we heard a rumor that she was in the house all the time, in the upstairs bedroom, because she didn't want to meet Norman.

Norman had a thing for actresses and even wanted to make me one. I can remember the first time he brought it up in the middle of our usual bickering, bickering that was turning ugly. "You should become an actress, Adele," he said. "With all that emotion, you'd burn up the stage." I laughed. "Don't be ridiculous. I've been a painter all my life."

"But you're always acting. Why not put it to use?"

Now I was really angry. "I'm not always acting. My emotions are real, not like yours. You're always watching yourself from a distance." But he had planted the seed. Later on I discovered that Norman was right, not about the reality of my emotions, but the need to play different roles, to dramatize myself.

I was in my eighth month when we got a call from Mickey Knox. He was working in the States and asked if he could stay with us for about a week. Norman, as always, was delighted. Sure, we said, for as long as you like. Mickey was working as a dialogue director with Anna Magnani in the film *The Fugitive Kind,* the Hollywood title for Tennessee Williams's *Orpheus Descending.*

Magnani's costars were Marlon Brando and Joanne Woodward. Mickey invited us to visit the location, which was not too far away, in Connecticut. I was excited about meeting Anna and even more thrilled at the prospect of seeing her work with Brando. Mickey was really nice that day and took us out to lunch with Joanne Woodward. Joanne had a genuine warmth along with her beauty and was without the airs and subterfuges that go with being a rising star. I sensed a kindred soul. After lunch, we visited the set, and Mickey introduced us to Magnani. I saw a plain woman, wearing no makeup and with her hair in rollers. She was short and rather dumpy, big breasted, with spindly legs.

When the camera began to roll and Magnani and Brando got into the scene, I was amazed by the transformation from a plain, rather subdued, frumpy woman into a luminous beauty, with such powerful emotion in the way she spoke and moved, in her dark sad eyes and expressive face. Something magical happened between them that made that scene memorable.

Behind the set, the reality was rather sad, as Mickey, who knew everything that was going on, confided to us. Evidently Anna wanted to fuck Brando to the point of obsessiveness and had pursued him aggressively. But she was not his type in any way, shape, or form. Brando had been really rude and even insulting in his rejection. Of course, everyone on the set was aware of the drama going on, but Anna, being an instinctive actress, used it for the scene, and it was right. She was in an emotional turmoil throughout the entire filming, we were told. But in spite of her anguish, or perhaps because of it, she was wonderful in the part.

Chapter 34

Norman and I made love almost up to the day of my delivery. He was not turned off by my big belly. Rather he was tender and gentle, telling me how beautiful I was and how much he loved me and the baby, getting as excited as I did when the baby moved inside me. How sweet he could be at those times. He made me happy, and I was more in love with him than ever.

Some weeks before my due date, we moved to temporary quarters in New York. I took classes in the Lamaze method. I practiced the exercises faithfully since I was determined to be awake through it all. Norman went to the special sessions for fathers-to-be. He made me laugh, telling me about someone asking the instructor what a woman felt like right before labor. "Like a big grapefruit stuck up her ass that she had to push out or be sentenced to go around like that the rest of her life," was the answer. Norman, for all his idiosyncrasies, was sweet during that last stretch, except for one scene at the very end. When the nurse came to prep me for birth, Norman refused to let her shave my pubic hair, giving her one of his long-winded theories about it not being natural, etc., etc. The nurse went into shock, but recovered instantly, saying the absolutely worst thing she could have said to my husband.

"I'm sorry, sir, but it's hospital regulations."

"No way," said the little bull. "I'd like to speak to the doctor."

At that moment, I had a painful contraction. "For God's sake, Norman," I gasped, clutching the bedpost. "Let her do it. It'll grow back." Even as I spoke, I felt another gut wrencher, and I tried to relax by doing my panting exercise. Norman was still arguing with the nurse. "Please honey, forget it. What difference will it make?"

I was in labor for six hours. It was a normal, healthy birth, and the baby shot out of my defuzzed vagina in twenty minutes.

Norman demanded to be in the delivery room with me. In those days, that was unheard of, so the doctors refused. I don't remember if I was even consulted. I was so busy with my contractions, I wouldn't have cared either way. On the other hand, I was feeling scared, and it would have been comforting to have him nearby. Norman insisted and talked the obstetrician into giving his permission.

Instead of two coaches, the doctor and his assistant, there was a third, my husband, holding my hand and encouraging me. It was wonderful. Thank God for the other side of Mailer, the sweet loving side, not the demonically crazy one that I was having to cope with more often than not.

I can still see my beautiful little girl with a full head of black hair as I held her in my arms for the very first time. Like so many mothers, I wept with joy, sharing that incredible moment with my husband. I was incredibly happy with my new baby, happier than I'd been for a very long time. We named her Danielle. In a couple of days, we drove back to Connecticut with our small entourage, to begin what I thought would be a new life.

For the first few months, I was totally absorbed in the baby, so I couldn't pay that much attention to my husband. I sensed some resentment on his part. I was tired all the time even with our nanny, Mary, to help. I guess I was spoiled because I really missed her when she was off two weekends each month.

When the nanny was away, I don't think I got out of my bathrobe, struggling with breast feeding for the first three months. It was not easy because my nipples were painfully sore. When finally I did not have enough milk, I gave up. After that, my life seemed to be made up of making formula and boiling dozens of bottles. Dandy was a colicky baby. There were nights when I would walk her up and down for hours trying to get a burp. It didn't help that I was so tense then, trying to be a perfect mother.

Norman, always generous about hired help, gave me a cleaning woman three times a week, and of course, there was dear Mary who was so wonderful with the baby.

As soon as I was up to it, we had weekend guests, and with the end of my breast feeding, my desire for liquor returned. We began entertaining again. I was enjoying my beautiful kitchen, cooking more, making as much of a mess as I wanted to because there was a maid to clean up after me.

With all the help I had at home, I was able to do what Norman had been suggesting all along, study acting. Mickey Knox had taken Norman to the Actors Studio where he met Frank Corsaro, who besides teaching, was a director and a member of the studio. Norman would talk to me about those sessions, but I listened with half an ear, having enough to deal with like a baby, my painting, the new house, and a husband whose behavior, to put it mildly, was becoming more *erratic*.

While I had always enjoyed the theater and films, acting was part of that other shadowy world, far away from the life I had to deal with now. But Norman loved those sessions, telling me stories about artistic director Lee Strasberg, Elia Kazan, and Tennessee Williams. He talked about this talented guy Frank Corsaro, about his sense of humor and his abilities as a director.

Norman said, "I told Frank you had talent, that you had the potential to be a very good actress. He said to get in touch with him if you were interested in the class." I think that was about the time Norman was workshopping his play *The Deer Park* at the studio. He was getting more and more involved with that, and I could see how important it was to him.

Perhaps my wanting to be a part of that might have influenced me. Anyway, I finally said yes. Whatever it was, I thought why the hell not? If I didn't like it, I could always quit.

At first I was scared and shy, the way I was when I began my art classes with Hans Hoffman. Here was a new medium, a new language that would introduce me to a new world, made up of people even more insecure than I was.

However, as frightened as I was, I enjoyed being up on a stage saying my first line.

I was not very good in the beginning, but I stuck it out, working hard, liking the challenge, excited by Frank and his creativity as a teacher. Even though I felt awkward, Frank was patient, guiding me and suggesting scenes for me to work on. I was there about six months, and I remember one scene I worked on at that time. It was from Ibsen's *Hedda Gabler*, where Hedda burns her former lover Eilert Lovborg's manuscript.

In my scene, Eilert has lost his only copy while on a drunken spree. Hedda's husband finds it in a roadside ditch. He shows it to Hedda saying there is no other copy, and he would give it to Eilert in the morning. Instead he gives it to Hedda, at her request. Hedda has an encounter with Lovborg, who is distraught about losing his manuscript. Hedda says nothing about having it. When he leaves, she burns it in the stove, jealous of Thea, Eilert's lover. As she throws the packet into the stove, she talks to herself. "There's where your child is, Thea. With its beautiful flowing hair." She throws in more pages, saying "Eilert Lovborg's child. Yours, I'm burning it. Burning."

I said these lines with gusto and believability. It was good material for me to work on. All I had to do was remember how angry I'd been at my husband and put it into those words.

I didn't mind the two-hour commute from Bridgewater to Frank's class. I had really fallen in love with acting and maybe a little in love with Frank. I thought his insights were brilliant and loved working with him. I would watch an actor or actress struggling in a scene, trying to make it work, and not succeeding. Then Frank would give the actor a suggestion, and the scene would come alive. The change would never have occurred to the actor. But Frank had a creative imagination and wasn't afraid to take chances.

I was becoming as passionate about acting as I was about painting. Dually talented and loving both arts equally was a mixed blessing. In the end, I spent many years trying to have two careers at the same time, something that wasn't possible, at least for me. I've exhibited my painting and managed to have a small career on the stage, but on a professional level, there wasn't the development there might have been in either field.

I was happy with my baby, who was blossoming and getting more and more beautiful every day. I was right about Connecticut being the perfect place for her. I was not so sure about me. I loved the beauty of the country, but I missed being near water and sometimes felt landlocked. Summer and autumn were easy, but the winter months were bleak and endless. Of course, there was less social activity, fewer weekend guests, and we were more isolated, a natural part of country living. From time to time, we would drive more than three hours into the city for a party and back the same night. God knows how we survived, with Norman drunk and driving those icy roads.

We were becoming more and more involved with Styron and the Roxbury clique. If I had felt inadequate about the New York intelligentsia, this new environment was where I really needed booze to cope with the sneaky, backbiting, one-upmanship that was gradually beginning to reveal itself. In the first year or so, Norman and Bill got on well together, swapping stories, talking about writing, each being as charming as the other and as drunk as the other. I never saw Bill without a drink in his hand, no matter what time of day we visited. I thought New York was a drinking town, but compared to this New England community of literary types, it was a kindergarten.

One thing I noticed abut Norman almost from the beginning was how impressed he was by other celebrities, especially if they were rich and Waspy. There was something deferential in his behavior toward them, and it was even more pronounced when he was drunk. He would go out of his way to get their attention by saying and doing outlandish things. I don't think he was even aware of it, but I was. Once after we had come home from a party, he was being particularly nasty and critical of something I'd done during the evening. I remember screaming back at him, "Why were you kissing so-and-so's ass? You're a big celebrity yourself. You're famous, remember? Your were knocking yourself out carrying on like an asshole with that stupid Texas accent. Christ, get some dignity." That's not to say I had much dignity when I was drunk, to put it mildly. But I didn't kiss ass nor did I want my man to do it.

Bill, of course, was the pivotal figure in the community, but as time went on, the power began to shift to Norman, who true to his nature, had to be the big cheese. In a sense, he had the right since he was, as far as I was concerned, superior to Bill Styron in every way. I say this even in face of the terrible changes that were going on in my husband. Styron was smart, but he didn't have the intellectual energy or brilliance of my husband—that is when Norman wasn't in the throes of his destructive excesses.

Old Van Wyck Brooks was never a member of Styron's court. The Brookses socialized with the Styrons, but were never a part of the political atmosphere of that elite literary clique. Maybe that's why I liked them. They were both in their late seventies, Van Wyck in his English tweeds and pipe and Gladys in her lace collar, looking like one of the *Arsenic and Old Lace* sisters. Van Wyck had known and written about Hemingway, Scott Fitzgerald, and many other famous writers of the twenties and thirties. They lived in Bridgewater, not far from us. We decided to be neighborly and invite them to dinner, but we changed it to tea, remembering that they went to bed at dusk. I'd never been to a formal tea. "What should I serve?" I asked Norman. "My mother served crumpets," I said, "but they were terrible." Norman didn't want to be bothered. "Don't get into a state. You'll think of something."

Norman loved my jelly roll. I'd learned to make it exactly like his mother did, it being one of his favorite desserts as a child. That seemed a likely choice, but it wasn't enough. Needing another dish, I looked up "tea" in my *Joy of Cooking*, a birthday present from Norman. Watercress-and-cucumber finger sandwiches were dull, so I abandoned *Joy of Cooking* for one of my Italian cookbooks, choosing of all things *Mozzarella in Carrozza*. I had never tried this recipe nor had I ever eaten it anywhere, including Italy, but my mouth watered as I read it. This is easy, I thought. It's just pieces of cheese stuffed into individual slices of Italian bread, deep-fried in olive oil, and served with an anchovy sauce. It sounded delicious, so that was it!

Lacking a silver tea set, I did the best I could pouring tea into cups that didn't match and serving the Brookses on china that was equally disreputable. In all the dinner parties we gave, beautiful china didn't seem to matter, but now it did.

When I brought out the *Mozzarella in Carrozza,* the look on this genteel couple's face was the same as if I had served them underdone slabs of calf's liver. I thought my dish looked delicious, swimming in its brown sauce. Gladys had a small piece of my jelly roll cake, but declined the *Carrozza.* Van Wyck, the more adventurous, gingerly cut into one, putting a large piece into his mouth. A long string of melted cheese hung from his mustache. It stuck there for quite a while, and I couldn't take my eyes off it. There was a pool of olive oil spreading on his plate and seeping into his slice of cake. He had mistakenly used the same plate for both.

Norman was busy talking, but I was watching every move the Brookses were making, checking every mouthful. I knew they hated that dish, and I was dying inside. Norman enjoyed it, eating three or four pieces, but I didn't care about him. What I cared about was the approval of those two Wasps. Norman was behaving himself, playing the young author, respectful to the elderly critic, who obviously esteemed Norman as a writer. In spite of the food disaster, the Brookses, though a little stiff at first, gradually relaxed and seemed to enjoy themselves listening to my husband, who had picked up none of my angst and was charming them. For that I was grateful. At one point, I tried to engage Gladys in conversation, but she was rather shy, so I gave up and mostly listened to Van Wyck and Norman having a fascinating discussion about Hemingway and Fitzgerald. After they left, I told Norman how upset I was over the food. "What possessed me to serve something like that, I will never understand." Norman just laughed and said I was making too much of it.

Thank God for the few people around us that I liked. There was Lewis Allen and his wife Jay Presson Allen, who were living in Roxbury near Styron. We saw a good bit of them. Of course, we knew Lewis from the Mexico days, before he met Jay. He always had that shy, boyish charm, and Lincolnesque craggy face I found attractive. Jay was tough and ambitious, one of those women who knew who she was and was very much in charge of her life. While I liked her, and while she was always friendly, I found her a bit intimidating.

The couple I really liked the most were the Gilberts. Ed was a fairly successful screenwriter and novelist, considered a bit too commercial by Styron and the snobs who surrounded him. I don't think Norman shared their opinion. He liked the Gilberts as much as I did. Ed's best-known novel was *The Beautiful People*. He has since died. I don't know what happened to Virginia, but I remember them fondly.

Of all the people up there, they were the least pretentious and the most fun. They lived in a charming 200-year-old house with the original floors and walls. Virginia was a terrific decorator and had fixed it up beautifully in the Early American style. She was a talented cook, and we were happy to get their dinner invitations on those long winter evenings. Virginia was a pretty blonde Midwesterner, with the delicate coloring of a Dresden china shepherdess. Ed was Jewish, and he looked a bit like Paul Douglas, the fifties movie star. He wore tweed jackets with the leatherpatched elbows and mixed a mean martini. God, did he ever. I didn't know what drinking was until I spent evenings with the Gilberts and discovered the martini. It wasn't Norman's drink, but it sure in hell was mine. I embraced my lethal enemy with all my soul. The martini and I were lovers for years, so much so that I was inspired to write the following monologue at one point:

It was there I developed a taste for martinis. All those Myrna Loy/William Powell movies. Rich, elegant, sophisticated Myrna. Mix me a martini, dahling. Never, never more than one olive—it isn't done. I always had five floating around in mine. Love to suck them, gin soaked and green.

Connecticut literati argue about how to make the perfect one. Should there be two stirs counterclockwise or three, gently, Goddamn it, don't bruise it. Mustn't upset the perfect marriage. Noilly Pratt, do you take Bombay Gin to be your lawfully wedded wife? I sure do, but just watch the vermouth,

*my God, watch the vermouth. How much? They almost came
to blows over that one. For Christ's sake, just use an eye-
dropper. If you don't have one, a twist of the wrist will do, or
you can let Tinkerbell piss in it. Well I had my ritual, no Noilly
Pratt at all, and I make the best martinis in town. Clear, tasteless, magic, frosted oblivion in a crystal glass.*

The honeymoon between Styron and Norman was waning and their
relationship becoming more and more competitive. Styron could
see that Norman was taking over the throne of his little domain.
I could feel the underlying bitchery and rivalry in the atmosphere
more than Norman, who was not quite aware of what was happening. And so, as I often did, I quieted my anxiety by drinking
too much, creating self-destructive situations, some unfortunately
occurring at Styron's house.

At one of these gatherings, we were sitting around the dinner table while a loaded Styron was going on and on about the
colored people this and the colored people that. While I cannot
remember his exact words, I can easily recall his patronizing manner and his perpetually smug expression.

"Hey Bill," I shouted, banging my fist on the table for empha-
sis, "I happen to be passing for white, so keep your fucking comments to yourself." There was a second of silence, then someone
snickered, and my remark was ignored as the conversation
resumed. My husband just grinned at me, raising his glass in a
half toast. I sat there feeling like an idiot, and even worse, my
lie hadn't gotten a rise out of Bill or anyone else.

On the drive home, Norman and I argued, having our usual
drunken lack of communication. When we arrived home and
were in the process of parking, I commented on the evening by

vomiting all over my black velvet coat. I didn't remember a thing after that.

The next morning, I made a horrible discovery. The ruined mess was not my coat. I'd taken someone else's. It resembled mine in fabric and style, but it was definitely not my coat. I decided to ignore it, but of course, I got the dreaded call from Rose the next day. She said the coat belonged to Mary Lee Settle, a Southern writer friend of Bill's. I vaguely remembered talking to Mary Lee, but I had to be cool. I said I was sure the coat was mine. Nevertheless, I would check it out.

I was in a panic and asked Norman what to do. "Brazen it out," he said. "Say it's your coat and you know nothing about it. After all they're almost identical. You can pull it off. You're a good actress." I called back and said that she was mistaken, that it was most certainly mine.

It wasn't just the coat; we could have paid for a new one. I just didn't want to admit that I'd thrown up all over it. That would have been embarrassing and would have given the Styrons more ammunition. A few days later, we were invited for lunch. I didn't want to go, but Norman insisted, saying it would look odd if he showed up without me. After lunch, at which Mary Lee was also a guest, Rose brought out the coat, and I knew that Rose knew that I knew that she knew. But my face was a blank. "Oh no," I said, "that's not my coat." They did look remarkably alike, and luckily there were no identifying marks or labels. Mary Lee and Rose looked at each other. "It's funny," Mary Lee said, "I could have sworn you took my coat. This is definitely not mine."

I stood my ground. "I'm sorry, Mary Lee, but it is. You should know your own coat."

It was not a nice thing for me to do, and to this day I can't believe I acted in that way. I should have owned up and paid Mary

Lee for a new coat, but I just couldn't give the Styrons the satisfaction. However, I'd made it even worse. Now, in addition to everything else, they probably thought I was a pathological liar.

Finally the tension between Styron and Norman exploded, with Styron employing one of his sneaky tactics. He'd been saying that I was a lesbian, and the rumor got back to Norman. That was Styron's way of taking out his jealousy of Norman—by attacking me. When Norman heard about it, he was in a rage and wrote Styron an angry, threatening letter. As far as the lesbian thing was concerned, Norman, in his drunken camaraderie with Styron, probably bragged about the few times we'd indulged in threesomes. Billy seized on the stories as an excuse to get Norman.

That little business was the *coup de grace*, and I was glad the relationship was over.

Now I could focus on the few people up there I liked and my beautiful baby, who was just beginning to walk. Norman was concentrating on his *Advertisements for Myself*. At the same time, he had set up a carpentry workshop in the barn. The first thing he did was to hang a punching bag and build a "screaming closet." It was something that looked like an outhouse—a six- or seven-foot-tall box just big enough for one person. He lined it with heavy carpeting and hung an electric light. You could sit in there and scream, yell, sing, curse, moan, masturbate, whatever. It was built for angst, which was in plentiful supply in our household. I used it a few times, once when I had a bad sore throat, which seemed to heal more quickly than usual. There were all kinds of strange-looking shapes in that barn made of wood that Norman had laboriously polished. He had also constructed a half-human-sized wooden egg. The idea was to get into this egg, curl up into a fetal position, and have someone rock you. Actually it was quite relaxing.

From the house, I could hear Norman's anger in the piercing whine of the buzz saw, as he labored over these nameless objects during those long nights.

Though God knows we needed furniture for the house, the only thing I asked him to build was a coffee table, which was all I wanted. But he kept making strange, useless shapes. One would have thought this would be therapeutic and calming for him. If it was, he certainly kept it a secret from me. Most of the time, I lived with a desperate stranger who was becoming more detached and more depressed. There were fewer and fewer glimpses of my charming, affectionate husband who still loved me and our baby.

When Dandy was six months old, she had a nasty virus with a fever of 105. The doctor came right away and told us to give her ice packs to lower the fever immediately. Norman was with me through the night, packing her little body in ice cubes till dawn. Thank God the fever broke. I was very frightened, and Norman was comforting through it all.

We hadn't done much entertaining during the two winters we lived in Bridgewater, but one spring we decided to have a special dinner party with some celebrated guests. I'm not sure, but it might have been Lillian Hellman, Gore Vidal, and Norman's publisher, and five or six other guests.

It took me about a week to plan the menu. I really fussed, trying dishes I'd never made before, like a chicken Gallantine, a fancy paté with a crust. It was a lot of work, but the result was worth it. Along with the paté, I served a shrimp curry with ten different condiments. The evening was going along beautifully with everyone enjoying the food. The conversation was brilliant and Norman a genial host.

I was serving seconds of curry, and he was pouring a third bottle of his favorite wine, Pouilly Fuisse. I was suddenly aware of an awful stink. It must have been one of those silent sneaky farts. We were all suspect, but I knew it wasn't me. It was getting more pungent by the minute, and it couldn't be ignored. I suspected a repeat. I took a big gulp of my wine and looked around at the faces for a clue as the conversation became louder and more animated. I exchanged looks with my husband, who took charge of the situation. "That damn dog. Tibo, what did you do? That's bad, very bad," he bellowed lifting a corner of my white damask tablecloth and peering below. I looked and so did the others, but the dogs were not there, nor were they even in the room.

Mary came in to clear the table, and I excused myself, to fetch the dessert from the kitchen. "Darling," I said in my best hostessy voice, "do open the window. It's quite stuffy in here."

My strawberry Bavarian had been in a mold in the refrigerator since the morning. I said a little prayer as I dipped the mold into warm water for a second and slipped it out onto a crystal dish. It looked so beautiful and professional after I decorated it with strawberries and whipped cream that I forgot what had happened. When I returned to the table, the smell was gone. Everyone admired the dessert.

Chapter 35

I invited my parents up to the house for a few summer weekends, and no matter how badly Norman and I were getting along, or how moody he was, he was always nice to them.

They would arrive in Daddy's beat-up Pontiac, and Norman would greet my father with a "Hiya champ." "Hey Paisan," my dad would answer, "how's it goin'? You still in training?" They would exchange punches like two old boxing cronies. Mama, as always, would roll her eyes.

"There he goes again," and she would wave her arms in exasperation, jingling all her bracelets, lighting up a cigarette, and blowing her smoke in my dad's direction. Norman took my father over to the barn to show off his punching bag and his crazy inventions, while Mama and I would play with the baby.

Afterward Norman would go all out for them. He hated making fires in the fireplace, but he would cheerfully start a charcoal fire to broil three-inch steaks, while I fussed over the rest of the meal, baking my mother's favorite lemon meringue pie.

Mama went into ecstasy over the fireplace since she had longed for one all her life. When I was a kid, we had a phony one with a red bulb lighting papier-mâché logs. A little revolving fan would create an illusion of flickering flames. I remember hanging my stocking on the mantelpiece every Christmas. Mama never got a real fireplace, or the house to go with it, but mine impressed her more than anything I had—including my marriage to Norman.

During those weekend visits, we never got drunk. I would never let my parents see me that way. I'd have one martini before dinner, and that was it. My mother, to my surprise and relief, had one glass of wine. Mama was on her best behavior, her sniping confined to my father. Now that I was a respectable married woman with a baby and a big house, I was less of a target.

Unfortunately our best behavior did not exclude our incessant bickering. One would think I would have been able by this time to ignore Norman's constant faultfinding. I suppose I would have if my sense of self had been stronger. But in spite of having gotten everything I wanted, a part of me still felt I was an undeserving impostor.

My parents were not uncomfortable in this abrasive atmosphere. After all, it was just like home. They were both genuinely happy about Dandy, their first grandchild, making a big fuss over her, which pleased me. Mama had calmed down a bit, or so it appeared, and Daddy was happy because Norman paid him a lot of attention.

I remember one particular weekend as if it were yesterday. It was early afternoon, and I was in the kitchen making the usual tuna-fish salad for lunch.

When I appeared with a tray of sandwiches and some lemonade, I was annoyed at the sight of both men in boxing trunks.

"My God, can't you have lunch first? You just got here."

"Nah," my father said, "we're goin' a few rounds first. I'll work up an appetite." Daddy, who had been teaching kids boxing at the Brooklyn YMCA, was in good shape.

I sat on the green velvety lawn with my mother on this lovely cloudless summer afternoon, playing with the baby, watching the boxing lesson, a jarring sight in such an idyllic setting.

It happened so fast, I didn't see the punch Dad planted on Norman's chin. He fell flat on his back and was actually out for a few seconds.

I yelled at my father, "Oh my God, Daddy, did you hurt him?"

"Nah, he's okay. He can take it."

Norman sat up almost immediately, shaking his head, rubbing his jaw. He was still groggy as my father helped him up.

"Jesus, young feller, sorry about that."

Norman was a good sport about the whole thing, and instead of being angry, he admired my father. "Not bad, Al, for a fifty-four-year-old." He touched his chin. "That was some punch you landed."

"Well, Norm," Daddy said, "you've got to be on your toes. You should've seen it coming. But that's the way ya learn."

It's lucky Fan Mailer wasn't there to see it happen.

We had purposely avoided having the two families visit at the same time. I don't remember seeing them together more than once, and I think it was for dinner at our Fifty-fifth Street apartment, for a rather strained evening. Fan and my mother did not like each other, having nothing in common. Mama was a Latin through and through, and Fan was proper and uptight. Mama was liable to come out with anything especially after a few drinks. You ran for cover if she started a sentence with "Can I be frank?" because it could be followed by a bomb.

But that night she behaved, sitting with Fan, being overly polite, her pinky sticking straight out from her teacup. Having little else to talk about, they stuck to one subject; at least Fan did, and that was her little genius and all his accomplishments. Fan did most of the talking, my mother nodding in agreement.

They both were tough women, Fan's toughness coming out of that enormous ego and my mother's a cover for her insecurities. That night Daddy was his most cavalier paying Fan compliments. Mama hid her annoyance at him, but I'm sure my father caught hell later. I could imagine my mother using her favorite phrase, "Who does she think she is, Mrs. Astas' pet hawse? I watched how you were kowtowing to that stuck-up old bitch."

And I'm sure Fan had an equally complimentary opinion of my mother. Mama had no complaints about Barney, who had been flirtatious with that twinkle in his eye I knew so well. She was able to chat easily with him, so, of course, she liked him best.

Another summer weekend, my mother arrived alone on Friday. It was Mary's time off, and since we had a party invitation for Saturday, I asked my mother to baby-sit. It was a New York party, lasting till three in the morning, after which we made our habitually drunk drive home. Norman had been horrible to me all evening, rubbing my nose in some blatant flirtation with a nothing woman.

I handled it in my predictably alcoholic, out-of-control way, hating him, wanting to pull his curly hair out by the roots. By the time we got home, we were really into a shouting match, with no thought of my mother in the upstairs bedroom in a house that was not exactly soundproof. The fight got vicious with us hitting each other and ended with Norman punching me in the face, giving me a black eye and a bruised mouth.

After that I was too frightened to sleep in the same bed with him. I spent the night crying myself to sleep on the living room couch.

I was up early to change and feed Dandy. She was standing up in her crib, and when she saw me, she gave me her sweet baby smile. "How's my precious darling?" I said, momentarily forgetting what had happened. I was hung over, with a black eye and hurt lip. I was terribly depressed, but I had to keep myself together for my baby and my mother. Mama was up early, too, and I could see by her face that she had hardly slept.

She was shocked when she saw my shiner and the black-and-blue bruised lip.

"My God, what happened to your face? Did he do that? I can't believe it. What were you fighting about? It sounded terrible, the way you were both cursing and yelling. Thank God the baby didn't wake up. I didn't know what the hell to do, whether to come downstairs or not. After all, I didn't want to interfere. But I should have, I should have," she wailed. "Look at your eye. I hope the bastard didn't blind you. It's a good thing your father's not here to see what he did. What the hell's wrong with him, anyway? Is he crazy?"

"Yeah, he is, Ma, when he's drunk. But then, I'm no picnic either. But he shouldn't have done it. He shouldn't have hit me, the lousy bully."

"You better put a piece of steak on that eye right away. I still can't believe he did that to you."

"Don't kid yourself, Ma. You don't know the half of it. Besides smacking me around, he has other ways of hurting me, like beating me up with words, constantly criticizing me. Humiliating me in public with other women. There are some women who can close their eyes to that. But you could never do that, and neither can I." I started to cry. "I just can't, Ma. It hurts too much, and it makes me feel like I'm a nothing."

She sighed and looked uncomfortable. I guess it was too close to home for her.

"I don't know what to tell you," she said helplessly.

"Forget it, Ma, I'll be all right after I get some coffee."

"What a gorgeous kitchen," she said. "Look at the size of it. I always wanted one like it, but your father could never put enough money together to buy a house." A few minutes later, Norman came in. I froze, refusing to look at him, slamming down his plate of scrambled eggs, restraining myself from dumping them on his head. He gave a sneaky look at my face, with no acknowledgment or apology. Mama busied herself at the stove. "Good morning, Mae," he said. "Did you sleep okay?"

Mama answered, "Sure, just fine." I felt her discomfort. She was really furious at him, but she was in an awkward position, and she didn't quite know how to handle it. A simple quarrel was one thing, but violence was something else. Furthermore, he was being his old charming self, as if nothing had happened, chatting to her about living in the country and the baby, asking about my father and what he was doing. She was confused, not knowing what to make of it or how to act.

When he finally mentioned my eye, he had the nerve to make a rotten a joke about it.

"Fuck you, you bastard. You hurt me," I said, not caring whether my mother was there or not. I had to get away from him before we started to fight again. I went upstairs to get the baby. When I returned, Norman had gone to his studio, and Mama was making more coffee. "I'm sorry, Ma, that you had to see all this shit. You came up for a nice weekend and this happens. You know how argumentative he is, you've seen it. He's not happy unless he's bickering about something. But this is the worst, because it's starting to get into something else, something scary. You saw what a bastard he can be, not one word from his mouth about being sorry he hit me, and I'll never forgive him, not ever."

I couldn't stop myself. I had to talk to someone. "He's getting more impossible to live with. Sometimes he's so Goddamn moody, and it's hard because we're stuck in this house together so much. But then he can change in one minute and be so sweet to me, so charming, and so goddamn bright. You know yourself how he can be, and then I forget the rotten side of him, until he reminds me again."

"Yeah, I know. Your father's the same, charmin' with everybody but me . . . You shoulda seen him bowin' an scrapin' over Mrs. Antoncucci down the block . . . 'How's Al,' she says to me the other day. 'None of your business,' I shoulda said. 'What do you want to know for?'"

I poured myself another cup of coffee. "Yeah, Ma, I know," I sighed staring gloomily out the picture window framing a beautiful sunshiny day. "Mama," I said, half to myself, "what am I going to do? I must be crazy because I can't leave him."

Here I sat in this pretty kitchen, where there was order and a peaceful quiet, broken only by the singing of the birds outside and Mama playing manitas, a Spanish baby game with Dandy. Her wonderful baby laughter was such a contrast to my inner turmoil. "God help me," I said angrily, "because I still love him."

Looking at my mother, she suddenly seemed physically smaller, more vulnerable, not like the fire-breathing dragon of my childhood.

She appeared bewildered by it all. This was a new side of Norman. After all, she hadn't seen us that often, and he had always been very generous to both her and my dad. And there I was, with my beautiful baby in my arms, the grand lady in my luxurious home that looked like a beatnik pad. As angry as she was at Norman, all she could say was, "Oh my God, a divorce, no one ever got a divorce in this family." She literally cringed at the word.

I hugged her. "No, Ma, I don't think so." Believe it or not, we love each other, and he loves the baby. Don't worry, we'll work it out." But even as I reassured her, I could feel that familiar fear in my gut. "But what about you and Daddy, you didn't get a divorce. God knows you should have."

She looked at the baby in my lap. "We stayed together because of you kids."

Her remark annoyed me though I said nothing. It was such bullshit, she was up to her old tricks again, trying to lay more guilt on me, the way they both did since I was a kid.

I wanted to cry when I thought of their constant fighting and Mama's relentless preoccupation with putting down my father in the same way Norman constantly chopped away at me.

I remembered how my father would threaten to beat up my mother every time she said she was leaving him.

I heard the familiar jangle of her bracelets, sliding on her thin wrists as she raised a cigarette to her lips. She shrugged taking a long drag. "Ahh," she said, "no matter how you cut it, they're all sons of bitches in the end."

Chapter 36

Bridgewater, like all small towns, closed down early. There wasn't much to do at night aside from the occasional movie or a visit with friends. Norman, as was his habit, would have a couple of Scotches after dinner, and we would watch television. While we weren't absolutely hooked on TV, we did have our favorite programs—the Sid Caesar show, Elaine May and Mike Nichols, *Playhouse Ninety*, and *Night Beat*, the Mike Wallace talk show.

Country living was definitely beginning to pall on us. We used to break up the winters with some weekend skiing. After I had the baby, I was afraid to ski, afraid I'd break a bone or something and be unable to care for her. Occasionally Norman would go skiing on his own, but he said it was lonely and he missed having me there.

Christmas in Bridgewater did not enrich Norman's mood. In fact Christmas anywhere threw him into a funk. I had always loved the holiday, a small miracle considering my childhood Christmases, but spending the recent holidays with Norman had diminished my enthusiasm. He went through the motions of the proper Christmasy things with me, but I sensed his underlying depression. "I've been that way about this holiday since I was a kid, feeling excluded because I was a Jew. Everyone else having a tree, Santa Claus, all that sort of thing."

Susie came to stay for Christmas again, and as always, I did everything to make it wonderful for her and my year-and-a-half-old baby. It was an F.A.O. Schwarz Christmas all the way.

Susie was now seven or eight. My heart went out to her, and I sensed her confusion and unhappiness. God knows what scenes she was privy to in Mexico, her mother married to Steve, that combustible, crazy Spanish Indian who, like myself, drank like a maniac. Their fights must have rivaled Norman's and mine, few of which Susie had witnessed.

I still remember a glum Norman and a depressed Susie, sucking her thumb, sitting before the television watching endless cartoons.

I shudder when I think about those wassail-cupped, one-upmanship Connecticut Christmases. A big Waspy fuss with mistletoe, plum pudding, and carol singing. I've always loved these traditional festivities anywhere else. I hated them in Roxbury, or for that matter, in the whole state of Connecticut.

Chapter 37

During the last months of our Bridgewater period, there'd been a dearth of party invitations, so we jumped at one involving a trip to New York on a Saturday night. It ended disastrously for us, due to our reckless intake of booze and hash, always in plentiful supply at any Village party. That night Norman smoked one joint after another. Since I was already flying on four martinis, it took just a few tokes, and I had my one-way ticket to outer space.

I could always measure Norman's state of drunkenness by his schizophrenic transformation from a mild pain in the ass into that sneering, squinty-eyed, drawling Texas bad man, a throwback to the time he was a nice Jewish boy/buck private in a tough Texas outfit, having his ass ridden mercilessly by a bunch of rednecks.

I could tell he was cooking up one helluva mess by the way the Texas bad man came on with a woman guest. The object of his amorous advances was a good-looking brunette wearing an absolutely spectacular black-sequined lace vintage dress.

Equally drunk and dazzled by his celebrity, her hips were practically twitching in response to his Texas drawl, and I knew he was about to draw his pistol and knock her dead. And I was ready to mount my broomstick, on the verge of initiating a hair-pulling match whilst fixing a glassy stare on her husband, a tall, balding, wimpy-looking guy wearing glasses and an impeccably tailored charcoal-grey flannel suit. He was not paying much attention to the whorish behavior of his wife. Instead he was trying to impress me with his credentials as a Wall Street stockbroker.

There were about twenty people at the party. Norman, the sexual revolutionary, decided to organize a mass fuck by haranguing everyone there. Most of the guests were too stoned and laid back to care. So the broker and his wife and I and my spouse floated into the bedroom.

By now I was so stoned, I felt a little crazy instead of being jealous about what was going on between my husband and the woman. I was obsessing about that black-sequined dress. I didn't see why she should have both Norman and the dress, especially since it would look so much better on me. With my husband's assistance, the stockbroker's wife removed her dress and flung it across the room. I had an impulse to grab it and leave, but I was distracted by my partner's fumbling fingers trying to find a zipper concealed under some ruffles on the back of my dress.

Mr. Stockbroker nervously cleared his throat. "Uh, well, do you think we should?"

"Why?" I asked.

"Because they are."

I giggled. "Well then, I guess we should."

He took off his pants, folding them neatly over the back of a wooden chair. I looked at his long, bony, white legs. He had more hair on them than he had on top of his head. "My God," I thought, "I'm going to get it on with Ichabod Crane."

I took off my dress and said, "You know what, I think you're getting the better of the bargain."

We went no further than my bra and panties and his shorts and socks, held up by garters. He ground his mouth into mine.

"Jesus," I said, "I'm so fucking stoned." We stared at each other, deciding that it wasn't worth it since I could barely stand. I knew that if I lay down, the room would spin, and I'd be sick. What I really wanted was another drink and a husband other than the one who was now pumping inside the brunette.

We sat watching this little tableau. By now I was on remote control, but my Wall Street friend wasn't. I watched him light a cigarette, take two puffs, and casually snuff it out on Norman's mechanically gyrating rear.

Naked Normie, with his sweating crazy man's face, let out a Mailerean bellow of pain. "Son of a bitch, what the fuck's the matter with you?"

Mr. Stockbroker was unruffled by Norman's rage. "Mr. Mailer, that's my wife you're fucking."

"Well man, that's my wife you're fucking."

"Your mistake, pal, we weren't."

Norman was ready to fight, looking forward to it, I would say. He rushed the broker, and there was a scuffle, with Norman landing a punch. The stockbroker's wife was hysterical, making a lot of noise, while throwing on her clothes. The host, hearing the commotion from the living room and worried that his place would be wrecked, separated the two men.

Norman demanded satisfaction, going on and on about his honor. Would the broker agree to a boxing match? Neither the broker nor his wife looked happy about that suggestion.

But Norman kept pressing, suckering this guy into agreeing.

"All right, just name the time and the place for this ridiculous meeting!"

"Tomorrow, Sunday at three thirty at our place in Bridgewater, Connecticut. I'll write down the address and the directions," Norman growled.

We went home that night in angry silence. Norman drove like a madman, but I was too stoned and sleepy to care.

I woke up the next morning with the familiar sick anxiety I always had after one of our fatal bacchanals.

"Norman, you're not going through with this ridiculous fight, are you? How do you know he can box?"

"If he can't, he'll learn in a hurry 'cause I'm gonna give it to the bastard."

I knew it was senseless to argue with him, so I let it go, hoping they wouldn't show up.

This was just another one of those asinine things we got ourselves into, and I wished it hadn't happened. What was the fight really about? Was it over the small blister on Norman's rear? It was a vicious thing for the guy to have done, but after all, Norman had initiated the whole thing, and I, Miss Drunko, played follow the leader as usual.

Our company arrived promptly at three thirty. I wasn't sure how to act. Was I supposed to be unfriendly? I wasn't angry at them. He shouldn't have burned my husband. But after all, when Norman gets that stoned, he takes his chances like everybody else.

In the sober light of day, we were all a little stiff, chatting about the weather, Sunday traffic on the highway, etc., etc. I wondered what the two of them had talked about on the drive to the country in their spiffy little sports car.

We sat on the lawn on a beautiful summer day, making polite conversation. I even offered them a drink, which they accepted. It was bizarre, like a scene from some screwy Woody Allen movie. Actually I rather liked them both, now that I was sober. Norman was very tense, but thank God, he dropped his Texas desperado act. I was hoping it would all blow over, but it didn't. Norman changed into his boxing trunks; the broker had conveniently arrived wearing tennis shorts. Norman had asked a friend to referee. He had an extra pair of gloves for his opponent, who looked grim. It was getting to be too real, and I was worried, as was his wife. Norman knew what he was doing, the other guy didn't, and he was getting the worst of it when they quit. The broker had taken a few punches, but there was no real damage. They even shook hands afterward, so I guess Norman evened out the score.

That episode was the last of Norman's Connecticut stunts. He was now gearing himself up for a new arena.

In 1959, we decided to move back to the city and put the house up for sale. We had lived there almost three years. We had become too isolated; and of course, there was always the curious belief that it would be better somewhere else.

We looked for an apartment in the Village. An agent found us a lovely two-bedroomer in an elevator building on Abingdon Square for $300 a month. I wanted it badly, and Norman liked it, but he balked because there was a doorman. I insisted, but he was adamant. "It's too fucking bourgeois. I don't want to have to have to say good morning to a doorman, whether I'm in a bad mood or not." We quarreled about it, but since he was in control of the finances, he got his way.

We ended up in a dark, dinky basement duplex on Perry Street, a sorry contrast to our big house. Its only saving grace was a scraggly little garden.

Nevertheless, I was back in the Village, and as far as I was concerned, there was no place in New York like it.

Chapter 38

In spite of the constant bickering between Norman and me, and his increasing volatile behavior, I still wanted another baby. Again I was naive enough to think it would help our marriage. But I also enjoyed and adored Dandy so much, I thought it would be wonderful for her to have a sister.

Norman didn't believe in birth control, a radical change from the time he made me wait so long to have Dandy. In the year before we made the decision to have another child, he would get angry because I was wearing a diaphragm. His anger seemed irrational, much less an overreaction. In the middle of making love, he would reach into me roughly, pull out the diaphragm, and throw it across the room in such a rage I thought he was going to hit me. "I hate those fucking things. They'll give me cancer," he would say. He would start to rant, going into long, convulsed monologues about the waste of his seed after its long journey from another life. On and on, not even hearing what I said in response. His blue eyes were icy and strange. I even wondered if he was on a drug I didn't know about. His behavior was so crazy. I tried to ignore it, keeping my anger in, just getting more depressed, turning away from him sexually more and more. In spite of his bullying, I managed our sex life so that I got pregnant when I thought it was time.

Norman was going to the studio every day, but I think he was having a lot of trouble writing. Even though I was pregnant, he dumped his frustration on me. Once we were quarreling about something that was inconsequential and without warning, he hit me in the stomach. I was six months pregnant and still recall the physical hurt and horror I felt. I started to cry, afraid he had done some terrible damage. Thank God the baby was all right. As usual, there was no apology.

I remember how quickly Norman could play the cavalier and apologize to persons outside our closest friends and family, if he felt he was wrong. And I was aware almost from the beginning how much on his best behavior he was with certain people in his orbit, like the Trillings, for example, and Irving Howe, the social critic and editor. He wouldn't exactly toady to them—he would still say his outrageous Norman Mailerish things—but he could be charming while doing so. He was well mannered, almost courtly, the brilliant and witty Mailer. These traits he was showing less and less to the ones closest to him, with the exception of his sister and probably the only woman he ever really loved, his mama.

The rest of us, more often than not, were treated to a spoiled, arrogant, grandiose, self-obsessed, little shit. His obsession with drinking and parties was stronger than ever. He was wild, making up for all those Bridgewater nights we stayed home, refusing no invitation, no matter how dreary. I tried to keep up with his frantic pace, but I didn't have the stamina. I wasn't drinking, so I stayed home more and more, and of course, he partied without me. Once I heard my husband's voice on the radio during an interview, extolling the value of pleasure and necessity of joyful promiscuity.

I was in constant emotional upheaval at a time when I should have been at peace with myself and the world around me. By the time I went into labor, I was physically and emotionally drained.

Norman asked again to be in the delivery room with me, and I agreed, but this time I couldn't help wondering why. It seemed to me it had more to do with his sadistic streak than any feeling of love and empathy. He got his money's worth all right because it turned out to be a painful, difficult birth. My darling Betsy must have known, with the psychic sensibility she had even then, that it was a dangerous and unhappy environment she was coming into. The contractions were so painful that they gave me a whiff of gas, and I had to work even harder than I had to with Danielle. I remember saying over and over, "Don't use forceps. I can do it myself," and I did, crying with joy when she came because my baby was beautiful and healthy. That was all that mattered to me.

Chapter 39

As soon as my energy came back, I wanted to party again. My love affair with booze being far from over, I took up where I left off.

After two months, Norman and I were making love feverishly. On my thirty-fourth birthday, he gave me a beautiful garnet cross, specifically to be worn when we made love. As the crucifix danced between my breasts, I made the sign of the Cross, hoping I would not be struck down on the spot.

We had not really christened our new apartment with a party. When Jean and Galy Malaquais were in town, we decided to give one for them. Knowing how much Norman wanted to please them, I went all out on the food, cooking it myself.

We invited about thirty people, a small number for us. Steve Allen came without his wife, Jayne Meadows. I had invited my old boyfriend, Jack Kerouac. This might have been his first meeting with Norman, and I liked the idea of my famous ex-lover and my famous husband being in the same room with me—especially since the duplex was a far cry from my cold-water flat in the days when Jack and I had been lovers.

I was disappointed in the historic meeting since Jack got very drunk and spent the whole party under the dining room table. I tried to coax him out, but he said he could hear better than he could see, so I left him there.

A week before the party, we had decided to landscape our little twelve-by-fourteen backyard. It was just a fenced-in dirt patch with a few rocks and some scrubby weeds. We called in a gardener, and for $800, he covered the ground with an instant lawn, planted some flowers, and put up a birdhouse. I was thrilled at the transformation, picturing us having our morning coffee in my lovely garden.

It was warm the day of the party. People spread from the living room into the garden. The next morning, I surveyed the wreckage. There was nothing left of our beautiful lawn and our flowers, which had been trampled by high heels. Having a party and letting thirty guests loose on a postage-sized patch of lawn was an example of our impracticality, on a par with housebreaking two puppies after installing white wall-to-wall carpeting in our apartment years before. Eight hundred bucks thrown away. We did find some use for the garden—the dogs had a handy john.

Though Norman worked every day, he was more restless than ever in his nightly wanderings, like a hound, relentlessly sniffing the gutter for prey, baying his cancerous poetry at the moon.

I could not keep up with him. We had a sleep-in nurse for the kids, but I still needed to spend time with my children. And as much as I loved to drink, I could not punish my body every night, sleep to twelve, and at the same time be a good mother, do any painting, and keep up my acting lessons with Frank Corsaro. I had always given my husband a long leash, but now there was none at all. His obsession with parties, or should I say with drinking and pot, was worse than ever. Most nights, there was a social occasion. But if not, he would sniff out women and a fistfight at any one of his favorite bars like the White Horse, Bradley's, the Fifty-five, or some of the downtown jazz joints like the Village Vanguard, Art D'Lugoff's Village Gate, and the Five Spot.

I was never really a bar drinker. I did my personal damage mostly at parties. However, I liked being high on grass and listening to jazz, but being with my husband would inevitably mean a brawl between us. Norman loved to bait people when he was in his cups, and being closest to him, I was fair game. Unable to think clearly, I would set myself up, and our endless tango would begin again.

Happily, there still were occasional evenings with just the two of us, when there was some semblance of civility, when we drank very little, and when Norman would allow a rare good mood to release all his charming qualities. He could be so nice, so kind that I would forget a lousy scene that might have happened the night before. There was a part of me, though, that was storing up a lot of anger.

Strangely, Norman's belief in my talents never wavered despite our stormy relationship. He would attack me about almost everything—except my kind of mothering or my abilities as an actress and painter.

There was enough of the survivor in me to know how important my children and my creativity were to me. Again Norman rented a studio for me, a floor-through in an old three-story loft building near Union Square.

Chapter 40

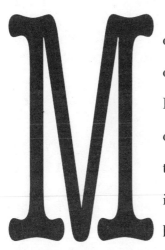oving to the Village did not mean peace on the home front, but in spite of that, I loved being there. We took advantage of everything Village had to offer. Over the years, Norman had talked himself into thinking he liked jazz—with the help of marijuana. Besides being a jazz joint, the Vanguard would feature guest comedians, one of whom was Lenny Bruce. We saw him through two arrests for

obscenity. Each time we watched him being led off the stage by
the police at the end of his act.

Lenny could talk about anything up there. Besides the political stuff, he would talk about fucking, coming or not being able
to come, or about pissing, shit, and assholes, cocks, tits, cunts—
and get laughs. There was one odd show I remember when Lenny
went all through the above and then made a sudden switch to snot,
describing the taste, the consistency, and different ways that people sneezed. The cool New York audience, who had laughed
through the earlier part of his act, was rather quiet, and except
for an occasional nervous giggle, no one was amused.

Inspired by his subject, Bruce was getting more creative, acting it out, digging into his nose with a vengeance. A few people
got up and left as it got more graphic. The cops, who were politely
waiting in the wings until he was done, came up and led him off
in handcuffs. It had happened so many times, Lenny was used to
it, cracking jokes as he walked offstage while we jeered and booed
the cops.

I think Norman was influenced by Lenny's irreverence and
his use of obscenity to shatter a few icons.

When Norman was in the last stages of his big crackup, he
was invited to read his poetry and prose at the Ninety-second
Street Y. He was very drunk, arbitrarily spewing out obscenities.
The program's director signaled disapproval from offstage, which
Norman chose to ignore. He raved on and on until the curtain was
lowered in his face. Even then he wouldn't shut up.

Unlike Lenny, Norman had no method to his madness. Of
course, the audience, made up of his beatnik fans along with a
sprinkling of literary types, loved the way he was making an idiot
of himself, egging him on under the guise of free speech. Incited
by Norman's antiestablishment rantings, the audience became so

rowdy that the police were called. Norman still wouldn't shut up, trying his damnedest to get arrested, not out of principle, but as part of his macho bullshit.

If I'd been sober that night, which I wasn't, I would have been terribly concerned about my husband's crazy behavior. Instead, I played the role of the great writer's hip wife, joining my voice with the crowd. I wasn't worried about an arrest. He was a celebrity, and I knew that if he wanted to, he could pull his psycho switch from manic to reasonable good guy and con the cops into letting him off.

His public stunts were destructive to himself and those around him. As bright as he was, he was becoming a bore in his incessant need to be the center of attention. It was, "Hey, look at me everybody, look how bad I can be!" In the process of what he so mistakenly called his self-analysis, he was denying his decent, kind, spiritual side. He was terrified of these aspects of his personality and went to extremes, drowning himself in booze and drugs in his desperate need to eradicate what he thought was the nice Jewish boy.

I was not helping him or myself by accepting his behavior, and that, too, was part of my alcoholic sickness.

My own self-destructive demons were riding hard. I remember, for example, that Norman came home at four in the morning after a night on the town, refusing to give even a polite explanation. I knew there was a woman, and I wanted to get even. I took a painting of mine that I loved, one that was his favorite, and put it outside with the garbage. He noticed the blank space on the wall over the couch. "Where is it?" he shouted. "I threw it out." He was very angry and rushed out the door to see if he could retrieve it. But it was too late. I'd punished him, but I'd punished myself even more, destroying a precious part of me.

No matter what, party invitations came in like an army roll call, and Norman always reported for duty. By now you would think I would have avoided going to any social gathering with my husband, but it was either that or being home alone wondering about what condition my husband would come home in or if he would come home at all.

However, I had an even more urgent need than being Norman's watchdog, and that was to get high. That's what I really wanted from those parties—an excuse to drink. It wasn't the people or the celebrities I met or even being the wife of a literary superstar. It was the anticipation, the excitement of getting drunk and with it the feeling of power, that I could do or be anything I wanted, that nothing could touch me. I was never the one to drink alone. I did that later in my life, when the party lights dimmed and went out, and I was by myself in the darkness.

One of the worst times was a party given by *Esquire* magazine. It may have been a special occasion, but that didn't really matter. The scenario was always the same for the Mailers. The only change was in the supporting cast and setting.

Norman was fond of quoting himself. "Repetition kills the soul," he would say in that self-righteous tone that would surface in spite of himself. His soul must have died long before that night, since his drunken behavior, like mine, was getting more and more predictable. He behaved like a shit at the party, staggering into the night, leaving me to fend for myself in a shark tank of literati. Angry and drunk, I was in no condition to go home alone. One of the editors played the gentleman and offered to escort me. Instead, he took me to his apartment. I was so drunk, he could have taken me to the middle of Central Park for all I knew or cared. It was a shitty thing for him to do, even if I had come on with him, which was a possibility since I came on with everybody when I was that drunk. Obviously I was out of control, and he should have taken me home.

At five in the morning, I came to, not quite knowing where I was or how I got there. I was alone in a bedroom, but I could hear dishes clinking in the kitchen. I had a terrible hangover. "Oh shit," I thought, "what the hell kind of mess have I gotten myself into now?" For the first few minutes, I couldn't remember whose apartment I was in, and I hoped it wasn't the person I thought it was. If so, I was in a lot of trouble, as was he. I tried to piece together some of the evening—my fight with Norman, his leaving the party. I remembered getting into a cab with the guy, crying my guts out. The rest was pretty much of a blackout.

Since I was nude, I assumed I'd gone to bed with the man who was making coffee in the kitchen.

I felt a terrible fear in the pit of my stomach, and I was in a panic. I had to get dressed. I had to get home before Norman. This time I hoped he did stay out all night. This is a first for me, I thought. I've never done this before. It's the beginning of the end. I broke out in a cold sweat. My kids, I had to be home before they woke up! The nanny was there, but they always came into my room as soon as they woke up. I had to be there, I just had to. I threw on my clothes, and then I realized I wasn't wearing my diaphragm. Oh my God, I hoped he used a condom. And then my rage at Norman returned. Fuck him, I thought. He's done it to me. I'll brazen it out, invent some kind of lie.

Norman was home when I arrived. There was a fight, and I ended up dropping my little bomb. I'd seen him angry many times, but this was the worst. For ten minutes, we did nothing but hurl insults and accusations at each other. The message was clear— that old double standard. He could do it, but I couldn't.

For days I was given the silent treatment, one of Norman's favorite punishments.

In the end, the episode caused major complications. Not so much between Norman and me, since we'd been steadily digging the grave for our marriage, but between an important magazine and an important contributor.

Sometimes I could create as much of a mess on one drink as I could on three. Mickey Knox was in New York and invited us along to see Sammy Davis, Jr., at the Copa. Mickey was a friend of Sammy's, and we got to meet the star after the show.

Sammy was as nice as could be, and I liked him a lot. He was one of those incredible talents who didn't need to give himself airs to prove anything. He introduced us to his bodyguard and some other friends. We all had drinks together in the lounge of the hotel where he was staying. I had my three martinis and was in my usual ebullient state.

Sammy's bodyguard looked the way I thought a bodyguard looked, big and tough, but smooth. I asked him if he carried a gun. "Of course," he said, but that's as far as it went, and he didn't offer to take it out. "Please," I said, "I want to see it." Norman glared at me, a silent signal for me to shut up, but my martinis had gotten there first. The bodyguard politely refused. "Come on," I insisted, "let me see your gun." He took it out and passed it around the table. It was the very first time I'd held a gun in my hand. I had a strange feeling of power as I pointed it at Norman. I grinned when I said, "I'm gonna kill you, you son of a bitch." My finger was on that trigger, and my husband wouldn't have to worry about his next novel anymore. That's how much rage I had inside me.

Chapter 41

More nights than I care to remember, I would be awakened by my sleepless, agitated husband muttering to himself, pacing the length of the room with that lumbering bearlike walk that had become more pronounced over the years. Holding his glass of Scotch and so unaware of my presence, he might as well have been the only one in the room. Suddenly I felt terribly lonely. Doesn't he ever stop? I thought. Why is he so driven? "Honey, what's the matter? Why don't you come back to bed?" He would look at me without answering, not seeming to hear me, his mind elsewhere. He took a long swallow of his drink. "Yeah, yeah, sure, sure," he would mumble and then there was silence, broken only by the sound of his teeth crunching ice cubes. His face wore that same angry look of anguish I knew so well but which no one else saw. God, I thought, it's gonna be a long night. Sometimes I would turn my face to the wall to try to blot it all out.

Norman gave a reading of his play based on *The Deer Park* at our Perry Street apartment. Kevin McCarthy, Mary's brother, was playing the part of the director Charlie Eitel; Monty Clift was Sergius, the protagonist; Rip Torn was Marion Fay, a pimp. Mickey Knox was Herman Teppis, the Hollywood producer, and Anne Bancroft read the part of Elena, the call girl. That evening we were waiting for Monty, the only one of the cast who had not yet arrived. The bell rang, and when I opened the door, he was there. I hoped my face didn't show my shock. It was the first time I'd seen Monty since the accident in Hollywood when he had totaled his car and was almost killed in the process.

It was not the same beautiful face I had known. Badly mangled in the crackup, it looked made over, and in the procedure, the fine features had undergone a slight thickening. Under the circumstances, the doctors had done a superb job, creating a facsimile of Montgomery Clift. But the luminosity, that special sensitivity in his face, was gone. He even talked oddly, with a certain stiffness in the way he moved his mouth.

We were genuinely glad to see each other, though I knew him only slightly, and he gave me a warm hug. There was something so lost and fragile about this man that my heart went out to him.

"Oh Monty, I'm so happy to see you." When he responded with a smile, I saw a glimpse of the face I had known. He was his sweet self that night, and it was one of the few times I'd seen him when he didn't get roaring drunk.

The reading happened some months prior to the Actors Studio production, which was to be directed by Frank Corsaro.

I was one of the guests in a party scene but had no lines. All I had to do was act as if I were having a marvelous time, an easy task for me. I didn't mind not having a speaking role. It was still fun, and I was grateful to be part of my husband's work.

During the rehearsals, Norman began to have a problem with the way the play was being directed. He was fighting with Frank as well as the cast—but then who wasn't he fighting with?

When I first met Norman, he told me that one of the comments in a letter attached to his honorable discharge from the army was, "This man has never learned to take orders." When Norman mentioned this to me, I didn't feel he was too upset about it. On the contrary, he seemed proud of it.

The final blowup came during a rehearsal with Norman constantly butting in and interrupting the actors, driving them crazy. He began to criticize Anne's interpretation of the character, infuriating her to the point that she quit, throwing her script at Norman. "Let Adele play it," she said. "That's what you always wanted." She walked out with Norman yelling after her, "Fine, because you'll never amount to anything," or words to that effect. It was a strange thing for him to say considering she had been a big hit in *Two for the Seesaw*. We had both seen the play and thought she was wonderful.

The *Deer Park* play never went anywhere, but my frustrated actor of a husband continued to create his own offstage dramas with my willing cooperation as his costar.

Chapter 42

I never came to terms with my drinking during this period of my life with Norman. And not until later, in any case. It never crossed my mind that I was an alcoholic. It wasn't even a question of being in denial. The thought just never occurred to me that I might have a problem. An alcoholic was somebody in the movies, like Ray Milland in *The Lost Weekend* or a Bowery bum lying in the gutter. I never consciously connected my drinking with the trouble I got into or with the fact that I needed to drink and couldn't imagine my life without it and that half the time I wasn't in control of that life.

But aware of it or not, I *was* an alcoholic with all the fears, dreads, and insecurities that my husband shared. Alcohol fed and ignited us, became the fuse that set off the million petty explosions between us, defusing my creative energies into a struggle merely to exist.

When I was drunk, my personality changed, and so did my face. There were times when I would confront my moment of truth in the bathroom mirrors of countless cocktail parties. It was not in my imagination that my features coarsened, my expression slackened with hopelessness. My nose looked swollen and my eyes, never large to begin with, were reddened and small, ringed by smudged black mascara. The faintest of lines on each side of my mouth deepened during the evening. I was thirty-five, but I could see the whisper of forty-five on my face.

"I don't know who you are," I would say to that stranger's reflection. "Am I allowed two guesses? You're not Ava Gardner," I would say sadly. "You couldn't be because she doesn't have beady little black eyes and a clown's nose. How about Mother Cabrini? Nah, she never got drunk. She had a boring life. I don't have a boring life because I'm Mrs. Norman Kingsley Mailer. He's the Kingsley and I'm Adele the Queensley of Morales, the envy of all. Christ, if only they knew the half of what living in the Mailer playpen is really like." During all this close examination and conversation with my image, I would stick out my tongue, scrutinizing it as if I could tell the future by reading the shape of the red and white splotches on the surface. At least I could depend on my tongue to tell me the truth and never age the way my face would. More often than not, I would cry my drunken tears of self-pity, wiping my black-smudged eyes on fancy monogrammed guest towels, the wreckage of my face staring back at me.

"Baby, you need fixing badly," and I would slap on a new mask of thick makeup base and heavy powder. I would repaint my mouth with my bloody red lipstick, comb my hair, and go back into the arena to float in my husband's orbit, my brilliant, talented husband who was wearing his own drunken mask. His handsome face puffy, that once-sensitive mouth tightened into an angry sneer, bleary blue eyes narrowed in a mean belligerent stare, the rumpled face of a bad drunk.

Chapter 43

Norman had gone to a party without me because I was truly tired and truly sick of booze, at least for this one night. He came home drunk and in an ugly mood, unwilling to say what was bothering him, but as always ready to dump it on the nearest person. But I was angry, too. It was four in the morning, and I was in my predictably jealous and anxiety-ridden state. Trusting was a thing of the past. I found myself making the same tired accusation and getting back the same tired lies.

"What happened? What are you so angry about?"

"Repetition causes cancer," was his reply.

"Damn it, don't give me your cancer crap. I'm sick of it." There was no reply, just a remote stare. I was near tears. God knows where he'd been, what filth he'd been into, who or what he had provoked in the state he was in.

His Brooks Brothers suit was dirty and looked slept in, and he was minus his tie.

"Where did you leave your tie? In someone's bedroom?"

"I'm home, aren't I?" and he made himself a drink.

"Should I get down on my knees and thank God?"

"Christ, you're stupid," he said with such anger that I shrank inside.

I looked at him wondering how I'd ever loved him. All I felt now was hatred and an overwhelming desire to claw that smart-assed mouth until the flesh hung in bloody ribbons. My instinct told me not to answer, that it would be dangerous to get into a screaming fight. Because neither alcohol nor pot was blurring my judgment, I could heed that warning voice.

I'd seen him wildly drunk before, but this time there was something evil and maniacal that had not been there in the past. I felt he was on the edge—of what, I didn't know. But I knew he was not above hitting me. He had done it before, not that often, but often enough to make me afraid.

I watched him fill his glass with bourbon, and then the fever-ish pacing began. The room was cool, but his face was clammy with sweat. Whenever I think about Norman's accelerating series of emotional crises that occupied him during most of our marriage, I think of his face, with those bourbon drops of sweat beading his forehead.

He was cursing aloud. It wasn't at me, but his invisible ene- mies, book critics and publishers heading the list. That frightened me more than anything else. "The hell with it," I said. "I'm going back to sleep. I'm not going to be a garbage pail for all your crap. The maid's off early tomorrow, and I've gotta get up with the kids."

"Sit down, baby, and shut up." He poured more bourbon down his throat. "Maybe you can learn something for a change."

I couldn't stand looking at that sweaty face, so alien from the face I knew. I've got to get away from him, I thought, not just to bed, but away from here.

I felt trapped. Where could I go with two little kids at dawn? My only escape was to go to bed and pull the covers over my head. But Mr. Hyde was blocking my way.

"Norman, I'm going to bed. You're acting crazy."

"Well, shut your mouth, you murderous bitch, and listen to me."

He'd been speaking in that silly Texas drawl, which in itself told me that he had gone into the Mailer twilight zone.

My God, I thought, will there ever be an end to this circus? Tomorrow my life might continue with Dr. Jekyll, but tonight I had to put up with a Mr. Hyde who was absorbed in punishing others, for pleasure and for relief from his own inner torments.

He stared through me with that distracted expression, as if he were listening to voices inside his head, that strange smile flicking across his face. I recall the essence of what he said, and the way he looked has always stayed with me.

It seemed to me that he'd taken the first step of his descent into hell, and I was the reluctant witness to a pact with the Devil, whose presence was stinking up the room.

Norman's Texas character drawled, "Baby, Ahh love ya, you're my woman, but if you wanna travel with me, it's gonna be a rough trip, you dig."

"No kidding," I muttered under my breath. He went to the drawer, took out his cigarette papers and some loose grass, and began rolling a joint. He inhaled deeply and held it out to me. I shook my head. That was the last thing I wanted. We sat in silence, and I might as well have gone to bed because he didn't know I was there. He had gone into his boozy, pot-filled head, mumbling sentences from his books, laughing softly to himself—alone in the room with his buddy, the Devil. By now, too keyed up to go back to sleep, I was hoping he would go out again so I could have some peace.

"I'm going to get those bastards," he said, "and I'm going to do it by being the biggest son of a bitch there is. From now on, it's just me and fuck everyone else. I'll do only what I want to, when I want to. If I have to, I will lie and cheat, no matter what the consequences." With these words, the nice Jewish boy was no more.

Chapter 44

It was March of 1960, and I tried to persuade Norman that it was imperative we get away from New York. For once he agreed with me. We decided to pack up and go to Provincetown till September. The kids were not yet of school age, so we didn't have that problem to cope with. Obviously, I'd had it with the insanity of the whole New York scene, but just as obviously, the New York scene was not the heart of the matter. Norman was really beginning to flip out, and I was trying desperately to hang in, coasting on the times when we were almost a normal couple. Yet again I deluded myself into thinking that a change in geography would have a calming effect on us.

We drove up to the cape in Norman's little toy car, a green convertible Triumph. In spite of shipping tons of our stuff beforehand, mostly cartons of Norman's books, we still looked like the Okies, with suitcases strapped on the back of the car, two babies and two enormous dogs, whose curly poodle parts protruded from every opening.

Since our family had grown, I was always after Norman to buy a station wagon, because we never traveled lightly, no matter where we went. I wasn't asking him to give up his beloved Triumph—we could have even rented a car—but he was adamant in his refusal. He seemed to think that station wagons involved plastic, cancer, bourgeois middle-class values, etc., etc. No amount of arguing could change his mind, so we drove for seven hours in total discomfort.

Much of the way up, I was brooding about why I was still with this man. Only now do I have some insight into what was going on in my mind and heart. There was my fluctuating self-esteem for one, going from thinking I was the greatest thing on earth to a total nothing, a part of the self-loathing of an alcoholic always seeking validation from the outside. There was the constant emotional seesaw with my husband, who either built me up or tore me to shreds. There was never any moderation between us. Behind all of this was the part of me that never wanted to grow up. I guess I wanted to be a dependent child the rest of my life.

I was a Depression baby, and I grew up in a culture in which my role as a woman would be to marry and have children. My prince would love me eternally, take care of me forever, and we would live happily ever after.

I think I was also acting out my love/hate relationship with my mother, who, like my husband, was a narcissist. After my shattering divorce in 1962, in one of my therapy sessions, I had a sudden realization that I had married a man who was significantly like my mother in his relentlessness and his controlling sadistic nature. I'd always been under the impression that women tended to marry men like their fathers. My therapist said that this was not always the case. Clearly, many women chose men who were psychically like their mothers.

In spite of the pain involved, I obviously was still fascinated by the Jekyll-and-Hyde facets of our relationship. Much of my identity was tied up with being Mrs. Norman Mailer, and I was frightened to give that up, no matter what the price. I also had become dependent on my lifestyle. I had no money of my own and two small children. Where would I go? What would I do? At least my miseries were predictable, compared to the more terrifying unknown.

Aside from my fear of being alone, I was also ashamed at the thought of a divorce. To me, it was a disgrace. It meant I was a failure, my secret voice echoing my mother's horrified remark, "No one ever got a divorce in our family."

I adored my girls, and I know Norman loved them, too. With everything that was wrong in our lives, there was still a little that was right, still some love between us. Even as I write this, I can feel the pain of that beat-up love again.

We rented the Hawthorne house on the crest of Miller Hill Road. Norman had stayed there with Bea in 1950. I wasn't hung up on stuff like that, so it didn't bother me. The house was at the highest point in Provincetown, with a panoramic view of the town and its lovely harbor.

Despite my increasingly negative view of our marriage, I was looking forward to our stay, naive in my hope that it would have a calming effect on my husband. As for me, the sea was always a tranquilizer. The town was a perfect place for children, and I was looking forward to spending hours with them at the beach. The house, too, was large, so we would not crowd each other. Provincetown had been good to us in the past. Perhaps it would be that way again.

I missed not being on the bay. I still felt that if you were not close to those mystical changes of light, sky, and water, you weren't on the cape. One might as well go to the Poconos. But it was Norman's decision, take it or leave it.

From the time we arrived in March until June's onslaught of the summer crowd, the town was dead, which was okay with me. We had a nanny for the children, giving me plenty of time for myself. I set up my easel in the glassed-in porch and went to work on a canvas or two in my hope that Provincetown would have a calming effect on me, as well.

I was sadly mistaken. Norman's moods were more erratic than ever, more about his writing than anything else. He wrote in a little shack that was part of the property, a little way down the hill. "Norman," I would yell from the kitchen window, "come and get your lunch." He would lumber up the path, walking like a rather fat bear. Sitting gloomily at the table, he would open his book immediately and begin to eat his perennial tuna-fish salad without raising his eyes from the page. I never tried to talk to him when he was like that, and I no longer felt responsible for his depression—as I used to.

His nights were as bad as the ones in New York, some worse than others. I would be awakened by his pacing, the clink of ice cubes in that goddamn glass of bourbon. He would mumble to himself, stopping now and then to scrawl a few words in his note-book. He didn't give a damn whether he woke me or not. He might as well have been the only one in the room.

Propping myself up on one elbow, not quite awake, I watched him with half-closed eyes. I sighed. Dear God, I thought, do we have to go through one of his nights again? Tomorrow I'm going to move into the guest room. I was annoyed and at the same time felt terribly lonely. I had a sinking feeling in the pit of my stom-ach along with a helpless anger at his inaccessibility. I wanted so much to help him, but I couldn't get through the barriers he put up. I thought, Why is he so fucking driven all the time? If this was the creative process, it was a pretty strange one.

"What's the matter, honey?" I asked for what seemed to be the thousandth time. Even as I asked, I thought, How can he tell me when he can't acknowledge or recognize the presence of his own demons?

"Nothing is the matter. I just can't fucking sleep." He took a long swallow of his drink, his face with that all-too-familiar, angry, wild look of anguish, one that no one else ever saw. He was look-ing at me, but his mind was elsewhere. I lay back, pulling the covers around my shoulders. I sighed and closed my eyes. Nei-ther of us spoke, and the silence was broken only by the irritat-ing sound of his teeth crunching ice cubes.

I sighed again. "Did you take your Seconal?"

"Yeah, but it's not working. I gotta step them up again."

He looked so tired and unhappy, and as tired as I was of these endless nights of his, I still tried to reach him.

"Baby, please come back to bed. I love you."

"Yeah, yeah, I love you, too," he said, but he was not really in that room. His lips were moving. He was having that silent dia-logue again. He peered into his glass, rattling those damned ice cubes. Picking up his notebook from the table, he looked amused at a secret thought.

"What's so funny. For God's sake, tell me."

"Shut up, I'm thinking," he said and reached for his clothes.

"It's four in the morning, Norman. The bars are all closed. Please come to bed." But his demons were burning his tail, and he wasn't going to slow down for anyone.

"Where are you going?"

"Just out for a drive to help me unwind."

"When are you coming back?"

"I don't know. Go to sleep. I love you," and with that he walked out the door, leaving me to lie there alone in the darkness, with my anger and depression for bedmates.

"I'll bet that son of a bitch has a date," I said to myself as I ran through the names of all the women I knew in Provincetown, Wellfleet, and Truro. In a minute or two, I heard the snarling sound of his Triumph's engine blasting the peace of the sleeping town. I felt more alone than ever. When the sound faded into the still dark night, I started to cry.

Chapter 45

he characters Norman picked for his entourage that summer were a reflection of his inner confusion and insecurity. They were from the sleaze of Provincetown and Greenwich Village, bums and losers. In particular, Lester Blackiston and Bill Walker were two beatniks from Washington who had attached themselves to Norman.

They were drunks and druggies, and I think both had done time, something that especially fascinated my husband. I never did find out what they did time for, but maybe that was just as well.

I believe both these guys were Irish, which gave them a certain cachet with Norman. He had a thing about the Irish. He loved them. Although he never denied his Jewish background, he wasn't happy about it. If there was such a thing as Jews Anonymous, Norman would have been a charter member. I sometimes thought he really wanted to be Irish; and if not Irish, Wasp and rich. He did get rich.

In his novels *The Deer Park* and *Tough Guys Don't Dance*, both protagonists, clearly extensions of Norman himself, are of Irish descent.

Bill and Lester hung around the house, kissing Norman's ass and mine, though I was not as eager a recipient of their attentions. They also supplied him with pot and plenty of it—for a price, of course. My husband still attributed this drug with mystical powers to heal his wounded psyche and as an aid in his self-analysis.

Lester and Bill freeloaded the whole summer, coming in and out of the house as if they lived there. The few times I complained to Norman, he told me to shut up, that they were his friends and that I was being petty and small minded. What's the use? I thought. It's his money and his time. But I knew they were a bad influence on him. I could see it from the way he behaved in front of them, trotting out his Texas accent, lapsing into his hipster pose, using words like "cat," "you dig," and "man." Not that I was above using the vernacular myself, but unlike my husband, I didn't go around butting my head against the chest of whatever man I was getting drunk with nor did I indulge in arm wrestling, staring contests, or other macho games.

With these guys around, there was plenty of the above going on. And to further ingratiate himself with Norman, Lester said he'd done some professional boxing. For Norman, that practically made Lester his blood brother.

Walker was bearded, very dark, with coarse, blunt features. He looked like a pirate and called himself a writer, though I never remember seeing anything he had written.

Blackiston claimed to be a poet. He was attractive with curly, light-brown hair and the face of a decadent cherub. In spite of myself, there were times I liked him.

But they were using Norman, and he was letting himself be used. Norman repeated his pattern of having nonthreatening losers and untalented second-raters in his court, and it was still driving me crazy.

Both of these guys ended up badly. Lester got stabbed to death in a prison fight, and Walker drank himself to death.

In his saner days, Norman used to rely on my finely honed bullshit detector.

One night, for example, while we were still in the city, Norman came home from Danny's Hideaway and talked about an ex-fighter he had met there and how charming he was.

This was a real find for Norman, since the new acquaintance, Roger Donoghue, was not only an ex-prizefighter, but an Irishman, as well. Norman went on and on to me about Roger, telling me how personable and interesting he was.

Roger, it seemed, had been a promising contender for the middleweight championship, but retired from the ring because he had killed a fighter by accident. Evidently, his opponent had had some kind of physical condition that was lethally accelerated by the punches he took during the bout. Roger was so traumatized by what happened that he never boxed professionally again.

Norman said that he liked him, but there was something a little off about him, and he wanted me to meet him to see what I thought. Was he a phony or not?

Shortly after that, we met him for dinner. I could see right off that Roger was a heavy hitter, so I knew he would fit in as a drinking buddy of Norman's. Besides that, he was charming, amusing, and quite ambitious socially, a young man who liked cultivating celebrities. I think he genuinely liked me, and I liked him, as well. In spite of my feeling that he was a bit of an operator, I gave him my stamp of approval. I didn't think he was a phony. There was something basically decent and no bullshit about him, and I felt comfortable with Roger from the beginning. I could see why Norman liked him. What especially endeared him to me was his sense of humor. God knows I needed that, since my personal life had gotten pretty heavy and not much fun anymore. In spite of the pleasure I got from my little girls and the creative part of my life, I felt I was under siege by the moody, threatening presence of my husband, whose behavior was becoming more erratic and hostile all the time.

Roger insinuated himself into our lives. We began to pal around with him, brought him to parties, and introduced him to our friends, whom he charmed with his anecdotes about celebrity friends and characters in the fight game.

Roger was Norman's current token fighter, a new addition to his entourage and a definite improvement over most of his appendages. My husband was in love, and I went along with it. Roger came to visit us in Provincetown that 1960 summer for a week. He was working on a book, and Norman was encouraging and supportive to the point I wondered who was really writing it.

Roger was pleasant company, returned our hospitality, and took us out a few times. Once we were going out for the evening, and we thought we'd fix Roger up with one of our women friends. I went down the list as Norman shook his head at all of them. Then I thought of Fay Mowry, a Provincetown artist, Waspy and from a rich family. She was a big girl, a painter with a gorgeous mane of red hair. Norman shook his head again. "Nah, it's not going to work." "Why?" I asked. "Is it because you've got your eye on her for yourself?" Norman let that one go by—which made me wonder.

"Yeah, maybe you're right. She's Irish, or part anyway. She's tough and bright."

"Yeah and rich, too," I said.

We invited her over, and the rest was history, ancient history. They're still married and even more rich.

One of the few remaining traits I loved about Norman was his generosity. Whatever else he was, he wasn't petty. But even that trait would disappear when Mr. Hyde took over. He helped aspiring writers whose work he liked, giving of his time to a fault and giving blurbs to writers he admired.

James Baldwin spent a week in Provincetown with us. I had known Jimmy since my early Greenwich Village days when I was going with Ed Fancher. We always got along, and I liked Jimmy a lot. Whenever Ed and I gave a party, he was invited. He wasn't shy, and he seemed relaxed, enjoyed himself, was bright and very articulate.

And now it was 1960, and Jimmy was a famous writer, visiting another famous writer in Provincetown, Massachusetts. Troubled and unhappy as Jimmy was, he was in much better shape than my husband and was much more honest.

At that time, there were no black owners of the upscale houses on the harbor side that we visited with Jimmy. The only blacks were the domestic help.

Jimmy did not feel comfortable in Provincetown. He didn't say why, but I could tell. After all, why should he? With the exception of some painters we knew and some individual members of the Wellfleet crowd, I thought he was above most of the people we introduced him to.

Of course, Norman had to show Jimmy some of his favorite watering holes in the center of town, which was rapidly changing, beginning to look like Coney Island, with streams of tourists and beats bumming around for the summer. Jimmy hated the sleaziness of it, and I didn't blame him.

In spite of that, he was a terrific guest, easy to have around. I knocked myself out cooking some good meals for him, and because he loved to eat, I enjoyed his pleasure.

Jimmy was not a phony. He was a brilliant, talented writer who didn't have to prove anything. He may have been a bit of a show-off intellectually, but why not? He had it, so why not flaunt it?

That was the summer I worked at the Provincetown Theatre, built on an old wooden wharf in the center of town, the very theater where O'Neill had done some of his early plays.

I was in a musical called *The Pirates of Provincetown*. It was the first and only musical I've ever done. There was a dance number I was in, and I remember how much anxiety I had learning a simple routine. The rest of the show was easy for me. I had no lines, except to scream once when I saw the body of a drowned friend on the beach. That was the moment that I looked forward to every night, and I gave it my all, putting my rage and frustration into that anguished scream to the heavens. It was a good "method" scream.

I can still picture the inside of that little theater with Norman and Jimmy sitting in the first row on opening night and how nervous I was. The play was pretty silly, but Jimmy was sweet about my appearance. What could he say about someone who didn't have one line? He did say he believed the scream.

I felt a little self-conscious in front of Jimmy about Netty, our maid, serving us dinner since Jimmy's mother had worked in white people's houses. But I felt more relaxed when he and Netty got to talking, and it turned out that she had met David Baldwin, Jimmy's brother, around 125th Street near where she lived.

Listening to both writers' conversation was an adventure. Though they admired each other's work, there was an underlying competitiveness; each one tried to top the other with brilliant observations and clever remarks about writing, about politics, about everything. Jimmy could be a little arch at times when he wasn't being arrogant or angry. He was ambivalent in his feeling toward my husband. A part of the subtext of his relationship with Norman was that he found him attractive. There was never a hint of that on the surface, but it's my feeling it was there in the thrust and parry of the duel of words between them. Jimmy hated Norman's essay "The White Negro," which had been published in *Dissent* magazine. He and Norman had a big fight about it. He did care about Norman the person, although he thought Norman's hipster pose was ridiculous.

Both men drank through that week, Jimmy as heavily as Norman. He didn't get crazy, as my husband did, just more gregarious and talky. I don't remember him getting nasty or hostile, at least not toward me. Curiously Norman, even at his drunkest, kept a lid on his tough Texan character.

I don't think he dared (even with his hazy, boozy, banged-on head) to trot that tired bit out because Jimmy would have laughed at him. (In looking back at that dreadful period, maybe it would have been better to have cried less and laughed at Norman a little more.)

Jimmy, in spite of his success, must still have thought he had a lot to compensate for. Though Norman and he were far apart in obvious ways, both were alike in the mixture of grandiosity and self-loathing, though Jimmy was more reachable than Norman and less cut off from his feelings.

I could identify with Jimmy's inner loneliness, his feeling of being an outsider. No matter how famous he became, those feelings would probably stay with him until he died.

I invited some friends along with Jimmy to a picnic at our favorite beach in Truro, a spectacular spot where mountainous dunes rose straight up from the shoreline. It was one of those cloudless, blue-sky, perfect days. I had made up a gourmet picnic basket with chilled wine and a thermos of martinis.

Norman was swimming, and I was setting up lunch on our blanket. I looked down the beach, and in the distance, I could see Jimmy climbing the steep incline of a sandy cliff. He was wearing bathing trunks, and there was something vulnerable about that painfully thin, spidery, black figure silhouetted against the sky-high sand dune, so isolated, so alone. From my own deep pain, I called out to him. "Jimmy," I said, waving a long-stemmed glass, "it's martini time."

any destructive things happened during that dreadful summer.

As the parties accelerated, so did our craziness. Probably the worst was an episode at a party in a shack on one of the back roads where everyone was packed into one big room. Norman and I were stoned even before we arrived, so we didn't mind the crush. The bigger the crowd, the more attention my husband would receive, and he needed that like a junkie needs a fix at any price. We were having a conversation (if you could call spaced-out jabbering a conversation) with a six-foot-one school-teacher, playing beatnik for the summer. She was smashed and hostile, ready to take off on her broomstick, and I suppose I was revving the motor up on mine. I'd seen Big Angelina around town, at all the Provincetown bars and the scroungier parties. She was wearing the only straw hat in that sweaty room, the biggest cart-wheel straw I'd ever seen. As she moved around, her hat seemed to float like a boat, bobbing up and down on the surface of the undulating sea of bodies.

Angelina and I bantered back and forth, and it turned ugly. She made some insinuating crack, so I snatched her hat and threw it on the floor. There was some shoving back and forth with a lot of cursing as we traded insults, with Norman telling me to go out-side and beat her up. She was so big, with the shoulders of a foot-ball player, drunk as I was, I was afraid of her and didn't want a fight. I turned away and tried to ignore both her and my husband, who kept taunting me with remarks like, "She's walking all over you, and you don't have the guts to stand up to her."

I tried to laugh it off. "You're full of shit," I said. "Why don't you fight her? You like 'em big, don't you?" But he kept on goad-ing me, joining forces with Angelina who was spoiling for a fight. "He's right," she said. "You are a fucking coward." The next thing I knew, I was outside on the dunes facing my big, gangling oppo-nent. Norman was right there, still egging me on. I was so stoned, I felt as if I were dreaming all of it.

If only it had been a dream, instead of a horrible reality. I don't know who hit who first, but we were rolling down an incline, punching and clawing and kicking at each other. I felt as if I were fighting for my life. It was an ugly cat fight, the first and last I have ever had—and it wasn't like the movies. Reliving the memory makes me sick at heart, but it is clear to me that the fight was the beginning of the end of that part of my life.

My husband should have stopped us, but he didn't because the sadistic son of a bitch was getting off, watching his wife degrade herself. I was told that Norman, along with the other guys, was taking bets.

It just ended, I guess with both of us crying and in shock. I woke up the next morning with my jaw swollen, a deep scratch on my cheek, and my body covered with black-and-blue marks. There were even bald patches on my scalp where clumps of my hair had been torn out by the roots.

My dear husband told me how proud he was because I was the winner. Evidently he had found out that she was in worse shape. I was too depressed to care.

I was getting sicker and sicker living with this man, allowing him to destroy me piece by piece. I look back and often wonder who that stranger was, so far away from the woman I really am. The person who did those crazy drunken stunts, that person who allowed those terrible things to happen to her. Like me, Norman was busy self-destructing, and I wonder if he has ever asked himself the same questions.

The Devil was keeping his part of the bargain with Norman. Even with the rotten things my husband was doing, he was still able to write, and on occasion write well, as in the *Esquire* piece on Kennedy. That he would even try to write every day and be at all coherent was even more surprising since he was becoming ever more irrational.

Chapter 47

That summer of horrors was far from over. I can recall the next event with even more clarity than that awful cat fight. And this time it was only words causing the blows.

I was sweeping the floor of the dining room while Norman ate his breakfast. I was talking to him about the bad influence Lester and Bill had on our life. I didn't want to put up any longer with their pot and their freeloading. I wasn't being possessive—they really were an evil influence. Of course, Norman took their side, kicking off an argument. In the middle of it all, and for reasons I can't remember, I could hear my husband saying, with that spiteful little smile, that he had had a mistress for the past year. Although I knew he screwed around constantly, he never really talked about the ugly details. But here he was calmly eating his scrambled eggs while he dropped his little stink bomb.

I looked at that hard expression and the once-beautiful face, now beginning to show the effects of his excesses and meanness of spirit. At that moment, aside from the terrible pain in the pit of my stomach, I felt fear, the same fear and lostness I had as a child. Now that lost little girl was with me again. Despite everything going on with what had been passing as a marriage, I still lived in that terrible fear of being left alone.

The first words that came out of my mouth were, "Who is she? What's her name?" He wouldn't say, so I thought it was probably someone I knew. His bloated face got even stonier when I started to cry.

"Is it someone I know?"

"No, it's not," and his eyes calmly went back to the book he always read at breakfast.

"Look at me, you lying bastard," and I began yelling out the names of all the women we knew, old ones, fat ones, ugly ones, pretty ones, was it this one, that one—until I ran out of breath. He was amazing. He just laughed. "Listen, I gotta go to the studio." As he was leaving, I asked the question I was afraid to ask. "Do you love her?"

"No," he said, "I love you," and he was gone into his inner sanctum, leaving me stuck with rage and pain.

As the days went on, he would taunt me about his affair when he was drunk and in an ugly mood. I was half mad with jealousy.

"Wouldn't you like to know her name?" he would say. I would try to ignore it, but I would end up screaming my hatred at him. I often felt capable of murder, but was also afraid to touch him, knowing how violent he was.

I didn't know it then, but Norman had secretly stashed his mistress far out in the dunes in a primitive little shack. It was completely isolated, and God knows what the bitch did, except wait for him to come to take her to bed.

A few months later when we had gone back to New York, I was sitting in a restaurant with a friend when she pointed out the mystery woman. She had seen Norman with her a few times. "So that was the one," I thought, "the woman who had caused me all the agony."

She didn't see me sitting there in that restaurant, but I saw her and wanted to throw my plate at the bitch right then. A good thing I was sober or I would have made a terrible scene. Instead, I felt sick to my stomach and just wanted to get away. There was no confrontation, but I did confront Norman with her identity, and he brazenly admitted it, not even making any excuses or attempts to deny the relationship.

I got my small revenge, though. At an occasional party, I would say, "I have to tell you, Norman, there's someone here I've gone to bed with. It wasn't great or bad, just casual, no way as good as what we have." This was an exaggeration on my part, since we didn't have much left anyway. "After all, you once made me promise to tell you, and that's exactly what I'm doing." None of it was really true. I had had one or two transgressions, but I was an absolute saint compared to Norman. He would get really agitated. "Who was it? Is it so-and-so, him, or him." I would laugh. "I'm not telling you. Find out for yourself."

Chapter 48

Norman had his share of fistfights that last Provincetown summer, but the one I really remember happened at the height of the season, and it turned out to be really costly for him. All his dopey stunts were costly, but this one was a real extravagance.

We had been out drinking at a party and then a bar. Afterward we walked home along Commercial Street at about two in the morning. The streets were deserted.

We could see a car a few blocks away. Even at that distance, we could tell it was a patrol car. But Norman, who was his usual drunken obstreperous self, began waving at the car yelling, "Taxi, taxi." I was tired and wanted to go home. "That's not a taxi, you asshole. Shut up, or you're going to get us into trouble."

As the car got closer, Norman jumped in front of it, waving his arms frantically, noisier than ever. The car pulled up to the curb, and one of the cops told Norman to quiet down. There was an exchange when Norman said something snotty, cursing the cops out. All of a sudden, he was shoved into the backseat, and the car roared off. "Hey," I yelled, "where are you going with my husband?"

It happened so fast that I couldn't quite believe it. It was an eerie feeling because the street was dark and deserted and suddenly I was left alone. There was a dreamlike quality about the whole scene, and then it hit me. They had arrested him. I was scared. Then I realized what he had said as he was shoved into the car. "Go home, honey, and I'll call you." Which is what I did.

After an hour of waiting and worrying, I was about to call the station when the phone rang. It was Norman. "Are you all right?"

"Yeah," he said, "but they arrested me."

"Oh my God."

"Don't worry, just come down to the station with as much money as you can find."

"Where is it?"

"In the top drawer of the oak bureau. And hurry."

I found the money, about $300. I took it and decided to take Tibo with me downtown. He was so happy about going out, he was jumping all over me. I looked around for his leash, but couldn't find it. In desperation. I grabbed two of Norman's beautiful expensive ties, knotted them together, and tied them around Tibo's neck.

By now it was 5 A.M. At the police station, I asked the officer at the desk where my husband was. He looked me over, and I sensed his hostility. I must have been quite a sight. Miss Rich Bitch from New York, dressed in her fancy party clothes.

"Who are you?" he said rudely.

"I'm Mrs. Mailer. You've got my husband, and I want to see him."

"Yeah, he's here," and he led me into a small cellblock.

I'd never been in a jail before, and I couldn't believe it was Norman locked in that tiny cell. He looked a mess. His suit was torn and dirty, a bloody bandage was wrapped around his head, and his eye was swollen. He smiled at me and looked almost happy, dazed, and still drunk.

"Oh Christ," I said, "not again. You told me you were all right. What happened to your head?"

"The bastard hit me with a fucking club, but it's okay. I don't think I'm badly hurt. Just pay the bail, and let's get outta here. I'll tell you about it later."

Norman said that when he and the two cops got out of the car, he wrestled one cop to the ground and threw a punch at him. That's when he was clobbered with a blackjack. He needed fifteen stitches to close the wound on his head.

A few days later, there was a trial that was more of a circus, something to entertain the Provincetown summer population. Norman decided to act as his own lawyer. The little rooster played Clarence Darrow, strutting around and hamming it up to a gleeful audience. The whole thing was ridiculous since all it amounted to was a stiff fine.

After one of the worst summers I ever experienced, it was September and time to go back to the Perry Street apartment. As glad as I was that it was over, I was still nervous about being in New

332 / *The Last Party*

York again. If it had been that bad in Provincetown, what was awaiting me in the city?

Our Perry Street lease was up, and we decided not to renew. I had always hated that dreary apartment, so it was okay with me.

A friend told Norman about a temporary sublet on the twelfth floor of a building on the Upper West Side. As far as I was concerned, it was the thirteenth floor, and I was not happy about that, nor was I happy about leaving the Village.

But we took it because the apartment was spacious, the biggest one we ever lived in.

It had two bedrooms plus a maid's room, a big eat-in kitchen, and two bathrooms. All the rooms were painted a dark, depressing green and furnished with a few sticks of ugly furniture. Even our few decent pieces died against the dark-green walls, a color that suited my depression about my life and the shambles of my marriage.

I wanted my husband less and less, and the specter of his drab-looking mistress hovered over me. How could I desire him when I was filled with an anger that was slowly turning to pure hatred?

He was beginning to disgust me, with his big belly bloated from boozy self-indulgence, so far from the slender, well-formed body I had once wanted so passionately.

When we did have sex, it was if I were doing it alone. On the edge of my orgasm, I would look into his face, with its detached expression of a stranger, clocking the sounds and movements I made. I felt as if I was being looked at through a microscope by a mad scientist. It was creepy, it turned me off, and I felt more alone than ever.

Once, when I refused to perform according to his demands, I thought he would hit me. I locked myself in the bathroom and could hear him shouting, "Goddamn it, I want a lady outside and a whore in bed, not the other way around." "Well," I shouted back, "I'm no whore, and you can get one of your so-called ladies to do your filthy business."

I was becoming more and more depressed just living from day to day. I felt as if I were falling apart, and my two beautiful little girls were all that kept me from unraveling completely. I was their mommy, and I adored them. They needed me, and I needed them. I did the best I could to shield them from the terrible things going on between Norman and me.

After the trauma and mess of moving for about the eleventh time, I put Dandy, my oldest, into a good nursery school. Our maid, Netty was still with us, so I tried to get back to my painting. But I was feeling physically and emotionally drained as if by a vampire who was sucking me dry. I tried to keep up with my husband and his innumerable selves, his desperately driven ego trips. I was living with a man who was living from one emotional crisis to another, on the edge of a complete breakdown. And we both were trying in every way we could to escape that reality. In spite of my desperate unhappiness, I was still riding that roller coaster with him, afraid of relinquishing my seat, lest I be replaced by someone else.

So far, Norman had the amazing ability to bounce back from whatever he had been going through and still write—a habit aided by a lifetime of discipline and expertise.

I was not so lucky. Though I was a good artist, I lacked the discipline and stamina to ride out those terrible days. In the end, neither could my husband, who was now producing nothing but chaos. If we continued to live this life, I thought we would end up in adjoining cells in a mental hospital.

Chapter 49

Although I didn't know it at the time, the fall and winter after that awful Provincetown summer began the final decline of our marriage—a kind of "last mile." There was no end to the messy episodes, not only between Norman and me, but out in the world, as well. He seemed, at last, to be spinning totally out of control.

A friend phoned in the middle of one November night to let me know that my pugnacious husband was being arraigned in night court on drunk-and-disorderly charges.

Norman had asked him to call and tell me to come at seven in the morning, along with a lawyer, to bail him out. I must have been used to this because I was more annoyed at having to get up at five-thirty to be in court at seven than I was concerned about my husband's night in jail.

I was told that he had been arrested at Birdland, the jazz nightclub, a place where Norman, who fancied himself a jazz buff, liked to get drunk. It all started over a $7.50 tab, or so I was told. Norman wanted to pay it with a credit card. (How could any bar tab of Norman's be that small?) The management wouldn't accept it. Evidently Norman made a scene, there was a scuffle, and the cops were called. I don't know what happened after that, but he was arrested on the familiar charge of being drunk and disorderly. His girlfriend, the one he'd been seeing, had the nerve to show her face in court. She'd evidently been with Norman in Birdland that night. I must have been tired, too drained to have a confrontation with the bitch who was sneaking around with my husband. Besides, what good would it do? When he filed out with the other prisoners, he looked over at me and smiled. At that moment with all my anger and annoyance, I felt sorry for him. He looked wasted, and I sensed, under the machismo, someone who was frightened and feeling lost.

He now had a police record with two drunk-and-disorderly arrests behind him, a nice Jewish boy gone bad.

On another night, a drunken Norman came home at 4 A.M., disheveled and reeking of cheap perfume and stale sweat. I had stopped pacing the room and worrying about accidents a long time ago. Sometimes I even wished he would get hit by a car. Instead it was jealousy that kept me awake, driving me crazy, because I was convinced he was with that bitch of a mistress of his.

He looked like hell that night, as if he had slept in his clothes. There were dark smudges under his baggy eyes, his face a dissolute mask. When he took off his jacket, there were lipstick stains on his open collar. I couldn't get the truth out of him by being calm, so I did what came naturally, I yelled.

"I can't take this anymore. Where the hell were you?"

"Baby," he said, "if I told you, you wouldn't believe it." He was using that stupid Texas accent again.

"You and that idiot accent! Speak normally, goddamn it!"

"Look," he said smirking, "if you'll be quiet, I'll tell you what happened. It's a good story."

He was in Prexy's on Sheridan Square in the Village when a good-looking black woman sat next to him. They got to talking, and she propositioned him, so they went to her place. "How could you do that?" I said. "She was a whore. How much did you pay her, you filthy pig?"

He was so engrossed in his story, he ignored the epithet.

"Shut up," he said, "and I'll tell you the rest of the story."

"I don't wanna hear it. I'm not interested," and I covered my ears.

"Yes, you do," and he continued, "we get to her apartment, and she undresses and turns into a he. She was really beautiful. I couldn't believe it." I sat there in shock afraid to ask the next question. "And then what did you do?"

Norman grinned. "I fucked her anyway."

My stomach lurched, with feelings of disgust. I knew I would never let him touch me again.

"Oh my God, how could you do that?" I got into bed and pulled the covers over my head. He went into the bathroom, and I could hear the shower going. He'll never be able to wash that one off, not for me anyway. I was exhausted. This is someone else's nightmare, it can't be mine, and I fell asleep.

Where was this madness of a marriage going to end? My soul was sickened and I was confused and trapped by my own ambivalent feelings, incapable of walking away. Living with him was hell, but what would living alone with two children be like? I wasn't strong enough to make that move. As strange as it sounds, I could not imagine my life, even the way it was, without my husband. He still had power over me, a power I hardly understood.

No one else lived with him, knew him the way I did beyond his books, beyond his writing. Acting impossibly weird one minute and okay the next, he could be so many different people, including the kind Norman, tenderly holding Dandy and Betsy in his arms.

Back in the fifties and sixties (and perhaps even now in the nineties), Norman had an obsessive need for power and the spotlight. He was a publicity hound. It didn't matter what kind of publicity it was, so long as he was center stage, sometimes making bizarre-sounding statements in his effort to be controversial. But unfortunately, it was often a means to an end, a cry loud and clear, "Me, me, me, everybody look at me. Attention must be paid to my brilliance, my audacious intellectual concepts." His convoluted rationalization was simple. "Praise me or damn me, but for God's sake don't ignore me."

When he announced his crazy scheme to run a campaign as a candidate for the mayor of New York City, I wasn't surprised, of course. I call it crazy, though, because it was a totally unrealistic fantasy connected to his grandiosity and self-idolatry, and what was worse yet, another way of running away from himself. I know how many layers there are to this complicated man, and running for mayor was the last thing he needed, considering the shape he was in. To add that kind of pressure to the tremendous inner stress and tension that had been building inside of him was bound to cause an explosion.

Norman got himself a campaign manager, a fat blond *shiksa* who had written a column for the *Village Voice*. I suspect she was more than his campaign manager, since after all, if it walked, talked, and had two tits, he was automatically in its pants, or trying to be. She had to be as crazy as he was or very ambitious to go along with him. Whichever it was, it didn't matter because the campaign never was a real political happening.

The next few months were a kaleidoscope of hectic events with Norman becoming even more frantic and writing very little. I was beginning to get caught up in my husband's fantasy. I remember talking to Dan Wolf about how I would redecorate Gracie Mansion and that I was looking for a beautiful silver tea set for the formal teas I would have. "I don't have anything to wear," I said. "I've got to get some new hostess gowns." Dan went along with me until we both began to laugh at the absurdity of it all.

Speaking of absurdities, an acquaintance told me a story about Norman that took place at the time. One night they'd been at a bar getting very drunk together and picked up two girls, who invited both men back to their apartment on Horatio Street. Norman passed out on the living room floor, and after some time, he woke up and staggered into the night. The girls, who were thrilled about meeting Norman Mailer, had chalked the outline of his body as he slept, with a sign, "Here lay the body of Norman Mailer." This was supposed to impress all of their friends.

"What idiots," I said, and I laughed.

Then there was that unattractive wimpy guy at a *Village Voice* party who drunkenly confided to me that he would get girls to go to bed with him because he knew Norman Mailer. Such was my husband's notoriety.

Norman adored his younger sister, Barbara, and she returned the feeling. In all his antics, he rarely directed any of his hostility at her. Of course, they occasionally quarreled, but he was always rather gentle and protective of her. They were very close, and she in turn was fiercely loyal to him and the family. Strangely enough, he was not hypercritical of Barbara, as he was of others close to him.

She was and still is special, and I'm grateful to her for the love and attention she gave to my daughters when they were growing up. She helped to create some stability in the crazy background Norman created for them, balancing the stream of stepmothers who went through their lives, helping to make them into the wonderful young women they are today.

Because of this, I was always careful, even in my rage and anxiety, not to say anything to her about Norman's excesses.

But being the intelligent, sensitive person that she was, Barbara must have been aware of what was happening to her brother, the terrible changes in him.

One afternoon, she came to the apartment bringing a typed assignment Norman had given her, something to do with the mayoral campaign. Norman looked it over, frowning and criticizing it in an odd state of agitation. They argued about it in a way I'd never seen before. He was being wretched and unreasonable, and she said so. Suddenly he did something unprecedented—he slammed his fist into her face, knocking off her glasses and breaking them as they fell to the floor. It was totally unexpected, and I was as shocked as she was. I could tell he had hurt her because she was holding her face crying, "What's the matter with you? Are you crazy?" He said something about her trying to sabotage him by doing a rotten job. With that, she picked up the pieces of her glasses and ran out of the apartment.

After she left, I asked him how he could have hurt her like that. He seemed to be without remorse, saying something like, "that stupid cunt." Another shocker, since I'd never, ever heard him speak like that about her.

I got mine the next day, during some petty squabble. Without any warning, he hit me in the stomach with his fist right in front of the girls, who started to cry. Norman looked so wild that fear took over. I took the kids and ran out of the apartment. I stayed away until I was sure he must have calmed down.

The next day, I called Barbara. She was okay, but still upset. "I've never seen him like this."

"Well I have," I said, "and it's getting worse." I told her what had happened to me, that he'd done it before, and that I was terribly afraid of him. I thought he should be committed before he killed someone—me or somebody else. We discussed it a few times, finally agreeing that it certainly would be better for him to get some help. Since we both knew how opposed he was to psychoanalysis and that he would never agree to seek help of his own volition, we both felt he should be committed. We discussed it a few times, but in the end backed off. Neither of us really wanted to face the enormity of what we were contemplating.

In spite of my tumultuous existence, I managed to take care of my children, giving of myself, the self I tried to keep separate from the me who was angry, afraid, and confused. I took the girls to the park and the zoo, with side trips to F.A.O. Schwarz. I played with them, read to them, and made them laugh.

All through my unhappiness, my hysteria, through my very existence, my darlings were the only certainty in my life. My love for them was the only thing I was sure of. They were my sanity, part of Norman and me, the love that, God help me, was still there for him.

In spite of all that was happening, in spite of my conversations with Barbara about committing my husband, I was still denying to myself that I, too, was in terrible trouble. Booze stilled that whispery voice that said, "Save yourself, take the girls and run away, run for your life." Norman and I were on a roller coaster. I couldn't and didn't want to get off. Then came that last terrifying drop into madness and near death.

Chapter 50

Norman decided to give a birthday party for Roger Donoghue on November 19. It would also serve another purpose. He wanted it to be a promotional party for his mayoralty campaign. I was so depressed by that time that the last thing we needed to do was to throw a big party. In fact, I didn't care if we never gave another one. But according to Norman, this was to be an important part of his campaign.

For the last few days before, and the very day of the party, he was frantically running around the city inviting all sorts of street people that he picked up in bars—Times Square bums, druggies, homeless, whatever he could get. He said they (the vast majority) would be his future voters, and he would be their representative. At the same time, he invited some influential people of power, to show his downtrodden flock that he had some serious backing for his campaign.

The whole business sounded horrible and nutty to me, but no matter how I felt or what I said, nothing could get him off this new obsession.

A week before the party, he was pacing the length of the room, with a bourbon-sweaty face, yelling into the phone, frustrated because he couldn't get through to Eleanor Roosevelt to invite her.

"What are you doing?" I said. "She'll never come here. The idea is ludicrous." Undaunted, he even tried to invite the Kennedys. Of course, he never got through. He was so angry, he became convinced that their inaccessibility was a plot against him. His insomnia was worse than ever, and he was a nervous wreck. Nothing suited him, and he found fault with everything.

In spite of all this, I still managed to do my part, getting the necessary things for this monster party, ordering the food, glasses, plates, a coatrack, and a bartender.

Norman, as always, took care of the liquor supply. Cases of it were delivered that afternoon, more than I'd ever seen at one of our parties.

The big event was supposed to start about nine, but Norman was on his own kick early in the afternoon, smoking pot and swilling bourbon. He was gone most of that day doing what, I don't know, most likely running around the Village campaigning, rounding up more of the sleazy downtrodden to invite to the party.

Years later, I ran into an actress I knew who told me a story about something that had happened the day of the party, something that may actually have contributed to what happened later.

Norman and John Cox, a Prudential Insurance lawyer and supposedly a friend to both of us, had spent the afternoon pub-crawling through Village bars. John decided to call the actress; since he had dated her a few times, he thought it would be okay to invite themselves up for a drink. She had never met Norman, and he thought, correctly, that she wouldn't be likely to turn him down.

After sitting around drinking and making small talk, Norman made a clumsy pass at her, speaking with that Texas accent, pawing her, and suggesting she go to bed with him and John at the same time. When she refused, he got angry and became verbally abusive. This was hardly the behavior of a man whose favorite phrase was "Cool it, man."

He wasn't kidding, and she was getting more frightened, not so much of John, who was so drunk he was out of it, but of Norman. She knew something ugly would happen if she didn't get them out of her place, which wasn't easy. They finally left, after she put on her hysterical act and threatened to call the police.

She couldn't get over this person, a famous author, in her apartment behaving like an animal. This was the man who in a few hours would be hosting a big bash for his fantasy as the future mayor of New York City.

y husband got home about eight. He had managed to sober up a bit, but he was still pretty drunk.

The children had been fed, and as always, I read them their bedtime story and tucked them in.

After that, I took my shower and got dressed, wearing an expensive black cut-velvet dress. Norman chose to wear a bullfighter's shirt, which he'd picked up in Mexico.

Two martinis before the party helped to quiet the feeling of dread that had been with me all day. By the time the rooms were packed with bodies, I'd had a lot more to drink, and I was overwhelmed by a feeling of impending danger. With my head in my hands, I tried woozily to think of ways to escape the party and my feeling of dread. Everywhere I looked, there were strange faces, especially my husband's. I felt spaced out, with nothing or no one to hold onto.

I spotted Louise, a friend who had come to the party with Shel Silverstein, who at the time was doing cartoons for the *Village Voice*. I was trembling, and she could see the state I was in even from across the room.

"Adele, what's wrong? What's the matter?"

"Oh my God, Louise, I feel like I'm coming apart. I have to talk to you. Let's get a quiet corner away from all these horrible people."

We tried to go into my bedroom, but there were some dirty-looking, bummy people sitting on my bed smoking grass. So all we could find was the bathroom. She tried to calm me down, but all I could do was cry and talk about all those terrible months, how scared I was of my husband, how evil he was and how he was trying to drive me crazy. "I can't stand it anymore. I'd like to kill myself."

"You've got to get away from him," she said.

"I know," I cried. "But where do I go? I have no money—and what about my kids. He's nuttier than ever, and I don't know what to do."

Meanwhile 200 people passed through those rooms. Crashers off the street came and went, cartons of liquor disappearing down their gullets. The sickly sweet smell of pot mingled with the odor of unwashed bodies. Canapés and cigarette butts were ground into the carpet. Nobody cared, everyone was drunk. It was a party that was like a twenty-headed, scaled monster sluggishly moving through those rooms, tracking filth, stinking of destruction.

My husband, whom I'd hardly seen or spoken to given the density of the crowd, had left the party out of his head on booze and drugs. I was told that Norman had run into George Plimpton on the street. George had had enough of the bad vibes at the party and was going home. Without any warning, Norman hit George across the face with a rolled-up newspaper because he had failed to fulfill Norman's request to bring some influential, moneyed people to the party.

By four in the morning, everyone had gone but me, Lester Blackiston, and a black guy who may have been one of the crashers. Norman was still wandering the streets, and along with attacking Plimpton, he'd been fighting some street punks and God knows who else. Lester and I and the other man were making stupid drunken chatter, when suddenly Norman appeared. What happened then was stamped in my mind as if in black and white.

Norman was dirty, his bullfighter's shirt as torn and bloody as his face. He had a black eye. I hardly recognized him, his face was twisted, and he was out of his head, so drunk I don't think he knew where he was. He charged into the living room like a crazed bull, looking for anyone, anything on which to vent his psychic pain and rage. I stared across the room at him, and for one insane moment, I became the matador waving my red cape, hating him, taunting him, my drunken anguish and fury matching his. "*AJA TORO, AJA*," I called, "come on you little faggot, where's your *cojones*, did your ugly whore of a mistress cut them off, you son of a bitch!"

Then we met in that last tango, our little dance of death tangled in that blood-red cape. He gored me near my heart and in

my back with a dirty three-inch penknife he had found somewhere. I stood still for a moment, very quiet, feeling nothing. I
put my hand on my side, and it was wet. Then I looked at my palm,
and it was covered with blood. "Oh dear Jesus, help me," I said
and I fell. I lay there in my blood-soaked dress unable to move,
conscious of this scene in hell indelibly stamped in all its grim
detail. Norman stood there and looked at me, while the black
stranger tried to help me up. My slightest move was agonizing,
and I screamed in pain. I could only lie still, too weak to stand.
The stranger saw my bloody dress. "My God, man," he said to
Norman, "what have you done? We've got to get her to a hospital." It was amazing how clearly I heard and saw everything—as
if it were happening to someone else.

I felt Norman kick me. "Get away from her, let the bitch die."

"Goddamn it, Norman, are you crazy? She needs an ambulance. She's badly hurt."

The black man tried to pick me up again to get me away from
my husband and out of the apartment. Instead, Norman shoved
him away, and I fell back still conscious. Norman grabbed the
guy, punching him, as they wrestled all over the room.

Blackiston had left, so there was just the madness of two men
fighting while I lay there, for all anyone knew, mortally wounded.
Finally my new friend knocked Norman to the floor, picked me
up, ran to the elevator, and helped me down to the lobby. There
was still a cluster of half-drunk party guests gathered there. Somebody called a doctor and an ambulance. By this time, my rescuer
disappeared into the night. No one knew who my dark angel was,
and I never saw him again to thank him for saving my life.

Donald Ogden Stewart, Jr., whom I will always remember for
his kindness, held my hand trying to reassure me. But another

voice hammered at me to shield my husband and tell the police I'd fallen on a broken bottle. I agreed through my shock and pain, too stunned to protest.

The police came before the ambulance, and a detective questioned me. They didn't care how sick or hurt I was. They wanted to know who did it. I can still hear the detective's voice saying, "Come on, Mrs. Mailer, those are knife wounds, punctures, no jagged edges. No broken glass did that. Now why don't you tell us who did this to you?" "I don't know," I cried. "There were pieces of broken bottle on the floor, and I tripped and fell."

As soon as the cops arrived, all of Norman's friends, literary and otherwise, disappeared.

The only one with me was Netty, our maid, who had left the children with one of our friends who had gone back upstairs. It was a miracle that the children slept through the whole thing. Even as I am writing this, I think of my poor babies, waking up with both Norman and me gone, gone with no goodbyes or explanations. I had never been away from them for an entire night. Netty rode with me in the ambulance, while my husband staggered out into the night.

In spite of the blankets, I was shivering, with Netty holding my hand, my voice a whisper, "I'm going to die, aren't I?" She had to bend close to hear me through the screaming of the siren. "Now, Mrs. Mailer, don't talk like that. Of course you're not. We're almost to the hospital." I wasn't in pain, I just felt remote, and even the sound of the siren seemed far away. When we got to University Hospital, they rushed me into the x-ray room, propping me up against the machine, and I fainted. I came to just before I was wheeled into the operating room. Somehow Barbara, my sister-in-law, had heard what happened and rushed to the hospital.

She walked beside me, holding my hand. I held tightly to it as if it were my last connection to this earth. She looked down at me, her face filled with worry and compassion.

"Barbara," I said, "I'm so scared. Please don't let me die. I want to see my babies again." "Of course, you will," she told me. "You're going to be all right." And then I was in that white room under a white sheet, white-masked faces looking down at me from under a white-hot light.

I was on the operating table for six hours, hanging on to life while a famous heart surgeon with the improbable name of Dr. Hacker and his assistant worked on me.

The x-rays did not reveal much, so the surgeons had to do an exploratory. They made an eight-inch vertical incision starting under my left breast and running down my stomach, then a ten-inch-long horizontal incision under the breast in the heart area. When they opened me up, I was hemorrhaging internally, flooded with blood. An angel's hand had stayed the knife, a whisper away from the heart itself. The coronary sac around the heart had been pierced and had to be repaired. Luckily the wound on my back was not too deep.

When I came out of the anesthesia, I vomited, the nurse wiping my face. I was alive, thank God, and in a hospital bed, catheters coming from every opening except my mouth. I was stitched together like a rag doll who had lost some of her stuffing. I had an incredible amount of antibiotics pumped into me, more than I would take in a lifetime, and I remember the terrible spasmodic cramps that shot through my body.

Afterwards when I was thanking Dr. Hacker for saving my life, he said that he had really sweated over me, that it had been a delicate operation. My will to live and my equally strong recuperative powers got me through. But what I also knew was that I was thinking of my babies, that I was not going to leave them.

Norman's mother wasted no time. She came to see me a couple of hours after I was taken from the recovery room. In spite of the painkiller, I was still hurting, so weak I could hardly talk. She could see that, but it didn't stop her from nagging me to stick to my story about falling on a broken bottle. She may have loved her grandchildren, but Norman might as well have given birth to them for all she gave a damn about me, their mother.

I was in intensive care for three weeks and on the critical list. Even then I was not spared the publicity. The first night I was in the hospital, I awoke in the middle of the night. My bed faced a glass partition, and I could see the intern on duty reading the *Daily News.* As he turned the pages, I saw the black headlines, "Writer Stabs Wife in Party Brawl."

Oh my God, I thought, make this nightmare go away. I'm not really in this place, with my torso wrapped in bandages. None of this is happening. We loved each other. Why, why, why did he do this to me? I know I'm going to wake up beside my husband, in my own bed, with the kids sleeping down the hall. I began to cry, and with every breath I took, I could feel stabbing pains from my wounded heart.

There were complications, and I developed pleurisy. I had days of forcing myself to cough, getting up the black phlegm from deep in my lungs. It was agony because of my clamped-together, raw flesh. The cheerful nurse handed me a jar ten times a day, saying, "Time for our coughing. You have to get it out." Bitch, I thought, what does she care how much it hurts?

There was another glass partition close to my bed, separating me from another patient, with just a few feet between our beds.

This weird old man with the face of a gargoyle kept making obscene faces at me, slobbering, his tongue lolling from his mouth. I thought it was death looking at me, and I screamed for the nurse to take me away from that apparition. They moved me to a different part of the room. The pain was getting worse, so they put me on morphine. After that I felt as if I were in heaven being carried on the wings of angels.

I've always been terribly afraid of dying, but whenever I'm plagued by my fear, I try to remember how I felt when I was given that blissful drug that spoke to me in God's sweet voice.

Don't hold on so desperately, let go, give yourself some peace, dying is simple, it's living that's complicated.

My feeling was one of painless floating warmth and light. No anxiety, no twisted thoughts, no dark dreams. If only death were like that. I would never be afraid again.

If I were ever to get hooked on hard drugs, it would be morphine. Not my sloppy sick puking, no more fun-filled-with-guilt booze addiction, forever paying a price for a few hours of release. Be it love, be it oblivion, but let it be morphine.

Chapter 52

Norman managed to slip in late the night after the operation. He had tried to come before, but I told the nursing staff I didn't want to see him under any circumstances. He must have found a way to talk his way as far as my room.

I panicked when I saw him. "My God, what are you doing here? I told the nurse that I didn't want to see you," and I reached for the bell.

"Baby, don't do that. I just came to see how you were."

"Well, you can see, can't you? Now get out," I said in a half scream, feeling a wave of nausea.

He bent to kiss me, and I recoiled from his touch.

"Why are you here?" I repeated. "I told the nurses to keep you away from me."

He sat on the edge of the bed, reaching for my hand. "I just want to talk to you."

"No, no, don't touch me, just leave me alone."

He looked haggard and strained, with dark circles under his eyes. There was a silence as he stared at me, frowning.

"You didn't tell the police did you? You're going to stick to the broken-glass story aren't you?"

"Yes, yes, now go away."

He tried to put his arms around me. He could see the fear in my face.

"Why are you so scared? That's the one thing I can't stand. Do you know that I watched you being wheeled into the operating room, and I'd never seen you look so beautiful. Don't you understand why I did it? I love you, and I had to save you from cancer."

I looked at him. He was hopelessly crazy, I thought. I couldn't believe what I was hearing. At that moment, I had nothing but loathing for this man in his goddamn Brooks Brothers suit, sitting there spouting his bullshit.

Who was this stranger? Once we had loved each other passionately, but now I hated that cold son of a bitch with all my damaged being.

I wept, hardly having the strength to do even that. "Save me from cancer?" I said. "Look at me, you almost killed me."

There was no apology, no sign of remorse. Only the rantings of a sociopath. Nevertheless, he seemed bewildered, and I knew he was scared. I felt completely alone then, and despite my fear and anger, I looked into his face and felt a momentary pity. We were both in such terrible, terrible trouble, Norman more so than I, because he had never been able to look at himself. Given his brilliance, he had many intellectually devious ways to hide, to bury his feelings so deeply, that he had to invent a surface reality. Not daring to admit to himself that the stabbing was just a drunken cowardly slop of an act that covered up his fears about his manhood, his anger at women, and his guilt.

I sensed a deep alienation in him, a terrible emptiness and aloneness, and out of my own desperation and loneliness, I felt sorry for him.

He cried, and yes, I held him, and we wept together, but even in my grief, I knew his were tears of self-pity. It was all gone between us, and I mourned the tears that were not for me.

It took twenty-eight years and a couple of bourbons for Norman to blurt out one sentence, "Adele, I'm sorry I trashed your life." It happened at our daughter Betsy's wedding party in 1988 at his Brooklyn Heights apartment.

I don't know why he bothered because there was something so grudging and a little condescending in the way he said it. I looked at him, and I didn't dare feel anything, nor did I trust myself to talk about it. Besides, his timing was lousy.

"Yes, you did, but you trashed your life, too." It was a thought that he had probably never allowed himself to have.

I had walked down the church aisle with Norman, at my daughter's request. It was a strange feeling for me and most likely for him. We had been strangers in the terrible time of the stabbing, and we are strangers today.

In a 1990 interview in *Esquire* magazine, Norman said, in reference to the stabbing, "A decade's anger made me do it, after that I felt better." It is a quote out of context, but its callousness makes perfect sense to me.

Chapter 53

The detectives came to question me again though I was in terrible pain and very weak. They nagged at me until I broke.

"Mrs. Mailer, we know your husband stabbed you. Why don't you tell us what happened?"

"Oh God, please leave me alone. I already told you what happened. I fell on some broken glass."

"You have a knife wound, Mrs. Mailer," they persisted. "Now we need you to tell us who did it." "All right, all right," I sobbed, "my husband did it."

At that point, the nurse came in. She was very angry. "You have to leave. Can't you see she's very sick? You're making it worse."

They apologized, and then they were gone.

Now began what must have been a complex plan to make sure Norman didn't serve any time in prison. Rather than be committed to Bellevue, he chose instead to have himself arrested. Arrangements were made that he be picked up leaving the hospital, presumably after visiting me. That day he actually did want to see me again, but I told the nurse it made me too anxious and I didn't want him near me. I don't know why he wanted to see me, knowing he was going to be arrested, but I was told by the nurse that he had sat in the waiting room for a long while and that the police picked him up on his way out. After his arraignment, he was sent to Bellevue for psychiatric evaluation.

Because I was on the critical list, I was allowed just a few visits from the immediate family. Norman's mother and father were staying at the apartment with the kids and came to see me. Fanny even brought chicken soup. All she could do was talk about Norman. She seemed bewildered, and she cried once or twice, but I know her tears were only for him. You can bet those visits were just to reassure her that I was not going to send her beloved Norman to jail.

How could I have let this happen to her son the genius, America's Number One novelist? She didn't say that, but I knew damn well that's what she thought. After she left me, she'd walk the few blocks to Bellevue to see Norman, bringing him some of the same chicken soup. I lay in my lonely hospital bed depressed and frightened, crying uncontrollably. I was having these spells more often now, never knowing when one would come up on me. I would wake up in the middle of the night in a sweat, weeping as if my heart would break. The night nurse would come in and ask me if there was anything she could do. I could barely answer, "What is this going to do to my kids? What's going to happen to my husband? We had fights, but he didn't have to do this to me. Why did this happen, Jesus God, tell me why?"

My own parents came to the hospital, and when they saw the shape I was in, they couldn't believe what happened. It was beyond their comprehension.

My mother wept with me, my father was angry, but quiet. They seemed to be in shock. "How could this happen?" They had always liked Norman, and he liked them back, as well. He had a special feeling for my father. How could he have done this thing to me and their grandchildren? How could he do this to them? What kind of animal was he? They wanted to know everything, but it was too painful for me to go into detail, and I didn't have the strength. "Ma," I said, "he was crazy drunk on booze and drugs. He didn't know who he was or what he was doing. He had a nervous breakdown." "I'll kill the bastard," my father said. "You make him pay for what he did. Let him rot in jail."

They really didn't deserve this kind of notoriety. Two middle-aged people who lived a quiet life on a Brooklyn street and now their daughter's life was spread all over the newspapers.

My father was still working for the *Daily News* as a linotype operator. He told me he had actually set the type for those two-day headlines. I can imagine how painful it must have been, not only his concern for me, but the humiliation, too. He had been with the *News* for thirty-one years, fighting hard for the printers' union in an atmosphere of prejudice and small-mindedness, and now this dreadful thing happened.

When I was nineteen, when I left home, I remember him saying, "Adele, whatever you do, don't make the headlines of the

Daily News," and he didn't mean good headlines, but big, black, bad ones. It was a strangely prophetic remark.

At one point, Norman's examining psychiatrist from Bellevue came to see me. He explained that under the circumstances, I could easily obtain a divorce from my hospital bed if I cared to. He said that Norman was diagnosed as being a paranoid schizophrenic with suicidal and violent tendencies.

"No kidding," I said.

He also said that in his opinion my husband was dangerous to himself and others, and he recommended a series of shock treatments.

"Hell," I said, "a frontal lobotomy would be more like it."

The doctor had the necessary papers with him, and he explained that I was the only one who had the authority to sign the release. Of course, I could think about it, he said, I didn't have to make up my mind right away. He almost made it sound as if I had to make a decision to buy a new house or a car, but I was horrified at the thought. I was tempted to sign, but in the end, decided not to. I just wasn't myself and couldn't trust myself to do the right thing.

I don't know how many people knew about this. I didn't mention it to anyone, least of all my family. Though I could just hear my mother saying in that inimitable voice, "Sign it. Let them fry the bastard's brains."

I was getting advice about pressing charges from all over. There were people who advised me to put him in jail for what he did, and it was even said it would be good for him, that he would be forced to work on that big novel he had been promising himself to write. A nice stiff sentence in jail, they said, would keep him from jerking around, indulging in his self-destructive behavior.

And then there were the so-called intellectuals and writers, some of whom were in that lobby while I waited for an ambulance, who were so afraid for their reputations that they fled as soon as the cops came, leaving me wounded, bleeding and for all they knew, dying, to ride alone in the ambulance with Netty.

Now they were here in my room, not out of concern for me, but for Norman. This little procession was led by the one who had created the broken-bottle story. Now they were shoving a petition under my nose, signed with their little chicken scratches.

I had to listen to the same old litany, what a tragedy it was for him, great writer, brilliant, blah, blah, blah. A tragedy for him? Well, what about me, my tragedy, my life that was in pieces? If he had shock treatment, they said, Norman would never be the same again, which was all right with me. I had been the one who had almost died. Even as I lay there, it was still all about him. They needn't have troubled themselves, since I had no intention of signing the release for the treatment nor had I ever intended to do so.

Chapter 54

I had been in touch with my little girls on the phone. Just the sound of their voices gave me hope. Afterward I would have one of my crying spells because I missed them so much. My mother-in-law had been taking good care of them, and we had decided that it was not a good idea for them to visit me in the hospital though I longed to see them. I worried terribly about the separation. They were just babies, waking up to find their parents had disappeared, told that their mommy was sick and had to go to the hospital but that I would be home soon.

So now it was time to go home after being away for a little more than a month. I would see my babies at last, but I was apprehensive about the future. I packed my things and said goodbye to my angels of healing, the nurses who tended to me during those terrible days. All the nurses in the intensive care were truly the best, they have to be. The surgeons came by every day, watching me carefully. I owed my life to them and the superb care they gave me. I remember Dr. Hacker telling me that I survived because I was young, because of my tremendous recuperative powers, and most important, a strong will to live.

I will never forget the greeting I got from Dandy and Betsy when I got home. I cried with happiness. Norman's mother had taken fine care of them physically, though God knows what she had told them about her son, the genius who could do no wrong, including near-murder. Of course, she wouldn't let anything happen to my kids, above all . . . no matter what she felt about me.

Norman was to come home from Bellevue in about a week, but for now I was alone, exhausted and still weak, in bed most of the day. Netty was great with the children and very good to me, and I was grateful she was there.

The day of Norman's release, I must have been living in a fantasy. I put on a pretty nightgown and carefully made up my face. In spite of my ordeal I looked beautiful. Because of my drastic weight loss, I even had my cheekbones back! But why did I care about how I looked to this man? I was home, I suppose, but not really back in reality. I was still in a daze.

The doctor from Bellevue had told me he thought Norman was still agitated and depressed, but there was little I could do about his state of mind. He was coming home to this apartment, and that was it. I told myself that if he were still dangerous, he would still be in the hospital. After all, he'd had three weeks to calm down, and seeing the children might be good for him. Whatever else had happened, I knew in my heart that Norman would never physically harm them. As for me, what more could he do that he hadn't done?

The day arrived, and I was still in bed when the doorbell rang. Netty opened the door. I could hear the girls' excitement. "Daddy, Daddy," and I knew they were in his arms. I could hear his voice, "How are you, my darlings? Did you miss your daddy?"

I tried not to cry, aware of my bandages, trying not to think of that terrible night. I had been so lonely, and a small part of me was wanting to have him back, even if it could never be the way it was that long time ago when there had been love between us. I was feeling very anxious, not knowing what to expect. I heard him greet Netty and her reply, "It's good to have you back, Mr. Mailer." "Where's Mrs. Mailer?" he asked. "Mommy's in bed, she's sick," Dandy said. Minutes went by. He wasn't rushing in to see me. Then I heard him again. "Is this all the mail, Netty?"

I started to feel angry again. Why is he looking at the fucking mail? Why is he prolonging the agony?

I readied myself as I heard him coming down the hall and into the bedroom.

We looked at each other, not touching. His eyes were angry and cold, without remorse. Mine were filled with tears. Neither of us spoke, the only sound was the ticking of the clock. He looked terrible, as if he hadn't slept in a week. His clothes were wrinkled, and he had lost weight. There was a grey cast to his face.

"Hello, Norman. How are you?"

"Lousy. It was hell in there. How are you?" he said mechanically. He bent to kiss me, and I shrank from his touch. I couldn't help it. His reaction was one of anger, just as it was in the hospital when he came to see me. What the hell did he expect?

"Goddamn it," he swore, "I can't stand you being afraid of me. That's all over with."

"I'm sorry," I said in a small voice. "I just have to get used to everything."

He stank of disinfectant, and he was still wearing his slippers. "Where are your shoes?"

"I don't know. I guess I just left them at the hospital. I was in a hurry to get out of there."

We made casual conversation, as if nothing had happened— and still not one word of remorse. He talked about some of the characters he had met in the hospital, asked if I had seen anyone we knew, about how the kids were, anything but feelings. It was very strange. There was so much going on between us that neither of us dared to talk about. And I didn't know if I would ever stop being frightened of him.

The grand jury investigation was pending, and Norman asked me to testify on his behalf. I was to say that I did not know who stabbed me. "Of course, I will, but that's perjury," I said to Norman's lawyer. "Don't worry about it," he said, assuring me that I would be protected.

My grand jury appearance was not for Norman. I was doing it for my kids. They loved their father, and I didn't want to cut them off from him, to have them grow up with a father in prison.

Testifying before that grand jury was one of the scariest things I have ever done. I was still not well and unable to stand up without feeling pain. I remember dressing that morning, choosing my most demure outfit, and wearing very little makeup. Norman's lawyer had coached me, assuring me again that I was protected against being charged with perjury. I wasn't prepared for the angry grilling of the prosecuting attorney, but I gave the performance of my life, and Norman was all admiration.

In the end, my husband changed his plea from not guilty to third degree assault. It's amazing, he almost stabbed me to death, and they called it third degree assault.

I saved his neck. I could have put him away for fifteen years if I had chosen to testify against him. All he got was five years' probation.

Before Norman was released from Bellevue, I was told that the psychiatrist had tried to work with him, but could not break through such a tangled series of defenses and rationalizations.

Years later, I remembered something that occurred in Provincetown at the end of that terrible summer, which I think might have unconsciously touched off his psychotic break. We had gone to see the Hitchcock film, *Psycho*. The killer in that movie was called Norman Bates, who poisons his dominating possessive mother and stabs a young woman.

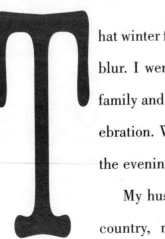

hat winter following my recovery was a timeless blur. I went through the motions and had my family and his to the house for a Christmas celebration. We even made some home movies of the evening.

My husband got fan mail from all over the country, most of the letters repeating his lawyer's comment, "Talent like his must be protected." There was little mention of me, not even a P.S., by the way, hope the wife's okay. He was the celebrity, I was not. That was the bitter reality for me and so much for my reflected glory. All the friends who had kissed my ass, telling me how wonderful my cooking was, my looks, my hair, my children—everything vanished.

Norman's social life escalated. He partied incessantly, invited everywhere. I say *his* social life, because it certainly wasn't mine. I was still in bed, barely able to get around. But Norman could and did so with a vengeance. He was back in the bosom of his sympathetic literary friends, to whom he had always presented his gentlemanly side, the sweet Norman. He had always been on his best behavior with people like Lillian Hellman, the Trillings, the Irving Howes, and the Dwight Macdonalds. He was careful not to let them see the obsessive, crazed side that I knew so well.

An invitation came one day to come by for cocktails at Lillian Hellman's. Although I wasn't quite aware of it, I was close to the breaking point, very close. On the surface it was just a feeling of depression, along with the continuing physical pain.

I tried to get dressed and simply couldn't make it.

"Honey," I said, "I still don't feel well enough to go tonight. I don't want to be by myself. Couldn't you stay home just this once?"

"I have to go," he said, choosing a tie from the rack in the closet. "She's invited some people who want to meet me."

"The hell with Lillian, what about me? It's just another party. You've been running all over town. I need you. I don't want to be alone tonight."

He looked at me with that familiar cold, fish-eye look, and I'll remember these words until I die. "Tough," he said. "Don't wait up for me," and he was gone.

That night after I read to the girls, I took some painkillers. It wasn't morphine, of course. That had ended when I left the hospital, but God how I wished it was.

I lay there sleepless. I was tempted to take one of Norman's sleeping pills, and then I thought, why not the whole bottle? I also needed a drink, but my doctor wouldn't permit it, not yet.

Not so my husband, he was drinking for both of us. I took neither the pill nor a drink, and I slept fitfully, waking at four to see his empty bed. Pacing in the deadly quiet of the bedroom, with just the ticking of the clock, I was consumed with a rage that was beyond anything I had felt before.

Back and forth, back and forth, thinking, thinking terrible thoughts, murderous thoughts. I don't have a gun, but there's a big knife in the kitchen. I'll stick it in him in exactly the places he stuck it in me. But instead, I took a big suitcase from the closet and crammed it with his fucking clothes. It was six thirty when I heard the click of the front door and then his footsteps down the hall and into the bedroom. He was there looking at me across the two beds, still drunk, holding a package in his hand wrapped in white paper. "I brought you a present," he said.

The dam broke, and my whole body shook with the force of my rage, so strong that I knew if I had been drunk and holding a gun, I would have shot him again and again until I emptied my hatred into his body.

"Where were you all night?" I screamed. "Don't you ever stop? Haven't you done enough? You're not human, you're a fucking vampire."

I could smell him from across the room. "You stink of pussy, you disgusting pig. Do you know how much I hate you? I packed your fucking bag, that's how much! Go on, move in with that hag of a mistress, that ugly whore you've been screwing all year. You tried to kill my body, you bastard, and now you want to kill my soul. Well, you can't do it, do you understand. I won't let you, you hateful son of a bitch. I should have let them put you away. But that's okay because I'm getting a divorce, and you'll pay, oh yes, you'll pay. I'll get you for everything you own. I'll take the kids away from you, and if I can help it, you'll never see them again. Do you think I want them to be around a crazy murderer?"

He stood there with a drunken, supercilious grin on his face. "You'll never make it without me, baby."

"Fuck you, you son of a bitch." Rage gave me the strength, stitches and all, to lift that heavy suitcase and hurl it across the room at him. He narrowed his eyes, reddened from the pot he'd been smoking, slipping into that schizophrenic Southern accent he used when he was drunk.

"Oh yeah, well let's see which one of us has the muscles."

"Is that all you have to say?" I screamed. "Just get out of my life. Who wants a man who needs a three-ring circus to get it up, you fucking male whore?"

The next day I called my lawyer.

Coda

Where in what cemetery of the heavens do the true words of lovers rest when they love no more.—FROM *THE DEER PARK* BY NORMAN MAILER

ost divorced women, if they choose, never have to see or hear their ex-mates again. Not so in my case. In the years following my divorce, Norman was in the media constantly, still performing his demented stunts. He was his own greatest publicity agent.

There were endless talk shows. He spoke to Dick Cavett about the psychology of murder; he thought that violence

would prevent cancer; and he had wanted to experience the act of murder.

I can recall watching that interview, mesmerized, unable to turn it off. There was still no expression of remorse, not a glimpse, only an icy detachment and, as always, a total preoccupation with himself.

For a hundred Sundays, I drank my morning coffee, reading the *New York Times,* another wife, another book, kudos, Pulitzer Prizes, million-dollar contracts, one of the highest advances for a book since Hemingway, all of this bounty while my wounds were healing. Faust was indeed reaping the rewards of his evil contract with the Devil. I knew because I was there when he signed on the dotted line. I was trapped in my purgatory of hatred, indulging my wildest fantasies, happily scooping out those baby blues like spoonfuls of cantaloupe, slowly slitting his fat, bourbon-soaked liver. Pulling nails out one by one. But the best was cutting out his lying tongue, chopping off his hands, dooming him to write the great American novel with his feet. Beat the bongos while I make a fat Norman doll wrapped in a thread from his Brooks Brothers suit.

I felt the powerful voodoo in myself sticking pins into all of his vital places. This one, my darling, is for what you did to me. This one is for the children. And this one for my fucking soul.

I remembered a fragment of a dream one night facing my reflection in the mirror. "Mirror, mirror on the wall, who is the fairest of them all?" The voice that answered me was my mother's. "You ain't, baby. You're drying up. You look terrible. A couple more grey hairs, mean lines around the mouth. Watch those frownies, they're getting deeper. You'll have furrows soon. Ya better get rid of that hatred, or it'll get rid of you."

My face was my vanity, so I said goodbye to hatred. I was a survivor, and I had to make a choice. Live with hatred and die, or live with love and survive.

I chose to live and learn to love myself again.

Index